Civic Jazz

Civic Jazz

American Music and Kenneth Burke on the Art of Getting Along

GREGORY CLARK

The University of Chicago Press Chicago and London

GREGORY CLARK is University Professor of English at Brigham Young University. He is the author of *Rhetorical Landscapes in America: Variations on a Theme from Kenneth Burke* and coeditor of *Trained Capacities: John Dewey, Rhetoric, and Democratic Practice* and *Oratorical Culture in Nineteenth-Century America: Transformations in the Theory and Practice of Public Discourse*.

The University of Chicago Press, Chicago 60637
The University of Chicago Press, Ltd., London

Printed in the United States of America

24 23 22 21 20 19 18 17 16 15   1 2 3 4 5

ISBN-13: 978-0-226-21818-2 (cloth)
ISBN-13: 978-0-226-21821-2 (paper)
ISBN-13: 978-0-226-21835-9 (e-book)
DOI: 10.7208/chicago/9780226218359.001.0001

Library of Congress Cataloging-in-Publication Data

Clark, Gregory, 1950– author.
Civic jazz : American music and Kenneth Burke on the art of getting along / Gregory Clark.
pages ; cm
Includes bibliographical references and index.
ISBN 978-0-226-21818-2 (cloth : alk. paper)—ISBN 0-226-21818-X (cloth : alk. paper)—ISBN 978-0-226-21821-2 (pbk. : alk. paper)—ISBN 0-226-21821-X (pbk. : alk. paper)—ISBN 978-0-226-21835-9 (e-book) 1. Jazz—Social aspects. 2. Music and rhetoric. 3. Rhetoric—Philosophy. 4. Burke, Kenneth, 1897–1993. I. Title.
ML3508.C53 2015
781.65'11—dc23

2014023238

♾ This paper meets the requirements of ANSI/NISO Z39.48-1992 (Permanence of Paper).

To Linda, for swinging along.

Music . . . would be the song above catastrophe.

KENNETH BURKE

Contents

Acknowledgments

The College of Humanities at Brigham Young University has supported this project with consistency, generosity and considerable patience. I am deeply grateful.

People working in rhetorical studies who have been particularly helpful as I have moved along through this project include Jerry Hauser, Michael Halloran, Debra Hawhee, Michael Leff, Carolyn Miller, and Jack Selzer. Anthony Burke and Michael Burke have been generous with their time and their memories as I have rummaged through their father's work. Jeanette Sabre and Sandra Stelts have been invaluable in facilitating my use of the Kenneth Burke Papers held at Penn State University. Amy Lafave guided me through the archive of the Lenox School of Jazz at the Lenox Library. Tara T. Boyce and Lisa Nielson Thomas assisted me in finalizing the manuscript at about the same time as Robert Bullough was providing me with a thorough reading that made the book much better.

Jazz people who have been helpful through the years include Wess Anderson, Jonathan Batiste, Stanley Crouch, Nat Hentoff, Laura Johnson, Sheila Jordan, Steve Lindeman, Wynton Marsalis, Albert Murray, Marcus Roberts, Wallace Roney, Harvie S, and Loren Schoenberg.

Douglas Mitchell at the University of Chicago Press has offered me the confidence I have needed to complete a slow and difficult project, and selected reviewers have been both rigorous and encouraging in critiques that have helped me along.

Linda Clark has been my companion at concerts and clubs, for backstage conversations, and in workshops and archives, helping me process it all in our own long talks. She has welcomed into our lives the musicians and critics this project has allowed us to meet, and made them our friends.

Foreword

I met Greg Clark in 2002 when my trio was serving as artists-in-residence for the Salt Lake City Winter Olympic Games. Since then, Greg and I have had many conversations about jazz and its potential influence on the people who come to jazz concerts and/or listen to jazz recordings. But when Greg approached me about writing this foreword, I did not really know what to expect, since I had not yet read the book.

I considered that the book might contain some anecdotes about jazz and democracy, with references to some nice concerts he had attended, or perhaps a philosophical treatise on how he felt about jazz. Instead, I found a carefully laid out set of principles showing the relationship between the rhetorical writings of the great literary theorist Kenneth Burke about improving civic life in America and the way in which jazz actually works during performance. At that time, I had never heard of Kenneth Burke—and hadn't read any of his books. Secondly, I had not expected such a thoughtful analysis of the parallels between group jazz improvisation and civic life in the United States. In short, the book wasn't at all what I thought it would be.

I asked Greg why he chose jazz as a model for getting along. He said, "In jazz, people for whom the American promises of equality and freedom and cooperative self-government had been broken from the very beginning made those very three things that they were denied into an art. They took equality and freedom and the idea of working voluntarily together to create better lives, and made music from them—music that expressed what they knew they deserved."

When asked why he found Kenneth Burke's work to be such a compelling model for positive civic dialogue, Greg explained that Burke was a man who could have led a privileged life on the basis of his race and class, but who instead examined throughout his long lifetime the damage that is done to people by adhering to old beliefs—particularly the belief that somehow they deserve the place they are in. Whether that place is good or bad, it is where they belong. In his writings Burke tried to understand how that happens, how to prevent it, and how to undo the damage. Jazz at its best creates moments when people can connect in ways beyond agreement, when souls can share a feeling, when they can comprehend communion.

This book provides very helpful insights into strategies and concepts that illuminate better ways for us to get along. It uses principles and ideas proposed by Kenneth Burke, as well as by jazz music, as rhetorical tools for showing how the art of jazz can move people and play a role in changing their attitudes in ways that may lead us in the direction of better civic communication.

The concept of collective group improvisation is the aspect of jazz that is most directly relevant to the civic work of individual and group participation in a democratic society. It's essentially what we all do every day: we spontaneously react to life's situations and challenges by making up what to do. We improvise in the moment to create order and stability in our daily lives. If the usual road to work is closed, we find another route to get there; or maybe we stop along the way and someone gives us helpful directions. Resolving the problem requires us to use our own resources in combination with the help and good will of others.

John Coltrane once said during a mid-1960s interview that he wanted his music to be a force for good. That was an individualistic agenda grounded in wanting to do something selfless that would uplift his audience. Coltrane wanted his music to function as a source of comfort and inspiration to heal and encourage the people who heard it. And that's not all. Playing jazz music properly requires each performer to try to turn a mistake or unfortunate occurrence into something good or even great. Sometimes you have to sacrifice what you wanted to play so that you can protect what someone else was trying to play, because you see the value in what they're trying to do. Quite often, it takes much more imagination, ingenuity, and energy to fix something together than to just move ahead with your own plan. This is true both for a jazz ensemble and for a community of individuals attempting to find ways to get along with each other.

The difference between what happens on a bandstand and what happens in a community of people who are expected to treat each other as equals is that the people on a bandstand have a common project that is very concrete—and that is to make the music work. The people in a community don't always have that clearly defined concrete project to bind their energy and efforts together. But the way jazz works is still a good metaphor for finding potential solutions that can be applied to problems among diverse individuals in civic life.

Another very important aspect of improvised jazz is that you can go anywhere in the world and say to jazz musicians you've never played with, "We're going to play a blues in B flat," and everyone will know what you mean, yet every time a jazz band assembles and plays a B flat blues, it sounds completely different; there will always be unexpected events that help shape each individual performance. In this aspect, jazz mirrors life—because we never know what each day will bring, and there are many moments and situations in which the outcome is unknown until it is negotiated through civic dialogue, or by choices made on the spot by the participants.

There's a profound moment in this book where Greg, through Burke, shows us a way of looking at conflict situations in a more positive light. Burke says: "Are things disunited in 'body?' Then unite them in 'spirit.' Would a nation extend its physical dominion? Let it talk of spreading its 'ideals.' Do you encounter contradictions? Call them 'balances.' Is an organization in disarray? Talk of its common purpose. Are there struggles over means? Celebrate agreement on ends. Sanction the troublously manifest, the incarnate, in terms of the ideally, perfectly invisible and intangible, the divine." That's what good jazz does.

In jazz we support each other at all times. For example, many times while playing with my trio I'll get lost in the form, and my drummer, Jason Marsalis, will play a strong downbeat on beat one so that I can find my place. Or if bassist Rodney Jordan gets a little off with the harmony, I will play a subtle bass note to help him get reoriented; he does the same for me. We are constantly listening and evaluating in order to make sure that we support each other all the time.

Another exciting thing about this book is its view of jazz as an active force in persuading and influencing people to evolve and change because of what they hear in the music. This is summed up eloquently by Burke: "Once you grasp the trend of the form, it invites participation regardless of the subject matter. Formally, you find yourself swinging along with the succession of antitheses, even though you may not agree with the proposition that is being presented in this form. . . ."

I always view jazz as a symbol of how things should be, not of how things actually are. Unfortunately, this means that most of the great jazz artists throughout history recognized that when they got off the bandstand, they would return to the same wretched and difficult social and political circumstances that they were using this music to get away from in the first place.

It's like the blues. The blues as circumstance is always bitter, sad, hopeless, and hard. We play the blues as an active antidote to cure the blues in life; not to escape it, but to directly confront it with "attitude." As Greg points out, most people think that being rhetorical is about getting people to do things by direct persuasion, but Burke teaches us that art gets people to change their attitude, and that is the antecedent to actual change. Burke says, "Our basic principle . . . is our contention that all symbolism can be treated as the ritualistic naming and changing of identity," a necessary process that proceeds as "a man fits himself for a role in accordance with established coordinates or for a change of role in accordance with new coordinates which necessity has forced upon him."

The experience of music or art in general can lead to change brought on not by direct persuasion, but by the experience that prompts an individual's change in attitude. Duke Ellington once said that "nothing great happens without forethought," and often the most productive forethought occurs in form of intense shared experience.

We need more people to be engaged both in jazz and in civic activities in this country. Why? Consider the fact that most high school students in the United States are required to read Shakespeare, though many will never pick up and read or study his work later in life. Still, as a society, we have decided that students should have the experience of being in touch with such a profound genius of literature. Do we suggest that young people should not take geometry, calculus, or physics, just because many of them will never use those skills later in their life or work? Isn't the goal to develop a student's general intelligence and ability to use a range of knowledge and skills in different areas to solve seemingly unrelated problems? *Civic Jazz* describes quite precisely how this music can contribute to the achievement of that goal in ways that suggest that everyone, not just aspiring musicians, could benefit from jazz education.

That, of course, would benefit the musicians in another way, by building a bigger audience for jazz.

At this time, many musicians are more divided than ever in both purpose and belief. This is one of the problems that this book could help us to address. Some jazz musicians espouse freedom and individual liberty without taking responsibility for helping others to experience that same freedom and independence. Some of our jazz musicians want to solo all night but fail to appreciate it when other musicians do the same. One trend that has been present in the music for the past few decades is that musicians want to play their original music and make their own statement, but see no value in investigating the music of the legendary figures who created the music in the first place. If we don't really value the music of Duke Ellington, Thelonious Monk, or Jelly Roll Morton, how could the music of any modern jazz musician be of any lasting cultural relevance?

In every field, we have pioneers who first built the field. Each subsequent generation builds on what came before. This is our common heritage and it sets the standards for our field. This guides the field as it grows and changes in response to our modern environment. Different artists have different views of how their cultural heritage informs their art. It's good to listen to different styles of jazz whether you like them or not, because it challenges your willingness to be open to different views. Even if your choice is not to be open to a particular view, that's fine as long as it's an informed choice you are making. As Greg Clark points out, when you are confronted with the unexpected, you have to either embrace it or reject it. In my view, neither choice is better than the other. Embracing change for its own sake is not necessarily preferred. But our shared heritage, both in music and in civic society, gives us a foundation upon which to evaluate the unexpected.

To me, one of this book's most profound concepts is that "art is not experience, but something added to experience." The American philosopher John Dewey once said, "We do not learn from experience . . . we learn from reflecting on experience." It is this reflection on experience that creates great art. As jazz musicians, we make it our goal to provide the public and each other with a meaningful encounter with great art—art that holds the power to stimulate change. In its earliest roots, jazz functioned in this role. It stimulated change, though that change was often painful and met with enormous resistance. At times we may fail and quit trying; we may even lose our enthusiasm and hope. But when we have a profound experience, that experience gives us the courage, inspiration, and will to change.

Throughout this book, Greg shows us that democratic cooperation is not easy to come by. People are not necessarily open to hearing another person's point of view that differs from theirs. As with jazz music, democracy is about fighting for everyone's right to be heard. When we're on the bandstand, we all have a right to be heard, whether or not we agree with what each person is playing at any given moment. But to create this great art, we must recommit ourselves to being open to one another every time we play. It's that constant recommitment that gives me such faith in the music and in the power of what it can do for each of us, as individuals and as citizens.

I found this to be a fascinating book. I read it with the same openness with which I approach music, and I was not disappointed. I made no assumptions or judgments before I picked it up, and I found seven provocative chapters starting with the first page. Reading it has given me a whole new set of strategies that could help to bring about meaningful change in our approach to jazz music, to each other as artists, and as citizens of this great country.

Participating in something that requires individual investment in a group agenda helps us to acknowledge that there is something greater than ourselves from which we can gain inspiration. How can jazz music be used in civic life? As a model for cooperation among people from different backgrounds? As a metaphor for resolving the many conflicts that will arise during group improvisation? As a representation of the speed with which things in life can change from moment to moment, from good to bad and back again? It's all of these things.

This book builds the case that for democracy to work, on the bandstand and in our society at large, it is not necessary that we agree on everything, or even on most things. For our culture and our political society to thrive, we must only learn to respect and listen to one another from a position of being willing to adapt or even change in response. Greg Clark shows us that the very act of listening and valuing opposing viewpoints can serve as an agent of transformative change.

Marcus Roberts

ONE

Setting Up

For what a Constitution would do primarily is to *substantiate an ought* (to base a statement as to *what should be* upon a statement as *to what is*).[1]

KENNETH BURKE

That a prominent British cultural critic from the left finds a good candidate for the meaning of life deep in what is unique in the culture of a United States that leans to the right merits our attention. When people play in a jazz ensemble, writes Terry Eagleton, "the complex harmony they fashion comes not from playing a collective score, but from the free musical expression of each member as the basis for the free expression of the others." That's why musicians who play jazz can lose themselves in the project of the group in ways that sometimes carry them, separately and together, well beyond the capacity of their own voices. What is meaningful in that is the "medium of relationship" within which people combine to make this music. "Is jazz, then, the meaning of life?" Eagleton asks. "Not exactly," is his answer. But the "practical, social form of life" jazz demands of those who play it just might be.[2]

The great jazz critic Martin Williams pointed directly toward that when he wrote that "the high degree of individuality, together with the mutual respect and cooperation required in a jazz ensemble carry with them philosophical implications that are so exciting and far-reaching that one almost hesitates to contemplate them."[3] We *can* contemplate them, though. And we should, starting from this essential point that the pianist Marcus Roberts has made more than once about jazz: "None of this music is about you by yourself. It's about you with other people."[4]

In New Orleans one late December we ran into Wess Anderson. We were there for an academic conference and Wess, an alto sax player known for his distinctly warm sound, was a guest at a panel on literature about jazz. He was based in New York, playing with the Lincoln Center Jazz Orchestra, and we had met him a couple of times at concerts there. But his home was in Baton Rouge, close enough during the holidays to come to New Orleans and talk about jazz. When we greeted him afterward, he suggested that we find him later at a place called Donna's Bar and Grill. Donna's was on the farthest side of the French Quarter from the convention hotel, and the streets we walked to get there, usually noisy and brightly lit, were mostly dark in the aftermath of Christmas. We walked in the chill thirty minutes or so until we found Donna's, looking like a rundown neighborhood bar on North Rampart Street. We hesitated outside but the live music we could hear coming through the door invited us in.

The room was warm, bright, and crowded. It was somebody's birthday, so balloons hung with the white Christmas lights along the walls. The air was thick with cigarettes, hot food, and fragrances worn on a night out. We walked through the door into a line of four horn players weaving improvised lines into a framework maintained by an old man on an upright piano behind them, a kid on a drum kit, and a big guy on a battered string bass alongside. Wess, in his dark New York suit, played his alto next to a small man in overalls and T-shirt playing tenor, and a trumpeter who looked like a college student. A tall man stooped over a trombone on the far end. It looked like a neighborhood pickup band. Wess grinned at us through his mouthpiece as we walked past the band toward foil pans of fried chicken and biscuits, and red beans and rice on the bar. Someone gave us plastic plates to fill and, following a wave from Wess's wife, we settled in at the space she had made at her table, eating and chatting and cheering the music on from one virtuosic surprise to the next, having forgotten that we were the only white people in the room. Enmeshed with the rest in the jazz being made there, we felt only welcome.

This book explores the jazz "form of life" that let us feel welcome that night. It examines the idea that jazz music demands from those who make it as well as those who listen a way of living that, as the student of conflict and communion Kenneth Burke put it in the epigraph that opens this chapter, "substantiates" the seemingly impossible American "ought" that is *e pluribus unum*.[5] That's what happens when jazz music works. It happens among those who listen, as well as among the musicians themselves; it happens as this music prompts them to interact as the sort of citizens the American Constitution demands people be: strong individuals combined in a common project they must sustain to serve their separate interests and their common purpose both at once. So, however diverse the interests of people who find themselves together, they share the necessary purpose of getting along. And there is more to "getting along" in what is at stake and what it takes than the phrase might lead us to think. To get along, individuals must change in response to each other, must listen as well as speak, and must learn as well as teach. They must revise and adapt. Kenneth Burke went a very long way toward describing how that happens, what can go wrong, and what it can be like when things go right. And what he described is more or less precisely what jazz enacts as this music is made in the kind of exchange of assertion and response that constitutes what Americans are taught to understand as civic interaction. Jazz music and Kenneth Burke never claimed each other as counterparts, as a theory and a practice of the same kind of thing, but they could have. Bring them together in that way, and in the substance and shape of the form of civic life that one models and the other describes, you can see the profound lessons in getting along they provide.

Throughout his life, Burke developed fresh conceptions of rhetoric and art that expand the reach of both by rendering them interdependent in the work that distinct and diverse individuals must do to get along. Explaining that was the focus of all of Burke's writing. Similarly, the music-making project of jazz proceeds from the very civic mandate that Americans' constitution demands, from the predicament people share when together they are charged to become *e pluribus unum*, the very form of life Burke tried to show us how to manage. To play jazz, musicians must be both distinctly themselves and one with an ensemble, because this music demands both their cooperation and their separate distinction. So sometimes musicians with little in common beyond a tacit agreement to submit for a time to the constraints of this kind of music making find themselves together on a bandstand. And that's enough. They decide on matters of process—tune and chord changes, key and rhythm, order of participation—and then proceed to make music moment by moment from the pooled resources that each one has brought. Like most every other music, a performance of jazz enacts a community, but the community this music enacts is one that demands greater individuality. To make jazz, musicians must change and adapt to each other, making judgments all along about what is and is not good for the music they are making. Watching jazz being made, we learn that *e pluribus unum* is more complicated than we might have thought. This book is about how jazz and Burke both explore those complications, how the demands of democratic culture prompted Burke to consider art rhetorical, and how jazz is an art form that turns toward lessons of civic life.

Constituting Identity

Kenneth Burke's statement about constitutions that starts this chapter describes as constitutional any situation that transforms the individuals it would encompass into the citizens it proclaims them to be. More precisely, constitutions prescribe for diverse people the attitudes and the actions that are substance of the identity, at once collective and individual, it would have each of them claim.[6] This project of substantiating of an "ought" is the core element of his "theory of constitutions in general"[7] that informs us that we are each subject to more constitutions than we might think. We live by the laws of our written constitutions, the ones that make their claim upon us explicit. But we also live our lives by other, implicit, constitutions. Both kinds of constitution are made from the same raw material, though: the situation shared by those to be constituted as a community. Burke called that situation the "Constitution-behind-the-Constitution"—or, sometimes, "beneath" it:[8] the given circumstances, mostly unchangeable, that both constrain and enable the sort of order that people can constitute there. One of those circumstances is the place: its physical characteristics as well as the histories that collide there. So the European immigrants who named the place they found "America" developed from what seemed a boundless land both an expansive individualism and a nagging sense of collective mission—for some sacred and for others secular—they felt destined to put to work there. Out of that situation came the aspiration of *e pluribus unum*, where each element checked and balanced the other, an aspiration they codified in the constitutions that would direct them in ways of life that could realize it.[9] Some of those ways of life are explicitly procedural, legalistic, or documentary. Many more, though, are embedded in shared experience, all but invisible. Jazz is one of those.

To call jazz "constitutional," in Kenneth Burke's sense of that term, is to claim that it shapes people's perceptions, aligns their aspirations, and directs their attitudes and actions. It is also to say that jazz is rhetorical. To say that is to suggest that music, even art, is rhetorical. And to say that will seem odd to anyone who understands the term "rhetoric" to refer to an act of persuasion that proceeds systematically from a stated set of good reasons. That's how we are taught to expect to encounter rhetorical attempts to influence us. We expect them to come at us frankly—as Burke put it, "from without." But Burke put it that way as he was proposing that our most powerful influences may well come to us "from within," at least seemingly so.[10] To explain the opportunities for, and the threats to, getting along that follow from that, he developed a powerful concept of rhetorical aesthetics that he first stated in print in 1924 and then elaborated over the next sixty-five years or so.[11]

Burke is difficult to categorize among American thinkers. Born near the turn of the twentieth century, he came into his own in his and his nation's twenties. And just as he was emerging as an important new voice in literary fiction and poetry, he began turning his published work toward criticism of a particularly rhetorical sort. This shift seems to have been in response to, among other things, the expanding capacity of mass media to influence his compatriots at a time of notable erosion of a sense of unity among Americans. By 1930 Burke was best known as a critic who explored the ways and means of rhetorical effect in his literature and music criticism, locating those arts in civic if not political contexts. This stance was notable at a time when, among writers and musicians at least, the idea that art had practical purposes and effects was unfashionable. During subsequent decades, Burke's civic concerns mounted as a relentless sequence of crises surrounding the Great Depression and World War II left him questioning whether Americans could ever do what their Constitution was calling them to do: pay constant and critical attention to any and every attempt to shape in them attitudes or actions that determined whom they understood themselves to be. To guide his fellow citizens in that project, Burke developed through those years a rich explanation of how a sense of identity is made and changed within communicative interactions of all sorts. This was his revision of conventional concepts of rhetoric that had much to say about how art affects the ways in which people think and act.

Jazz was also born with the American twentieth century. Its antecedent in African American communities was a pervasive, participatory music that people would improvise together on a strong rhythmic foundation. Jazz developed as elements of that music combined with bits and pieces of music from other Americans. It combined African rhythmic patterns, an African American intensity of expression, European instrumentation and convention, and the form of American popular song in a hybrid sound that became immediately recognizable as an expression of this unwieldy national culture. So from its beginning, jazz accommodated a national mandate that by now seems that it should be undeniable: that Americans in all their differences be accepted and respected as full participants in the civic endeavor of living and working together as a people. This music was distinctly American, as well, in the way it was made. Musicians skilled on their instruments, generally acquainted with a jazz sort of sound and fluent in chords and scales, can play good jazz by submitting themselves to what the music requires of them. Agreement on key, sequence, and rhythm is enough for them to begin. From there, they do what it takes to combine their separate voices in a coherent musical statement where separateness can be still heard. And they do so improvisationally, without knowing precisely what that statement, fully realized, will be.

Burke described how that process proceeds when he located aesthetic form not in the work of art itself, but in the experience that an encounter with it provides a person.[12] He explained that an aesthetic artifact takes form in the purposeful sequence of prompts it provides to move that person from one state of mind to another, with "state of mind" understood as integral to one's sense of identity.[13] So aesthetic form works on us like the plot of a story that comes to life for us as we see, hear, or read it. Plot moves us along with it by prompting expectations. If what comes after is what was expected, we remain in a state of mind that is mostly unchanged. But if something unexpected happens, we are surprised, even disturbed, and must choose whether to adapt and change perspective or reject the story altogether. That experience of change, whatever its extent, becomes the story for us.[14] For Burke, a work of art composes a sequence of these experiences. It's like music. Hear a dissonant chord or a harmonic progression that is incomplete; that's what anticipation sounds like, feels like. Burke once shared with a friend in a letter what "exquisite enjoyment" it was "to tantalize oneself with dissonances, and then resolve them" on the piano.[15] That enjoyment was not in the resolution alone, but also in what its anticipation required of him. A mystery novel offers the same sort of enjoyment as it leads us through increments of uncertainty and discomfort to a new comprehension of the whole situation. It is what we learn as we move through it from the changes we make that gives the narrative its substance. It's not the answers at the end we enjoy so much as the changes we make along the way.

Changes are why musicians like to play jazz, and why audiences like to hear it played. Jazz is music of changes—certainly of the chord sequence, which gives direction and structure to a tune, and which musicians call "the changes." But it is also a music made of the changes of plan and expectation that follow from the improvisations it requires of those who play it, changes that provide those who listen with surprise and challenge. The face and posture of one who plays jazz show the stress and the joy of that kind of change, as the smiles shared by those who listen show that satisfaction can follow from an encounter with something new. These are individuals progressing in harmony: something encouraging to witness and to experience. Maybe that's why people are often still smiling after a good jazz performance ends, why strangers speak to each other about the music as they move toward the doors, extending the feeling of this music that has taught them something about getting along.[16]

Constitutions, Explicit and Implied

"Getting along" is one way to describe what Aristotle designed his concept of rhetoric to help people do. In the Athens of his time, agreement was the currency of power shared among a ruling class—agreement that he thought ought to be established through disciplined, deliberative discussion. Aristotle did acknowledge other kinds of influence, though, like the profoundly rhetorical art of theater he described in his *Poetics*. But when we use the term "rhetoric" we don't often think about that. To most of us, "rhetoric" still means mostly the kind of influence that operates by direct and explicit proposition regarding what someone should believe and do. People who want others to agree with them, who want their cooperation, assumed in Aristotle's time and assume now that accomplishing that involves some sort of persuasive argument.

On his common-sense observation that getting along requires more than agreement alone, Kenneth Burke pronounced Aristotle's conception of rhetoric incomplete. Getting along requires people to find and even feel a connection with each other, to recognize something of themselves in each other. It is a felt sense of being bound together by some sort of commonality that opens us to the influence of others and to change. So Burke proposed a broad conception of rhetoric that includes direct persuasion but encompasses other communicative interaction as well. Change, after all, is what occurs when we communicate with each other. We can't help but come away comprehending things differently than we had, regardless of how small the change or its consequence.

What changes is some element of one's sense of self—self in the sense of how one understands things, and with whom one is partnered in comprehending the world. That's what is rhetorical.

Burke's point about rhetoric is that to be persuaded we must be able to identify ourselves with the persuader, to recognize in that identification some commonality of beliefs, values, or purposes. Such recognition binds people together. We can enable that recognition in each other by what Burke called "deliberate design," but there are other ways, indirect and even, as he put it, "unconscious." We encounter those subtler prompts almost constantly and sometimes even seek them out, "earnestly yearn[ing]," as we tend to do, "to identify [ourselves] with one group or another" as compensation for the alienation we feel in the face of very "real differences or divisions."[17] For Americans, doing just that is a matter of civic duty. That "the individual identity is formed by reference to his membership in a group,"[18] as Burke put it, is what their Constitution counts on.

Burke discussed all this in explicitly civic terms in the section of *A Grammar of Motives* that he titled "A Dialectic of Constitutions." Written constitutions direct us in substantiating the "oughts" they would have us together embody by prescribing ways of interaction that, for the period of that action, transform us into citizens. As prescribed in the American Constitution, those interactions are rhetorical in the conventional sense of deliberate attempts at persuasion that set to work shaping identity. That Constitution would have Americans understand themselves as "a *plurality* acting as a *unity*" in a project of making what it proclaims "ought to be" in their nation into "what is."

Burke noted that a constitution expressing the "fundamental, organic law or principles of government of a nation, state, society, or other organized body of men" can be "embodied in written documents" *or* can be "implied in the institutions and usages of the country or society."[19] Either way, the work at hand is to "[suggest] what coordinates one will think by." An explicit constitution states those coordinates, while one that is implicit in a community's "institutions and usages" makes them available for individuals to experience. The writer Ralph Ellison was a close reader of Burke who used the concept of implicit constitutions to respond to a young African American scholar who once asked him if he didn't agree that "'the Harlem Renaissance failed because we failed to create institutions to preserve our gains.'" The "we" he was referring to was African-Americans, and no, Ellison didn't agree. "'We *do* have institutions," Ellison said. "We have the Constitution and the Bill of Rights. *And we have jazz.*'"[20] That young scholar, Robert G. O'Meally, later recounted the exchange to introduce the collection he published of Ellison's writings on music. Jazz, he wrote, is "an institution in the sense of that word's Latin root, *statuere*: 'to put in place' or 'to stand' "—the very Latin that Burke had used to introduce his discussion of constitutions in *A Grammar of Motives*.[21] "With its insistence on individuality of sound . . . and on the capacity to swing with and against one's fellow players; its accents on improvisation and readiness for changes; and its connections with the comedy laced by tragedy that defines the blues," O'Meally explained, "jazz is a musical language that reminds us what and where we are as US citizens. . . ."[22] This is civic jazz.

If a constitution is, as Burke said, "a structure of motivation" that "propounds certain desires, commands, or wishes," and if it does so as if "by the first person to the second person" in order to "[lay] down the environment for future acts,"[23] then jazz is indeed constitutional. Among Americans, at least, jazz can operate rhetorically as what Burke called an " 'idealistic anecdote' " that expresses a "Constitutional wish."[24] At its best, this music resolves conflicts between individual and collective, resistance and cooperation, and division and communion by placing each opposition in the service of a common project. So it asserts individuality *in* community rather than against it, privileging diversity in order to advance unity, and realizing *e pluribus unum* in the process—at least for the time it takes to play the tune. To participate in that process onstage, or at the one remove that is a seat in the audience, is to encounter the American identity that "ought" to be: the identity that Ellison remembered encountering among the African American musicians who passed through the Oklahoma City of his childhood:

> Their driving motivation was neither money nor fame, but the will to achieve the most eloquent expression of idea-emotions through the technical mastery of their instruments . . . and the give and take, the subtle rhythmical shaping and blending of idea, tone and imagination demanded of group improvisation. The delicate balance struck between strong individual personality and the group during those early jam sessions was a marvel of social organization. I had learned too that the end of all this discipline and technical mastery was the desire to express an affirmative way of life through its musical tradition, and that this tradition insisted that each artist achieve his creativity through its frame.[25]

In 1945, deep in the writing of *Invisible Man*, Ellison posted a fan letter to Kenneth Burke.[26] He wanted to thank Burke for freeing him to make "writing" and "politics" inseparable, to write a novel that was art and rhetoric both at once.[27] "My greatest debt to you," he told Burke, "lies in your courage in taking a position and making your 'counter-statement.'"[28] *Counter-Statement* is the book that presented Burke's challenge to the proudly impractical aesthetic that had prevailed in American art and criticism for some time. Burke issued that challenge by proposing his profoundly rhetorical theory of aesthetic form that treats art as assertion of influence, and that focuses on its effect. Art is always a matter of form, but the form which matters in art is that of the experience it provides for those who encounter it. That experience is immersive, emotional as much as intellectual, even spiritual when it lets two or more people feel themselves transcending the differences that divide them for a moment or two. Rather than showing us something or even explaining it, art enables us to inhabit it. Ellison's childhood memory of the jazz he heard coming up from the open doors of bars along the street describes how the music worked on him in terms that apply to the effect of art in general: it "gets beneath the skin and works into the very structure of one's consciousness."[29] That's the rhetorical power of aesthetic experience: its "ability," as Burke put it, "to make us feel such shifts of attitude not merely from without but from within."[30] Sharing that experience with others, we can locate ourselves "as a person in groups or movements"[31] around us, identifying ourselves anew. "Only the arts," Burke added, "can saturate themselves with such changes of attitude imaginatively, personally."[32]

Quoting

When they improvise, jazz musicians often "quote" from other musicians whose phrases their listeners will recognize. Quotes provide those listeners with points of connection to what they already know, which can help them find a place for themselves in new, unfamiliar music. Just as important, though, quoting honors those who have come before by acknowledging debts. I do that kind of quoting throughout the chapters that follow. But sometimes quotes aren't enough. Sometimes a musician needs to explain something about the music, about where it comes from, before performing it. So what follows in this chapter is my explanation of where this book has come from.

This exploration of the civic work of jazz has roots in a broader inquiry into art as aesthetic expression *and* rhetorical effect. I explore jazz in that context as an art that not only expresses the identities of individuals and cultures but also shapes them. To explain how that happens, I rely on Burke's thoroughgoing rhetorical aesthetic and his insistent point that the rhetorical power he finds pervasive in our experience, particularly in art as broadly defined, demands of those who encounter it close attention and a persistent practice of critique. I read Burke as developing that point throughout his work, operating as something of a civic theorist who would educate Americans in their ongoing constitutional project, recognizing in their interactions what to embrace and what to resist, what to confront and what to let go by.

On Music in Particular, and Art in General

In his *Politics* Aristotle worried about "the effect of music," asking: "Must we not rather regard music as a stimulus to virtue capable of making a certain kind of character?" Kenneth Burke would ask that kind of question much later about rhetoric and identity. After working his question through for a few pages, Aristotle could conclude that "it follows from all this that music has indeed the power to induce a certain character of the soul. . . ."[33] That music can affect identity is explicit here, though Aristotle didn't develop that concept of rhetorical effect in what we have of his *Rhetoric*. Still, reading what he did develop there, we can see that something like the shaping of identity was at the heart of Aristotle's conception of rhetoric. But it is only in this brief discussion of music in his *Politics* that the suggestion becomes explicit.

Burke's contemporary, Suzanne Langer, picked up something of that thread when she wrote that "the great office of music is to organize our conception of feeling into more than an occasional awareness of emotional storm," and, in doing so, to connect that feeling "intimately and self-evidently to life"[34]—a statement that clarifies a bit of what Aristotle might have been getting at. Our contemporary, Mark Johnson, has picked up that line of thought too, using music to explain how a rhetoric that shapes identity might proceed. Johnson writes: "Music captures us, carries us along on a sensuous, rhythmic, tonal adventure" for a while, "and then deposits us, changed, in a different place from where we started."[35] Read this as a vivid description of Burke's concept of form in action, and you'll see music as rhetorical and how, quite specifically, it influences identity. Daniel Levitin has described what is at stake here in terms that follow from his studies of brain science. "We surrender to music when we listen to it—we allow ourselves to trust the composers and musicians with a part of our hearts and our spirits," he writes. "We let the music take us somewhere outside of ourselves." It is as if, Levitin confesses, we are allowing the musicians "inside" us, allowing them "to control our emotions and even our politics—to lift us up, to bring us down, to comfort us, to inspire us." And then he puts us on notice, as Burke would, to be wary: we don't often leave ourselves "so vulnerable with a total stranger."[36]

In almost any well conceived and performed aesthetic encounter there is, according to Burke, potential for this kind of transcendent effect, whether it works on people for better or for worse. The reach of that effect was extended through the twentieth century by mass media that made "art," in that term's broadest conception, available to disparate and diverse Americans who might have little else in common, by providing them with increasingly vivid experiences of what could present itself as a national culture. And though he probably didn't have jazz in mind, Burke could have had it in mind when he described the sort of art at work in this context as being so "thoroughly integrated with the national life" that it "must represent, form, confirm, utilize, and project the national values, ideals, and expectancies." That's a constitutional statement of art's civic work. Rather than making a political or ideological argument, art wields its influence most of the time in what Burke called a "'Whitmanesque'" way: offering palpable images of an American way of life that enacts its "oughts" rather than asserting them. And in making such art, artists take on a civic role not unlike the one Walt Whitman claimed for himself in his poetry: a representative citizen "'be[ing] himself'" while at the same time "act[ing] as a public spokesman. . . ."[37]

It may be necessary that artists of every sort do this in the United States. Read in response to the fact that some Americans may have little in common beyond their residence within the same boundaries, *e pluribus unum* is a summons calling them all to civic action, but precisely what that action can be is ambiguous. It might be this ambiguity, combined with their insistent urge to direct each other, that leads Americans to enlist even their art in the rhetorical project of promulgating the particular way of life that they would have everyone share. The need for such sharing has always been pressing in America. As he surveyed the rubble of the first republic in the aftermath of the Civil War, Whitman articulated the primary national fact: the absence of, in his terms, a "common skeleton," a "reliable identity" shared by the citizens of the nation. In 1871 it looked to him as though politics and government had demonstrated themselves inadequate to the task of providing that. So Whitman announced that he was looking to American art for that function.[38] A few decades later, Kenneth Burke came to see things much the same way, observing that any "complex social organization" must be "maintained by a state of mind," and that states of mind must be "constructed out of art."[39] A few decades more, and Terry Eagleton, that persistent student of America, would locate art "at the very root of social relations" as "the source of all human bonding," and would write that only by means of an "imaginative exchange" that enables "appropriation of each other's identities" can diverse individuals ever unite in common cause. So art *must* do rhetorical work but, Eagleton added, "if the aesthetic must bear the burden of human community, then a political society . . . must leave a good deal to be desired."[40] That's precisely what Kenneth Burke had come to think as early as 1930, and why he attended so closely to the rhetorical power of art.

On Jazz

The idea that jazz might do this kind of rhetorical work helps explain what Ralph Ellison might have had in mind when he said that "we know much of jazz as entertainment, but a mere handful of clichés constitutes our knowledge of jazz as experience."[41] One of those clichés is what got me into all this. It began when, at a concert of what was then the Lincoln Center Jazz Orchestra, I heard Wynton Marsalis say that jazz is the sound of democracy and then use the next two hours of music to show some of the ways that is so. Marsalis is not the only one in jazz who has said something like that. Most of the musicians I have talked to in the years since find compelling ideas about freedom, equality, and cooperation to be inherent in jazz. But Marsalis may be the most insistent and explicit. "Great [jazz] musicians," he writes, "demonstrate a mutual respect and trust on the bandstand that can alter your outlook on the world and enrich every aspect of your life . . . from individual creativity and personal relationships to the way you conduct business and understand what it means to be a global citizen in the most modern sense."[42] That is because "jazz . . . reminds you that you can work things out with other people. It's hard, but it can be done." By playing jazz, and even by listening to it well, you come to understand "*the importance of expressing the core of your unique feelings*" as you develop, at the same time, "*the willingness to work things out with other people.*" Doing that is the work of everyday life, particularly when life is lived upon democratic assumptions. "When a group of people try to invent something together, there's bound to be a lot of conflict," he says. "Jazz urges you to accept the decisions of others. Sometimes you lead, sometimes you follow," and that exchange is a satisfying way to "make something out of whatever happens—to make something together and *be* together."[43]

Other jazz musicians have offered similar lessons. For example, implications of Bill Evans's well-known statement that "jazz is not a what, it is a how" resonate through the chapters that follow. "If [jazz] were a what, it would be static, never growing," Evans said. "The how is that the music comes from the moment, it is spontaneous, it exists at the time it is created." In a democratic culture in which people presume themselves equal and, so, cooperation is necessary, civic participation must proceed along these lines.[44] Duke Ellington once answered a question about his own artistic purposes in terms that stated very simply the very kind of getting along that Evans implied. "I play for the audience," he said, for the purpose of providing them an experience that was, in his words, "rather like that word 'swing': when two people are together, and my pulse and your pulse are together, then they're swinging."[45] Here Ellington refers to "swing" as the organic syncopation characteristic of much of the music that members of a jazz ensemble must sustain together. That is difficult because you can't really count out the rhythm of that rhythmic pattern. You have to feel it and hope that others feel it with you. So Ellington's intimate description points beyond rhythm alone. Marsalis helps us see where it pointed when he says that swing is the "how" of jazz. "Swing demands three things," he writes. First, "it requires extreme coordination, because it is a dance with other people who are inventing steps as they go." So it requires participants to sustain each other in this rigorously intuitive rhythm they can't maintain together by will alone. They must sustain it through every uncertain moment of their improvisation. That's true of this particular sort of swing, but it's also true of swing in the sense that is an essential element of any music we call jazz: the rhythm of insistent momentum that is a sonic symbol of getting somewhere new, of progress. Submitting yourself to that rhythm, as Marsalis puts it, "tests your inner resources; it can make you question who you are, make you reach deeper, make you respond more freely," perhaps as a new and better sort of self. This requires individuals and groups to change—perhaps the most vibrant form of getting along.[46]

It's common for jazz musicians to treat jazz as rhetorical in the sense that they compare the music to conversation. In his extensive study of jazz improvisation, Paul Berliner describes an improvised ensemble performance as "a musical conversation" to be maintained among the performing musicians as well as with their "predecessors within the jazz tradition." And it's a conversation that must encompass each player's own "inner dialogue" about his or her place both in the particular group and the music in general.[47] That's why, as Berliner also notes, many musicians who consider playing jazz to be "moral and ideological" action even think about their musical performance as a way to "make a mark on a world plagued by social conflict and preoccupied with materialistic values."[48] Nicholas Gebhardt expresses a similar understanding in terms that point jazz toward an identity rhetoric like Burke's when he insists that "the meaning and value of the jazz act is inseparable from . . . the changing character of the musician's social and political relations."[49] The way musicians embody those relations and give them voice, and the place in the community that expresses them, are, as he puts it, "deeply ideological."[50]

Ingrid Monson offers a broader image of jazz performance as a fully formed civic parable. "A small jazz band," she writes, "provides a framework for musical interaction among players who take as their goal the achievement of a groove or feeling." So playing the music is a matter of each individual making musical choices that combine in "a satisfying musical whole."[51] Upon that generalization, she then cuts to the core of the civic problem:

> There is an inherent tension within the jazz ensemble between the individual and the group. On the one hand, the aesthetic of the music is centered on the inventiveness and uniqueness of individual solo expression; on the other, climactic moments of musical expression require the cohesiveness and participation of the entire ensemble. In an improvisational music, such as jazz, the interaction between the group and individual greatly affects the ultimate composition and development of the music.[52]

The lesson of her parable becomes clear when Monson follows that description with a suggestion that we consider jazz improvisation "an apt metaphor for more flexible social thinking" that would require people in any situation to do the equivalent of "listening to the whole band if you ever expect to say something."[53] As Gebhardt puts it, "The meaning and value of the jazz act is inseparable from . . . the changing character of the musician's social and political relations."[54] Since those relations are themselves essential elements of one's ever-developing identity, it is only in the process of careful listening that saying something that matters enough to others to prompt them to change becomes possible.

On America

Identity, said Ralph Ellison, is "*the* American theme."[55] That's because much of what Americans do share doesn't combine into common identity. What they share are expectations of an equality and freedom that individually they can't fully enact, as well as aspirations to a unity and community that collectively they can't fully realize. This predicament follows from what historian Ann Douglas calls a "tangible and unique mission concocted of unlimited natural resources, theological obsessions, a multiracial and polyglot population, and unparalleled incentives and opportunities for democratization and pluralism" that is their common inheritance.[56] That makes life in America, in the archaic terms from William James to which Douglas turns, "a plural and heterogeneous affair of simultaneous affects" that individuals must improvise together out of what they can share: a " 'will to personate.' "[57] That "plural and heterogeneous affair of simultaneous affects" is the aggregate of separate striving, and the will to "personate" is an insistence that shared identity be realized in the image of the American imagining it.[58] Personations are proposals, enacted rather than articulated, of what the identity shared by the collective ought to be. In its native diversity, America encompasses many of those but has no good way of adjudicating among them. No wonder Whitman couldn't find what he was looking for.

Issues like this are explored in poetry and prose about jazz that tries to articulate what the music lets us feel. For T. J. Anderson, the project of this body of American literature is to "testify" to the difficulty of performing conflict and conformity both at once.[59] Reading across these texts is an encounter with what he calls "the united testimony of the community."[60] What that testimony expresses is, as Anderson puts it, an "attitude."[61] And for Kenneth Burke, attitude is much of what identity is made of. "Personal identity comes to a focus," he wrote, "in the complex of attitudes . . . that constitute the *individual's* sense of orientation," of one's location in relation to others and the circumstances they share.[62] An eloquent description of how that is so, of the particular ways in which individual identities are not only interdependent but also enmeshed in tensions of attitude, is James Baldwin's story "Sonny's Blues," which we can read as a study of the development of identity in the context of shattered relationships that only profound changes of individual attitudes can repair.

Langston Hughes wrote about that sort of thing too, and in one phase of his career he wrote quite deliberately toward the purpose of changing Americans' attitudes about race. During the 1950s he supported himself at least partially by writing five children's books for the Franklin Watts *First Books* series that was filling the bookshelves of young baby boomers across the nation. The purpose of the series, as stated clearly on the jacket of every book, was this: "When boys and girls FIRST start asking *why?* . . . *what?* . . . and *how?* FIRST BOOKS are the <u>first books</u> to read on any subject."[63] So Hughes wrote *The First Book of Negroes* (1952), *The First Book of Rhythm* (1954), The *First Book of Jazz* (1955), *The First Book of the West Indies* (1956), and *The First Book of Africa* (1960), each offering gentle descriptions of aspects of African America to "kids" he knew were most likely white.[64] In his *First Book of Jazz,* Hughes located the music's roots in the rhythmical songs that hardworking people would sing in order "to work together better."[65] Illustrations accompanying that phrase depicted those people as black, with tools in their hands that suggested slavery, as the words themselves turned the work song toward the kinder idea that singing together in rhythm helps bind individuals together in their separate efforts. What Hughes didn't explain to these children about the work song was the loss and pain it expressed. Rather, he described the jazz music that he told them had developed from it as a kind of music played "as one feels like playing . . . for fun at that particular moment," as a "happy sound that makes people want to get up and move in time to the rhythms."[66] Hughes didn't tell them the rest. But he did try to prompt attitudes about this music that might open the way for those children to recognize something of themselves in those hard workers and their descendants, to see them as fellow citizens with whom they could share common ground.

On Kenneth Burke

Kenneth Burke's concept of a rhetorical aesthetic is what holds this book together. It's a concept that combines not only art and rhetoric but also identity and experience in ways that offer insight into how we influence and change. So Burke's theory of aesthetic form describes how people adapt themselves to each other's portrayals of the way things are, how an "*individual's* sense of orientation (sense of 'reality,' with corresponding sense of relationships)" can be transformed each time situations demand that the alignments and attitudes that give identity so much of its shape must be changed.[67] Similarly, Burke's concept of rhetoric treats identity as the "substance" of ourselves that we make from our "motives" that, in their moments of change, must "shift" both self and society.[68] "Our basic principle," he wrote early on in a statement that can contain all his work, "is our contention that all symbolism can be treated as the ritualistic naming and changing of identity," a necessary process that proceeds as "a man fits himself for a role in accordance with established coordinates or for a change of role in accordance with new coordinates which necessity has forced upon him."[69] This changing and fitting can occur in response to direct persuasion, to an assertion of terms that are primarily conceptual and abstract as conventional rhetoric prescribes. But it can also occur through the responses that constitute the form of an experience that an artist has composed. We communicate by symbols, necessarily, but we best comprehend the meaning of those symbols in the "arousing and fulfilling of desires" they prompt in us—an experience that is lived and not symbolic at all.[70] That's the first step in the process of finding for oneself a fit in a shared situation.

The next step is change. It helps to understand, as Burke put it, that "one's notion of . . . personal *identity* may involve identification not just with mankind or the world in general, but [with] some kind of congregation that also implies related norms for differentiation and segregation."[71] And "identity" for Burke, as Timothy Crucius suggests, is not a state of being but a "process, a social, symbolic, linguistic process."[72] Dana Anderson describes it as a process of "articulating 'who I am' " in ways that can "address, and perhaps even transform, the scenes it inhabits and the other selves therein."[73] That's what making jazz is for those who perform it, and what "saying something" requires of them: contributing substantially to the highly disciplined, intensely collaborative project of ensemble improvisation. It marks in the music they are making with others the moments when a new identity, their own and maybe even a shared one, "*comes to be*," as Anderson puts it.[74]

Burke wrote *Counter-Statement* to confront the fact that "the artist discovers himself not only with a message but also with a desire to produce effects upon his audience."[75] After all, as Jack Selzer explains in direct reference to Burke, art develops out of artists' "emotional need to articulate emotional states" and "evoke emotion in their audiences."[76] When Selzer and Ann George note that Burke generally used the term "artist" to describe those who practice "art in its widest aspects," including "an *art of living*," they point to the fact that Burke would always "treat art not as self-contained or self-expression but as a socially engaged moral and civic force"—as, in their phrase, "a form of civic action."[77] And often, when you read what Burke wrote about these matters, it seems as if he might have had music in mind. He did study music intently as a young man, and he was for a time deeply conflicted about whether to devote his career to music or literature.[78] Even as a middle-aged man deep in a career in letters, Burke would still improvise on the baby grand that dominated his living room almost daily in search, he once suggested, of his own identity. "For several hours a week," he wrote Malcolm Cowley, "I pound away at these, thus indirectly repeating, 'I am I,' until I wonder who I am. . . ."[79]

And there is much in his work about music. Debra Hawhee's study of Burke's early music criticism focuses on what he called "the appeal of form," that rhetorical aesthetic he explained in *Counter-Statement* most vividly in terms of rhythm. "A rhythm is a promise which the poet makes to the reader," Burke wrote there, "and in proportion as the reader comes to rely upon this promise, he falls into a state of general surrender that makes him more likely to accept without resistance the rest of the poet's material." Burke went on to say that this pattern applies as well to other "sounds" that offer "analogy to actual movement, since sounds may rise and fall, and in a remote way one rises and falls with them." This—in Burke's vivid terms, which Hawhee finds and quotes—reaches toward "one's 'muscular imagination' "[80] and so "lays us open."[81] Jeffrey Carroll's extensive study of music as it appears throughout Burke's work attends to what I consider a civic consequence of that effect.[82] Carroll finds Burke treating music rhetorically, as analogous to oratory. After all, Carroll writes, music and oratory are both "device[s] of the moment to capture the spirit not of the composer's mind, not of the form's own capacities, but of the dreams and wishes of the audience." And he finds all this implicit in Burke's statement that "music deals minutely in frustrations and fulfillments of desire." That is how art operates as what Burke called a sort of "waking dream" in which audience is the dreamer and artist the manager of "the conditions which determine this dream." In this way the artist becomes "manipulator of blood, brains, heart, and bowels which, while we sleep, dictate the mould of our desires"—a virtuoso of influence and rhetorical effect.[83]

Calling the Tune

A band sets up and an audience assembles. Then someone calls the tune. Each musician can play it his or her way, as long as each one adjusts and adapts that way to the evolving ensemble sound. We watch and listen, and we might even learn something new about how to hold ourselves together. It's not the harmonies, the chord changes, the shared rhythms that keep this music from flying apart. It's the attitude with which jazz musicians play it. Kenneth Burke would call that attitude "piety," his name for a "desire to round things out, to fit experiences together into a unified whole."[84] While that sort of piety might be innate in all of us, most of the time we suppress it. But when jazz musicians do that, their music doesn't come together. If the jazz is going to work, if it is going to provide its audience with a coherent and moving experience, piety must dominate ego. That, as the essence of the identity being shared by the group, is what makes good jazz possible at all.

It may be this attitude of piety, this motive to make things whole and complete, that gives art its power. Art is inherently rhetorical to the extent that it addresses others and aims at effect. But its rhetoric becomes compelling for others when the art brings to life in them the idea that, in the face of constant fragmentation and creeping incoherence, people can bring order and purpose to their life together. Burke hinted at something like that in "The Calling of the Tune," his essay on the economics of art's effect. He opened the essay with this statement: "A piper who had insisted upon the right to call his own tunes became unhappy when everyone began saying to him, 'I don't care what tune you play.' He discovered that he wanted them to care tremendously. . . ."[85] Ultimately, that desire has little to do with economics. It has to do with a sense of something like a calling to move others toward a better life. To matter to people, art must address the potential that is inherent within them to progress. Burke once wrote, "The artist, as spokesman, does not merely represent his subject; nor does he merely represent himself; he also represents his [audience], in the sense in which a legislator is said to represent his constituents."[86] A good legislator works to bring dissonance into harmony, contention into cooperation, toward the end of enabling constituents to realize some aspect of their collective potential. It is in that sort of work that art is not only rhetorical, but also civic in purpose and effect.

Something like that is what Ralph Ellison had in mind when he said that jazz does constitutional work. And Stanley Crouch has explained how that is so, in terms that treat jazz as something that can remind us of "grand human possibility with the same clarity that it does human frailty."[87] The provision of amending the Constitution reminds us of that, calling upon those it would constitute to improvise their own solutions to emerging problems. So to accommodate change, Americans can change their Constitution in what Crouch describes as an exercise of the "freedom to constantly reinterpret the meanings"[88]—I'll add the identities—it provides them. "Perhaps no society so significant has emerged over the last five centuries that has made improvisation so basic to its sensibility," Crouch concludes.[89] Jazz works in the same way, operating on "an aesthetic rejection of the preconceptions that stifle individual and collective invention"[90] that are necessary to advance the "ought" of unity in diversity in America and continue the process of developing among us a better form of life.

This is the tune I have called. It might resonate at this time when civic life in America seems more a struggle than usual. I'll play this tune out a little like jazz, moving it forward in something like the way Burke described aesthetic form. Discussions of Burke's ideas will lead into discussions of jazz, stories about jazz will connect to explanations of America, explorations of civics will develop into descriptions of getting along.

The next chapter, "A Rhetorical Aesthetic of Jazz," further explains Kenneth Burke's experiential concept of aesthetic form as a way in which people influence each other to change. Any encounter with art takes the form of experience, and as we know, experience affects how people think and feel, how they understand themselves in their circumstances. This is identity being made and maintained—for Burke, the project of rhetoric. Chapter 3, "What Jazz Is," locates that project in the moments of participation that constitute diverse people as community, and presents jazz-making as a model for civic participation of a very American sort. Chapter 4, "Where Jazz Comes From," examines the tension of individual and community that is persistent throughout American cultural history, so that we can understand how that conflict can be made constructive. Jazz and Burke both suggest that resolving the conflict is not the goal. The goal is to learn that sometimes we can understand opposition as interdependence. Chapter 5, "What Jazz Does," uses Burke's work to examine jazz as a response to constraints and opportunities among Americans who tend to embrace democratic privileges but resist democratic responsibilities. Jazz not only models productive democratic interaction but also practices it, doing at times its own political work. Chapter 6, "How Jazz Works," explains jazz as a sort of summons toward an individual way of life that is necessarily communal, and explores how the same sort of summons comes from Kenneth Burke's work. Chapter 7, titled "So What?" brings jazz and Burke together to show how they both matter. Both focus on the ways people identify themselves, separately and together, as they participate in what is the primary civic act: getting along.

Kenneth Burke lived his long life through a century that seemed to him made of mostly dark times. But you can read what he wrote during that long life as an ongoing reminder to his American contemporaries, as well as to himself, that for all the disappointment, injustice, and sorrow, there remains in America "also the humanity of our people, the fountain of good will that keeps welling up anew. And with this we would be identified, with this we *must* be identified."[91] Jazz reminds us of that as well.

TWO

A Rhetorical Aesthetic of Jazz

Once you grasp the trend of the form, it invites participation regardless of the subject matter. Formally, you find yourself swinging along.[1]

KENNETH BURKE

The statement above picks up Kenneth Burke midtheory, at the place where for him the rhetorical and the aesthetic combine. The insight that we communicate best by reaching beyond statements of concept to provide each other with experience, though he didn't put it quite that way, is Burke's center of gravity. In *Counter-Statement,* Burke used the term "experience" in ways that aligned with what, at about the same time, John Dewey was calling "*an* experience" in *Art as Experience*. "Experience" is a continuous "inchoate" flow, while "*an* experience" is something "composed" in a way that develops meaning and purpose as it "runs its course to fulfillment."[2] That is the core idea of Dewey's aesthetic theory. If art is experience given meaningful and coherent form, then, engaged as we always are in making sense of things, we are all being artists all the time. Those whom we call "artists" distinguish themselves from the rest of us by doing this common work with uncommon insight and elegance. By Burke's theory of aesthetic form we are also all artists, but Burke focuses on the fact that we are as intent upon communicating our sense of things to others as we are on making that sense for ourselves. That makes his concept of art rhetorical in a way that Dewey's is not: "Experience is less the *aim* of art than the *subject* of art," Burke said, so that "art is not *experience*, but *something added* to experience."[3] That "something," his theory of aesthetic form suggests, is a pathway through experience for others to follow. In Burke's other words, art's rhetorical work is to get people "swinging along" through the experience an artifact offers. It's unlikely that Burke had jazz in mind when he used the phrase "swinging along." But because jazz claims to work on us in precisely that way, I consider his use of it to describe the effect of aesthetic form fortunate for my purpose, and in this chapter I may as well follow it to where it leads.

You could say jazz is made by ensembles of individualists. Early jazz—sometimes dubbed "Dixieland," but better described as New Orleans music—was played by people who brought their distinct voices together in a simultaneous improvisation that involves something like weaving separate solos together all at once. Louis Armstrong learned to play jazz this way, but soon began separating his solos out so they could be more distinctly heard. But through his years as the preeminent soloist in jazz, Armstrong always held himself accountable to the collaborative flow of the ensemble and his solos were always integral to the sound of the whole band. On that set of values, jazz took on the shape of turn taking, of passing the solos around, calling on each musician to step forward for a time and then back again in alternating soloist and accompanist roles. Players in the band were still improvising, and simultaneously, but in ways that made space in the music for individuals to tell their own separate stories. For all the great soloists who mark the high points of jazz according to its canonical history, jazz is hardly jazz at all if it is not played with others. So when the pianist Bill Evans made a solo album, he overdubbed his own tracks to make a trio performance and called the album *Conversations with Myself*. Even playing alone, jazz remained, for him, a project of "swinging along."[4]

Characteristic of jazz is the fact that the mandate to swing along extends to those who listen. In a classical concert people listen by sitting still; listening to jazz, people move along with the music. To witness discrete individuals combining together in ways that create music that could not be composed, performed, or even imagined alone is to move along with them and to share in the surprises that make them smile. At its best, the experience shared by a jazz audience feels like a kind of communion, a renewal of commitment and conviction that people really can, as jazzman Loren Schoenberg put it with profound simplicity, "get along."[5]

Kenneth Burke used the phrase "swinging along" to denote giving the self over to the experience of an aesthetic form. Used in the context of jazz, that same phrase would describe the effect of the infectious rhythmic groove—whether it is technically a swing beat or not. It's what holds the music together, however extensively the music is improvised, and what that gives listeners is a sense of forward momentum in response to which, most of the time, they can't help but physically move. In principle, these two versions of the phrase really describe the same thing: getting along. Socially, getting along requires suspending distrust, overcoming resistance, and letting yourself join with others while you are still uncertain just where things will go. It is a democratic sort of choice, intimate and interpersonal and only eventually a practice of politics. It's the basis on which people who acknowledge each other as more or less equal and more or less free consent to work together, regardless of what else might divide them. Musically, it's what keeps the music coming, an aural and physical manifestation of a faith that people can indeed continue to make music together from one moment to the next and keep that music coherent as they move it along. Because jazz improvisation is always a confrontation with uncertainty, faith at the front end is the best we can do until we can look back at the fact of the music we've played or heard. It's not hard to apply all this to social and civic life. Watching and hearing it happen in jazz, it's hard not to. That's how this music can help people keep believing that they can live and work together after all.

Americans are generally not well prepared for such swinging along. Most of us are enculturated as soloists who must to learn how to improvise with others. That's why we are taught at school the social science of civics and some of the social arts of working and playing together. Still, what we come out of school knowing about civics and citizenship is mostly the political part. To become the kind of people that jazz suggests we can be requires climbing onto a learning curve that is as slippery as it is steep. But the music can help us. As Marcus Roberts puts it, jazz proposes that people can live honestly and harmoniously together despite their differences. It's a proposal he asserts without words each time he performs. For Roberts—as well as for his occasional ensemble partner, Wynton Marsalis—people make jazz together from the very materials of swing, with "swing" understood again here as that propulsive rhythmic pattern that is so intimate and organic that it is difficult to explain, and that requires selves giving up something for a group to maintain it. When the music is good, musicians and audiences feel in their bones and mark with their bodies that whatever has been required to get to that point is well worth giving. That's when you know, as Roberts puts it, that somehow "things are going to be ok."[6] But, as Marsalis reminds us, "it's hard to be truly swinging":

> Swing is all a question of how long you can maintain equilibrium with other musicians. Anyone can do it for one measure. But two or three minutes, or ten, that's a different story. You have to adjust to what everyone else plays whether you like it or not. Don't judge it or fight it. Work with it. Because the music is not going to stop for you to get your head right.[7]

Good jazz is made on the fly in response to this demand that individuals hold nothing of themselves back from the act of joining with others to make the music. It requires them to risk giving the self over to the music they are making together, music each one can help shape but cannot control. And in that situation, in Marsalis's words, "genius" can occur.[8]

This happened once at our own piano. The members of the Marcus Roberts Trio were at our table one winter night. With our thirteen-year-old daughter and two or three friends, we were hosting them for a quick dinner from our favorite Thai takeout after a long day in their short residency at the university where I work. They came late, slowed by shared head colds. Marcus was tired and quiet, but he brightened when he discovered our daughter. He began to quiz her about her interests in music. He learned that she had tried and given up piano and then violin, and was now trying jazz singing. When he asked about songs she knew, she told him that she'd been singing along with Natalie Cole on her *Unforgettable* album, particularly the uptempo standard "Route 66."[9] He got up from the table and had her guide him to the piano—Marcus is blind—and then told her to stand close by the bench. Then he began to play rich and elegant chord progressions that evolved out of quiet complexity into disquieting tension and then, as if in release, settled into the stable rhythm and familiar changes of a slow blues. By then we'd left the table and were sitting around the piano, moving with the music. None of us could hold still. Even Rebecca in all her adolescent selfconsciousness was beginning to move along with music as it gathered her up. Then, as Marcus approached the end of a chorus of blues changes with the emphatic clarity that signals a singer to be ready, she looked toward us wide-eyed for confidence. His accompaniment started her: "If you—get the chance—to motor West—Take the highway—travel my way—that's the best." Her voice was breathy, a little shaky, missing the pitch here and there. But as Marcus pushed her into the third line chord by chord, her voice found energy she didn't know she had: "Get your kicks, on Route 66!" That was when she began to forget herself. Her eyes closed and her voice strengthened. He brought her around to the second verse, through the part about winding from Chicago to LA, and then into the bridge, where she took off on her own momentum through St. Louie and Joplin, Missouri, and on through the Southwest to Kingman, Barstow, and San Bernardino. By the time they came back to the third and last verse, she and Marcus were a duo, swinging along deep in the same groove. When she sang, "Get your kicks, on Route 66!" that last time around, in her child's voice we could hear a woman.

What we heard emerge in our daughter's voice that night was something of the cheerful defiance that is always present in jazz that is played on the foundation of the blues. It's an assertion of the authority of your feelings, propelled by the courage that follows from the knowledge that someone else who is feeling and saying something similar is performing right there with you. Jazz *is* an act of hopeful defiance of the alienation and fear that makes us hold ourselves back to avoid judgment or rejection. It asserts an attitude that resides not in the tune or the lyrics, but in the performer—one that, most of the time, it's hard to muster all alone. So Marcus played through that song in a way that met our daughter exactly where she was and took her where she didn't know she could go. For Rebecca to find herself there, and for us to witness her there, was a moment of transcendence, of consummation. Both of these are Burke's words for the communicative experience toward which all of his work tried to get people to aim. So while he's considered primarily a literary and rhetorical theorist, consider him more than that as he maps the way toward insights that so easily slip out of our sight. We might even consider Burke's work an accompaniment of the sort that Marcus Roberts provided for our daughter: a composition, improvised from the circumstances we all share, that provides his compatriots with momentum and direction that they can begin to claim simply by swinging along.

The Civic Problem

In Kenneth Burke's concept, the rhetorical and the aesthetic—argument and art—necessarily combine, and in America they combine in the project of shaping individuals in the image of the interdependent independence that follows from their civic ideal of *e pluribus unum*. That so many Americans seem unwilling to claim that interdependence along with their independence, even to admit to it, has always been this nation's basic civic problem. Burke's work can be read as addressing that problem by describing how that interdependence works in ways that urge his readers to embrace it as well. On this reading, his primary concern seems to have been rhetorical in the sense of the ways in which influence works: how we influence others as well as how we are influenced. Burke's primary purpose seems to have involved helping individuals—and, for him, individuals of a particularly insistent American sort—change their cultural pattern by starting to think of themselves less as adversaries and more as compatriots. Read through Burke's work, including his various magazine articles, and you see that this was a pressing problem for him, living as he did in a nation that he saw fractured repeatedly by internal conflict.

To find ways to transform conflict into cooperation was an even more urgent matter for Ralph Ellison, who, with African Americans generally, suffered far more than Burke could the pain of such fracturing. If he read it, Burke must have embraced this image from Ellison of the dystopian civic life so persistent in the nation they shared:

> Beset by feelings of isolation because of the fluid, pluralistic turbulence of the democratic process, we cling desperately to our own familiar fragment of the democratic rock, and from such fragments we confront our fellow Americans in that combat of civility, piety, and tradition that is the drama of American social hierarchy. Holding desperately to our familiar turf, we engage in that ceaseless contention whose uneasily accepted but unrejectable purpose is the projection of an ever more encompassing and acceptable definition of our corporate identity as Americans.

What values and principles, beliefs and aspirations, can unify a people for whom the concepts of self and community so contradict? Ellison offered no answer. He could only consider the consequences that follow:

> Here the most agonizing mystery sponsored by the democratic ideal is that of our unity-in-diversity, our oneness-in-manyness. Pragmatically we cooperate and communicate across this mystery, but the problem of identity that it poses often goads us to symbolic acts of disaffiliation. So we seek psychic security from within our inherited divisions of the corporate American culture while gazing out upon our fellows with a mixed attitude of fear, suspicion, and yearning.

This is a portrait of an America in full compliance with what its Constitution seems to say but not with what it means, an image of a people so thoroughly engaged in contending over their differences that they fail to do what is required to provide the common ground for their community. That ground can only be found within the perimeter of their points of connection with each other, places that the rhetorical project Burke described as "identification" seeks and finds. Identification is, in his concept, what rhetoric does: work that is both intimate and interpersonal, public and civic, and rigorously so, because to identify with someone or something requires "differentiation and segregation" as well as sympathy and connection.[10] Each of us makes and remakes an identity by choosing to connect ourselves with this idea or that value and, of course, separating ourselves from others. You would think the separation is the hard part, but what worried both Burke and Ellison was that Americans seem far more adept at separation than they are at connection. For Ellison, the concept of cooperation was inherently dissonant, rather than more or less harmonious, as it seemed to be for Burke[11]—you don't need to read far into the work of either one to sense a sort of weariness with the persistent contention that saturated American life as they knew it. That both of them looked hard at the capacity of aesthetic experience to bring people together suggests that each, like Walt Whitman, may have already given up on argument as a way to prompt the practice of *e pluribus unum,* looking instead as Whitman did for what Ellison described as "a system of aesthetics capable of projecting our corporate, pluralistic, identity."[12]

Burke proposed such a system in his theory of aesthetic form. Here, in one of his clearest explanations, is how he described language having that rhetorical effect:

> For instance, imagine a passage built about a set of oppositions ("*we* do *this,* but *they* on the other hand do *that; we* stay *here* but *they* go *there; we* look *up,* but *they* look *down,*" etc.). Once you grasp the trend of the form, it invites participation regardless of the subject matter. Formally, you find yourself swinging along with the succession of antitheses, even though you may not agree with the proposition that is being presented in this form. . . . Thus, you are drawn to the form, not in your capacity as a partisan, but because of some "universal" appeal in it. And this attitude of assent may then be transferred to the matter which happens to be associated with the form.

What makes this sort of experience different from an encounter with rhetorical argument is that it is the form more than the content that calls for assent. Rather than addressing the reader, this kind of text engages her in "not merely receiving, but . . . creatively participating in the poet's or speaker's assertion." There is, of course, danger here. Burke warned that in any aesthetic encounter "you are drawn to the form" with an "attitude of assent" that "may then be transferred"—and without much critical attention—"to the matter which happens to be associated with the form." But if we learn to watch out for that, we will find that there is good to come from sharing such experience with others, not the least of which is the "awaken[ing of] an attitude of collaborative expectancy in us"[13] that binds us together with the others who share the experience.

That's how Burke theorized art doing the civic work of "projecting," and even promulgating, a shared identity. And it seems to be what Ellison was looking for when wrote that he sought "a system of aesthetics capable of projecting our corporate, pluralistic, identity."[14] But like Whitman before him, Ellison was looking for more than a theory. He was looking for a particular practice of art that would enact aesthetically an American identity engaged in an American way of collective life. Burke's own stated project was one level up in abstraction from that: to explain *how* art works to form a "corporate" identity in those who encounter it. Still, it seems Burke should have found in the jazz music Ellison proposed as the paradigmatic practice of American art a realization of his own theoretical project.

Jazz Civics

I noticed all this in Burke when I went looking for a rhetoric of jazz—an explanation of this music's form and effect. As a teen trying out who I might want to be, I found music on the upper end of the AM dial that sounded more subtle and substantial than the Top 40 that dominated the middle range, and I liked the feel of myself listening to it. So I became a casual jazz fan. But it wasn't until half a lifetime later, when I was thinking about a concept of "rhetorical experience,"[15] that I heard anything more than that in jazz. It was at a concert where trumpeter Wynton Marsalis was performing with the Lincoln Center Jazz Orchestra (now renamed the Jazz at Lincoln Center Orchestra) that I began to hear in the music what this book tries to describe. The JLCO is a jazz big band, and was made up that night of fifteen musicians: a rhythm section, of drummer, bassist, and pianist, and twelve horns: seven on brass and five on reeds. They played mostly jazz standards, improvised anew, of course, in that moment. Between the tunes, Marsalis would step to the microphone to provide a primer on the idea that jazz is the sound of democracy. That was when I began to recognize in the making of jazz music a model for democratic interaction, for democratic citizenship.

Good jazz is made as unique performers find in their very differences musical ways to get along. There is magic involved in that, as together they invent on the fly music that none of them could ever create or even imagine alone. They make that music out of the diverse individualities that they come to the bandstand prepared to express, identities that come willing to develop and even change in the process of playing. Jazz requires individual improvisation, of course, so it demands a profound sort of listening. Individual musicians listen to each other not just to stay together, but with the necessity of responding to each other, in ways flexible and fitting, on their minds. That is how what one musician plays is determined, at least partially, by what the others have played. The performance proceeds like a conversation, but not the casual sort of conversation in which people just bat around their ideas. This is a conversation among individuals who together must accomplish something then and there, who must make their way as a group through a problem that none of them can solve working alone. The trajectory of that kind of conversation can't be predicted, because it requires each participant to adapt and change, to play and say things not thought of before, as each tries to fit himself into the music being made. What can follow from that can seem like magic as the musicians end up playing as themselves but beyond themselves—as each finds elements of a new self, maybe a better self, in the process of playing with others. This is getting along of a transformational kind.

I learned at that concert not only that every musician is a soloist in jazz, but that every soloist plays jazz in the service of the group. Each jazz musician must make, from the very material of her differences and conflicts with the group, new things to play that can belong in the music they are making together. When that happens, the audience can witness a working community that draws upon each member's unique resources to advance the common project. In the process, of course, individual players advance their own aspirations as well. That is precisely what they have all prepared to do. And this is what differentiates playing jazz from most other sorts of getting along. On the bandstand the task at hand is delimited and the participants, however diverse, share a particular skill set, considerable knowledge, and a history to which they hold themselves accountable. Off the bandstand, people often have much less in common with regard to preparation and purpose, and the less people have in common, the harder it is for them to find ground upon which to base cooperation. Still, what jazz musicians do on the bandstand can teach the rest of us much about our predicament and our potential, together as well as individually.

So there is much to learn from a performance of jazz. Consider a 1958 recording of the mid-century standard "Autumn Leaves" on Cannonball Adderley's quintet album, *Somethin' Else*.[16] The tune begins with piano, bass, and drum marking out in distinct rhythm a dark harmony that is augmented after a few bars by a sequence of slightly syncopated chords, played brightly by horns repeatedly, to answer in counterpoint. On that introduction, Miles Davis's muted trumpet pushes out the first phrase of this ballad's familiar melody, made of four phrases of four ascending notes, each phrase starting a step below the last. Davis plays it fragile and restrained, his rendering spare and aching. "Autumn Leaves" is a song about loss, and Davis cuts the sorrow of the song deeper than any performance I have heard when he ends the first verse not on the resolving note you expect, but on an unexpected note that lies three half steps down. It doesn't resolve, leaving the wound of the tune open. Other than that single note, he plays the melody as written, embellished only by the rhythm of a hesitant swing. But that last note is emphatically of Davis, the man who went into heroin addiction and then out all alone, and who—while taking a break outside a midtown Manhattan club where he was playing, under a marquee that blazed his name onto 52nd Street—was beaten bloody by police for being black in America.

Then it is Adderley's turn. His arpeggios on the tune's chord changes pour over what Davis has just played, as if his alto is letting loose what the trumpet pent up. Adderley's improvisations are raw, his song of loss and sorrow energized by an almost hopeful sort of anger. It's as if there's no relief or resolution at all on the horizon but there is, in the meantime, virtuosity. Adderley plays some choruses and then Davis returns. They play their separate ways together through a few more, bound together in the rhythmic and harmonic momentum of Hank Jones's piano, Sam Jones's bass, and Art Blakey's drums. Playing together, they all five begin to sound something like the way people sharing the same car on a train might look: each one deep in his own thoughts and feelings as the pulse of wheels on the rails and the landscape rushing past the windows encompasses them more than they know at that moment in the intimacy of the same journey. In this "Autumn Leaves," as each musician engages the others in the differences that divide them, they are bound inexorably together by the time, place, and purpose they share. So Davis's still anguish and Adderley's manic edge are both enveloped in what seems to be a single heartbeat that is finally exposed in Hank Jones's meditative piano, which winds the song down and leaves me comprehending things no other version of "Autumn Leaves" ever offered: that opportunities can follow from loss, that some things don't heal, that too much remains uncertain, and that we can smile when for a moment elegant surprises interrupt our deep sorrow.

These musicians both challenged and supported each other on their way through this sad song. Each time one pulled back to accompany another, his voice and its attitude remained vivid in the accompaniment he offered. In all their differences the two primary soloists, Davis and Adderley, found ways to make what they had to say separately something they could say in this song together, and that required each of them to open himself to the risk of what he might learn about himself that he hadn't known before. That's how they managed to transform a sentimental song about loneliness they had learned from what was then called the "Hit Parade" into an unflinching expression of the pain that is always a part of a life lived with others—pain that their music makes a thing of beauty. They did it in an intimacy of voice that suggest they were playing as much for themselves as for the rest of us. That intimacy invites listeners for a few moments beyond themselves to encounter something of what each musician has come to know.

John Dewey once called "the continual disclosing of truth through directed cooperative endeavor" the best candidate he knew for the primary tenet of an authentic American religion.[17] Religion is about transcendence, and *e pluribus unum* is an aspiration as transcendent as any. The civics it implies is the sort of doctrine that would enable people to achieve something like it. Religion is also about sacrifice, and jazz music can show us a kind of cooperation that demands a profound sacrifice of self, the kind in which a better self can sometimes be discovered. This is how jazz is intensely rhetorical in the very way religion is: its project is to prompt others to progress beyond selfishness by enabling them to comprehend in themselves a person whom joining with others might let them become. And like religion, jazz draws upon the resources of rhetoric and aesthetics to let those who experience it experience that self that rationally and emotionally, systematically and intuitively, all at once. All this is deeply implicit and mostly unintentional in jazz, rather than explicit and didactic, as it is in religion. Still, jazz and religion both do their rhetorical work by engaging people in experiences of assertion and deference, defiance and compromise—what Kenneth Burke tried to describe in his rhetorical aesthetic that sketches the kinds of interaction that would help Americans advance their shared civic project. Like the best of both religionists and jazz musicians, Burke believed that advancing that practice is possible—that, as he wrote in that very rough American year of 1967, when his fellow citizens were fighting over differences of race, class, and political values in the streets, among them there remained nonetheless "a fountain of good will welling up anew."[18] Again, jazz believes that too.

Kenneth Burke and Jazz

So Burke and jazz both locate people in situations where solving their own problems demands deep interdependence. His overlapping descriptions of rhetoric and aesthetics explain how that can happen in much the same way jazz music makes it happen. Burke wasn't much interested in distinguishing between rhetoric and aesthetics. Rather, he was "much more interested in bringing the full resources of [both] to bear upon the study of a text than in trying to draw a *strict* line of demarcation between [them]."[19] If we read the word "text" in this statement to denote any aesthetic artifact or act of expression, we have in that statement a framework for finding "*what to look for* and *what to look out for*" in the whirlwind of communication that is our way of life. For Burke, the phrase "way of life" had a particular meaning that connected with "identification," the purpose he assigned to rhetoric: "A way of life is an *acting-together*; and in acting together, men have common sensations, concepts, images, ideas, attitudes that make them *consubstantial*"—his vaguely mystical term for moments when people experience themselves as "both joined and separate, at once a distinct substance and consubstantial with another."[20] When Terry Eagleton suggested that the meaning of life might be found in the "form of life" of a jazz ensemble, he seems to have meant the same thing.[21] Burke's words describe the American civic ideal of *e pluribus unum*. But as the perpetual tension between individual and group demonstrates, such a way of life, such a form of life, can also lead people astray. So we need to understand how these moments of connection and separation occur as responses to what tries to influence us. Whether the influences that come at us are aesthetic, or rhetorical, or both at once, we must subject them to our judgment. Burke's work offers a thorough description of what that kind of critical judgment entails, and jazz provides a real and reliable enactment of its ideal practice.

But before I go further, there's an inconvenient fact to address. Kenneth Burke wrote almost nothing about jazz. This was in spite of growing up and maturing in America at the same time as the music, and in spite of being throughout his life a voracious reader of the popular press that covered jazz as a part of the developing national culture. So you would think that he would have recognized what in his work and in this music so nicely aligned. But I have found no evidence of that. There were, however, two moments in his work as a young music critic when he wrote about the strand of African American music called "spirituals" in ways that had rich resonance with jazz.

In 1933 Burke published in *The Saturday Review of Literature* a review of *Run, Little Chillun!*, a musical that played for three months at New York's Lyric Theater that year. That review later appeared as an essay in his *The Philosophy of Literary Form*, titled "The Negro's Pattern of Life." *Run, Little Chillun!* was developed for musical theater from the play *The Green Pastures*, by Hall Johnson, a prominent African American composer who drew upon the "spirituals" tradition to create and perform music with his African American choir that would have broad appeal among white audiences. Burke wrote about Johnson's work twice as a critic: in this review, and in an earlier one that mentioned a 1928 performance in New York of Johnson's Jubilee Singers. In both reviews Burke commented on the pleasant sort of power he found in this music, trying and generally failing to explain it in a satisfying way.[22] It remained, for him, music of a delightfully arresting sort, but that is about as far as his description went.

The 1928 review, published in *The Dial*, focused primarily on a concert in New York of what was labeled "New American Music," produced by the League of Composers to present experiments in contemporary music in the orchestral tradition. Burke's review recounts that performance confronting the audience with " 'new sound combinations, contrapuntal effects and rhythmic devices' " that seemed to him, frankly, like "a kind of 'stunt writing.' " By his description, this was highly self-conscious music, "excessively episodic," "solemn," and "cautious and formal"—precisely, he was to learn later that evening, what the kind of music Hall Johnson produced was not. The review makes it clear that Burke became weary of this "new music" by the end of the concert, and in this paragraph it suggests as well that by the end of the review he was weary of writing about it:

> Fifteen minutes afterwards we found ourselves translated—listening now to the Hall Johnson Jubilee Singers at the Embassy Club. Perhaps our difficulties at the League of Composers figured somewhat in the blossoming of our delight; but in any event, the zest, the unction, the physical undulations, the naïve Epicureanism of these singers overwhelmed us like a revelation.[23]

Hall Johnson was a classically trained musician and composer whose group, the Hall Johnson Negro Choir, was by 1925 performing frequently in New York, both in concert and on radio. The choir cut its first recording in 1928, the year Burke first heard them perform. Then they sang in *The Green Pastures* on Broadway, in the production of *Run, Little Chillun!* mentioned above, and later in a number of Hollywood films. In his introduction to *Thirty Spirituals*, a collection he published of his own arrangements, Johnson explained what Burke couldn't—how this music could speak so viscerally even to the most sophisticated and jaded listener:

> True enough, this music was transmitted to us through humble channels, but its source is that of all great art everywhere—the unquenchable, divinely human longing for a perfect realization of life. It traverses every shade of emotion without spilling over in any direction. Its most tragic utterances are without pessimism, and its lightest, brightest moments have nothing to do with frivolity. In its darkest expressions there is always a hope, and in its gayest measures a constant reminder. Born out of the heart-cries of a captive people who still did not forget how to laugh, this music covers an amazing range of mood. Nevertheless, it is always serious music and should be performed seriously, in the spirit of its original conception.[24]

This may be the "revelation" that "overwhelmed" Burke as he listened to this choir after enduring the concert of "new American music." Instead of conveying concepts, this music was inviting the audience to inhabit with the performers an intimate experience of "longing" and "hope." Burke tried to capture that experience a few years later in his review of *Run, Little Chillun!*, writing that the music had "a positive ability, exemplified with a conviction, a liquidness, a sense of aesthetic blossoming, and a gift for spontaneous organization which is capable . . . of actually setting the spectator aquiver as he participates in the vocal and mimetic exhilaration taking place before him."[25] To illustrate this, he described a particular "choric scene" that, in "allow[ing] for considerable improvising beyond the specified trend of the plot," had "so combined the planned and spontaneous as to offer the fullest opportunity for the workings of those hypnotic processes by which the cast, like migrating birds, could fall into a unity, and this unity in turn could absorb the spectators, precisely as one might, in observing the bird's movements, veer and deploy with them."[26] This is the kind of "identification" he called "consubstantiality" in action, an experience made possible for the audience by performers who could express themselves so freely that their performance seemed to Burke more a "calling" than a "job." He described himself coming away from that experience with "an aesthetic understanding"—rather than a conceptual one—of a version of "the 'good life'" in which "the demands of commercial and financial conquest are almost wholly irrelevant."[27] In 1933, the way of life that Americans had built around those goals was collapsing around them. It was as if these singers were summoning him to a better one—one that didn't make sense in the prevailing scheme of things, really, but the summons was compelling nonetheless. "Where does this fit?" Burke recounted asking himself as he left the theater for that night for the street. "Where does it apply as you elbow your way towards home?"[28]

Burke could not and would not try to claim as his own the African-American identity he had encountered in this music, but the fact that it was an *American* way of life seems to have started him examining and adjusting his own understanding of which values, ideals, and expectancies ought to constitute his nation. In the moment of the performance he had become as much participant in this experience as spectator, and he found his own conception of what America might be changed in the process. But by the end of this review, Burke had retreated back to the role of reasoning critic, expressing his concern that Americans who shared the way of life these people had performed in their music would not be able to hold their own in the "deadly quarrels" that people who live by a "commercial ethic" must sustain. So he concluded the review with a question about whether art could ever be "relevant to our present life" and, at the same time, still offer "somewhat of a corrective to too gloomy a view of the present.[29] Perhaps if he had used some subsequent New York nights to find more African-American music of many sorts—and there was plenty of it coming down from Harlem—the either/or that structured his closing question might not have seemed such a contradiction.

Born two years before Duke Ellington and four before Louis Armstrong, Burke circulated widely in New York City in the years jazz music was the new thing on radio, on record, and in live performance. And he lived not far at all from the jazz world. His eventual son-in-law, Jim Chapin, was a professional jazz drummer prominent in the big bands of the late 1930s who remained active in jazz circles until his death in 2009. Ralph Ellison, who wrote extensively about ways in which jazz was a glimmer of the hope in this country, was Burke's regular interlocutor and correspondent. Ellison's good friend, Albert Murray, who wrote pointedly about jazz and blues as enactments of an America as much African as European, spent many long evenings drinking and talking at Burke's New Jersey farm outside New York City. And my own rummage through Burke's record collection there turned up dusty 78s of Louis

Armstrong and Duke Ellington, along with first pressings of some early bebop from Dizzy Gillespie. Despite all that, I have found nothing in Burke's writing, published or unpublished, that has anything substantial to say about jazz. Even my query to Jim Chapin not long before he died regarding whether he and his father-in-law had ever talked about jazz resulted only in this: "No. I don't know why we never did. KB had strong opinions about everything. Just never got around to it, I guess."[30]

It's as if Burke and jazz lived parallel lives, engaged separately in the same civic project of resolving what seems unresolvable in the conflicting claims Americans find themselves making on unfettered freedom and an ideal of connection and cooperation more complete than any nation has yet achieved. I'm not surprised that jazz didn't acknowledge Burke—but that Burke didn't acknowledge the significance of jazz, experimental musician and wide-ranging cultural critic that he was, does surprise me. Still, I find that juxtaposing his ideas about identity and community with what is involved in the practice of making jazz exposes fresh ways in which to understand these very American problems and promises.

Swinging Along

Developing as an individual while engaging wholly in the common project of a group is the ideal of American citizenship. Conventionally, the development of any civic identity proceeds through the sort of public discourse that we readily recognize as rhetorical. But through the twentieth century, a mass media that became increasingly ubiquitous carried constructs of popular culture across the nation's diversity to provide people with vivid encounters in sound and image of what Americans are or were urged to be. Kenneth Burke may well have done his rethinking of civic rhetoric at least partially in response to that. Rather than the overt and even adversarial practice of deliberate persuasion, Burke did come to consider an experiential shaping of identity to be the primary rhetorical effect, and he described it occurring in a wide variety of ways that reach beyond argument.[31] This is the kind of identity that develops when we identify someone or something as like or unlike ourselves, as aligned with us or opposed in matters pertaining to particular "ideals, values, and expectancies"[32] we want to embody. If individuals share a bond, they make it from materials they encounter in their shared experience. And what Burke's work acknowledges is a fact that is very

American: It is shared experience as much as shared genes that lets us recognize kinship, and the lack of such shared experience that leaves us alienated.

So rhetoric, for Burke, is as much a matter of feeling as anything else. Feeling follows from experience and experiences are made aesthetically, with "aesthetic" understood as a design to bring a feeling into being through a sequence of encounters with perspective and attitude that culminates in a sense of oneself that is more or less different from before. That's how Burke's redefined rhetoric shifts the aim of influence from opinion to identity, and how his redefined aesthetic relocates art from the artifact to the experience of identity that an artifact provides. Most readers of Burke are familiar with a passage from his book *Counter-Statement* that we can read as his description of how an artifact provides such experience: "[F]orm is the creation of an appetite in the mind of the auditor, and the adequate satisfying of that appetite. This satisfaction . . . at times involves a temporary set of frustrations, but in the end these frustrations prove to be simply a more involved kind of satisfaction, and furthermore serve to make the satisfaction of fulfillment more intense."[33] What art provides for individuals is essentially a "way of experiencing"[34] that takes shape as sequence or a "pattern of experience" that has been composed in order "to make over [the one who follows it] in its own image."[35] Art is rhetorical to the extent that it gives "simplicity and order to an otherwise unclarified complexity," and rhetoric is aesthetic as it "codif[ies] a pattern of experience,"[36] a "way of life"[37] that binds disparate individuals in common cause.

So art—meaning here aesthetic experience in its broadest conception—works rhetorically by carrying people through an experience of enacting a particular shared identity as their own, of inhabiting the beliefs and attitudes that would constitute the particular self that an artist projects upon them. That can be a good thing, or it can be very bad. Writing *Counter-Statement* in a contentious nation as it careened into the Great Depression, Burke was sufficiently alarmed by the state of civic life to turn his work from the literary to the critical in an attempt to help his compatriots learn to discern which among the influences that were so relentlessly coming at them did indeed "represent, form, confirm, utilize, and project" a shared identity that was both purposeful and inclusive—one that was "thoroughly integrated with the national life," as it ought to be.[38] Burke tried to explain what that entailed, and to give Americans some ways in which to proceed. All of this saturated his description of where that process should lead: to a way of life that to me looks a lot like the way jazz music is made.

THREE

What Jazz Is

An art, to be most thoroughly integrated with the national life, must represent, form, confirm, utilize, and project the national values, ideals, and expectancies.[1]

KENNETH BURKE

Burke might have continued this statement by moving on from this insight about art to one about "identity," the connection he made in various ways throughout his work. "Personal identity," he wrote, "comes to a focus in the complex of attitudes . . . that constitute the *individual's* sense of orientation," including the "corresponding sense of relationships."[2] This offers an explanation of what, early on, Burke labeled his "basic principle": "that all symbolism can be treated as the ritualistic naming and changing of identity."[3] Rhetoric alone, as we understand it conventionally, is not sufficient for that task. To change in identity requires changing not only how we experience what is around us but how we experience ourselves there—experiences we often repeat to the extent of ritual, like going somewhere to hear music live. So I read in Burke's rhetorical concept of aesthetic form an explanation of how encounters with art, broadly defined, can lead an individual into and through a particular "orientation," a "way of life" that it renders palpable and vivid. And that, from Burke's perspective, is how rhetoric really works: through an immediate encounter with an experience that invites but also, by design, calls upon our identification. As far as that essentially civic act of identifying oneself with "national values, ideals, and expectancies" is concerned, art—in the expansive definition implied in his theory of form—becomes effective rhetoric as it enables people to share an experience when they encounter it together, and yet to feel that experience as intimately their own.

Walking along Houston Street toward the Rockwood Music Hall, we met the band we were there to see coming the other way. Jonathan Batiste was blowing his harmonaboard toward the sky in full dialogue with the young guy on alto sax beside him, playing in a New Orleans groove dug deep by two other guys on tambourine and tuba just behind. This was Stay Human, a band formed when the four—two black and two white—were getting started at the Julliard School. Their stated project is "social music." This kind of music, while "heavily rooted in jazz," as Jon reminds us, is not a genre. Instead, it is music played with a particular "intent": to bring people together who would otherwise remain separate while living side-by-side.[4] They were doing that along the sidewalk: bringing people together in an immediate experience of harmony and rhythm. Most of these people had seen Jon's announcement on the social media site Twitter and had joined the band along the Lexington Avenue Line down to the Lower East Side. As Jon has explained in an interview, "In a subway car, people . . . never converse or connect with each other" even though they are stuck "two inches away from each other" for the duration of their ride. So Stay Human boards subway cars and starts playing with such cheery rambunctiousness that even strangers have a hard time not joining in. It's "almost ritualistic" the way this can bring "people together like a community," he says.[5] And the band's very name, Stay Human, is, as he puts it, like a call to people "from all walks of life coming together to share an authentic and transformative moment through the power of music."[6]

The Rockwood Music Hall is a deep and tall storefront filled with small tables and stools that press against a corner bandstand. The place looked full when we got there, so we followed a set of stairs to a balcony were we found a space at the rail. Below us a rock band was packing up. This night a new band was taking the stage every hour, and most in the audience looked settled in for the full list. Others like us, who were squeezing in for Stay Human, had also found their way upstairs to the balcony. So we were two Westerners in our sixties standing between a well-dressed couple in their eighties and three teen boys wearing backward caps. We all cheered when the band walked on to set up. Joe Temperley was with them. Joe, a veteran of the Woody Herman and Ellington bands, was at the time the Jazz at Lincoln Center Orchestra's eloquent baritone sax. Standing next to him was another visitor, a self-conscious Asian kid with a silver tenor—a student Jon met at a summer workshop, we learned later, whom he invited to try this professional gig. It was a varied gathering both onstage and in the audience that night.

When Jon sat down at the piano he led the band through some jazz standards, a little Broadway, some rock and R&B and recent pop, all on the ground of a jubilant New Orleans groove. Then, thirty minutes into the set, they paused. The room fell quiet as Jon began to improvise an extended arpeggio that sounded like Debussy but then became increasingly blue. He paused again, and then started to play a single dissonant chord on the high keys, like a chime each beat in 6/8 time. Then the tuba slipped in underneath a four-note riff that cycled through every two bars, making a duet that sounded like an ominous marking of time. That's when Jon started singing the wrenching old ballad "St. James Infirmary." It's a song about identifying a body in a morgue, about the dissipation and death that is the underside of street life. Louis Armstrong's early recording moved the song at a faster tempo than a New Orleans jazz funeral march, but with no joy in voice or horn. Jon sang it slow, his piano voicings alternating tension and resolve, giving us the harsh lyrics with a restraint so tense that we were relieved after the last line when the band burst into a polyphonic scream that rose almost to intolerability, and then dropped hard into swing to support an aching sax solo. When Jon finally pulled the mike back to his mouth to reprise the lyrics' anger in his voice, and when he borrowed Cab Calloway's playful phrase for call and response with the audience, he used that exchange of *hi de hi de hi de ho* to get us angry too. When our singing was sufficiently raw, he brought the song down and ended it with a sadness so elegant that we were left gasping. On that crowded balcony we had all waited for Stay Human as strangers standing two inches apart. Still crowded, we now were standing together, having been called back to a shared sorrow no one in this room could ignore or deny.

Revisiting Burke on Rhetoric and Art

Kenneth Burke's work ranges widely and can seem beyond disciplinary category. But you would not be far off the mark to describe his topic as communication, the kind that advances the expansive project I am calling "getting along." For Burke, communication is the breath of life, the process by which we come alive to ourselves because we can only do it in interaction with others. Whatever its immediate purpose, any communication can to greater or lesser degrees urge upon others some values, ideals, and expectancies that shape who they believe they should be. That's where our opportunities and our troubles both lie. Much of our communication is innocuous, of course—though more of it than we readily recognize can put matters of identity at stake in its nudges toward what someone thinks we ought to be. But inherent in each nudge is a moment when, if we pay attention, we can see more clearly than usual the person we have been as well as the one we might be. In that moment of choice we respond. So we respond to every nudge, even if in flat rejection. And for a split second we reflect, sometimes almost involuntarily, on what we value and hope for, what we expect, and what adjustments we need to make in response to the unexpected. It is obvious that in such adjusting we change. But even in not adjusting, we come to understand better where we stand, and that too is change. The changes can be trivial or life-altering.

It is then in communication, broadly defined, that we do our work of identity formation. It's in our interaction with others that we become ourselves. That happens, in Burke's description, this way: "Where two opposed principles are being considered, each of which has the 'defects of its qualities,' what we want is something that avoids the typical vices of either and combines the virtues of both."[7] This is the refining process of genuine dialogue that does to identity what Burke described it here doing to "expression": subjected to dialogue, expression " 'purifies itself' in the course of its unfolding."[8] This process can clean up one's defects, but it can also create opportunities for identity to unfold differently than it otherwise would have. Whether communication is intimate or public, personal or political, much the same thing is happening. It is, in the abstract, civic work. On this conception of communication Burke brought the separate categories we call rhetoric and aesthetic together to suggest that, whether logically or artfully or both at once, we communicate in ways that enable us each to encounter something of the life of the other as if it were our own. And that experience enables individuals to reassert, adjust, change, and then to share once again the "values, ideals, and expectancies" that shape who they are.

As Burke told the story, he had started out as a fiction writer and poet whose focus, like that of any artist, was self-expression. But the events surrounding the descent of his nation into the Great Depression turned his urgent attention to "interdependent, social, or collective aspects of meaning, in contrast with the individualistic emphasis of his earlier Aestheticist period."[9] So he "made the shift from 'self-expression' to 'communication,'"[10] a term he understood as one of a "family of key words that includes . . . 'communicant,' 'community,' and 'communion.' " His concerns now focused increasingly on "humanistic integration and cultural reconstruction,"[11] as they were both advanced and retarded by "symbolic motivations and linguistic action in general."[12] Out of that came his "theory of form"[13] that explained how "a way of experiencing . . . made available in art"[14] could prompt people, whether they noticed or not, to understand themselves and their relations to others in new ways. In a summary of ideas from George Herbert Mead that he seemed to embrace, Burke wrote: "A social relation is established between individuals and external things or other people, since the individual learns to anticipate their attitudes toward him. He thus, to a degree, becomes aware of *himself* in terms of *them* . . . . And *his* attitudes, being shaped by their attitudes as reflected in him, modify his ways of action." This quite precisely describes Burke's concept of how an important element of identity is formed.[15]

Burke's purpose in all this was not just descriptive. He was always, he said, trying to portray "how, if all went as ideally intended, things would shape up."[16] What he meant by things "as ideally intended" was, of course, his own sense of the essential American "oughts." So Burke's work is theoretical as it gives us methods for doing that work of "humanistic integration and cultural reconstruction," and polemical in its persistent suggestion of where that sort of work should lead. In a nation of displaced people (even the original inhabitants of its land were displaced by the first immigrants) where roots are often not deep, culture and identity are both in perpetual process. That gives Americans trouble. Haunted as we are with calls to collective mission, we share an insistent need to identify ourselves around a stable set of "national values, ideals, and expectancies." But that is difficult to do for people who are always in the process of inventing themselves, of making and remaking their collectivity on the fly from the materials at hand. So no wonder life in America seems so intensely rhetorical and so persistently dogmatic, and why we so readily label each other "American" and "un-American." Even art in America does that sort of civic work—perhaps *especially* art in America.

The American identity crisis intensifies in contentious times. In late 1942, after a year of national effort to gain traction in a widening world war, Burke published a magazine article, titled "Government in the Making," to address the eroding of democracy he saw in the nation. If democracy is to survive, he wrote there, Americans must treat even this "modern total war" as a set of "democratic situations." Then he explained what he meant in the terms of labor relations. In a sustained emergency, government must take on the role of management and citizens the role of labor. But when management *is* the government, there is no channel available to citizens for arbitration. Any dissent or resistance becomes treason. So Burke proposed that citizens and government both quite deliberately identify themselves differently in this situation: as parties in a "consultative" relationship in which they must act as collaborators in the critical project of attending together to "'what to look for, what to look out for, how, and why?'"[17] After all, waging war is necessarily cooperative work—assuming, of course, that government and citizens share the same values, ideals, and expectancies sufficiently to do it.

Twenty-five years later, in the social turmoil of 1967, Burke could no longer assume that. So he pled with his contentious compatriots both within and outside government to fall back from what looked like unsolvable conflicts to more malleable images of themselves that they *could* share. His method, as he explained with just a hint of desperation in a theoretical essay on rhetoric published that year, was this:

> Are things disunited in "body?" Then unite them in "spirit." Would a nation extend its physical dominion? Let it talk of spreading its "ideals." Do you encounter contradictions? Call them "balances." Is an organization in disarray? Talk of its common *purpose*. Are there struggles over means? Celebrate agreements on ends. Sanction the troublously manifest, the incarnate, in terms of the ideally, perfectly invisible and intangible, the divine.[18]

This may look like avoidance or denial. But what Burke had seen of his nation's twentieth century—from Depression through Hiroshima and into Cold War, through class and racial conflict and the debilitating adventure in Vietnam—left him believing that such a practice was better than the alternative. So this was the instruction he offered in a strategy of symbolic if not practical "transcendence" that might allow antagonists to identify with each other just enough to keep them from violence or flying apart. If you can't see yourself in each other's actions, perhaps you can see something of yourself in others' abstracted attitudes. And, if you can be patient, that might just be enough.

So, in that angry summer, as Americans in major cities were burning their neighborhoods and fighting in the streets, Burke published an essay in *The Nation* that urged Americans toward an attitude that he thought might still unify them:

> True, there are mean places. Each day the news assiduously hunts them out, that we newsmongers may variously identify ourselves with some persons in those selected areas of victimage. But there is also the humanity of our people, the fountain of good will that keeps swelling up anew. And with this we would be identified, with this we

> *must* be identified, for otherwise the supersonic this or that, the moon shots, the great new realms of knowledge, the *sheer genius* of all such accomplishments, the whole thing becomes a damned lie.[19]

Burke had observed long before that people "earnestly yearn to identify themselves with some group or other," and when they act on such yearning they are prompted "by a partially dreamlike, idealistic motive, somewhat compensatory for real differences or divisions, which the rhetoric of identification would transcend."[20] At this fractious civic moment Burke took a step past the intellectual project of developing critical methods to the civic one that involved pressing his fellow citizens to acknowledge that yearning and to recover that motive—to adopt an attitude toward each other out of which more productive interaction might proceed.

What Burke was asserting here was an alternative American identity, a "way of life," an "acting-together" that would be sustained upon values, ideals, and expectancies that pointed toward an ideal he called "consummation." That was his term for the ultimate culmination of a civic quality of communication that must begin in self-expression. Self-expression, focusing on the self, is only incidentally communication. But, Burke believed, it ought to mature into motives that focus on addressing others. And what ought to follow from that, ideally, was an understanding shared by self and others together. That's "consummation."[21] We can't achieve that, of course, but we can interact with each other in ways that keep us at least looking toward it. Introducing his theory of form, Burke had written that "art is not *experience*, but *something added* to experience."[22] What is added is the shareable identity that the art enables diverse individuals to experience together. So when people hear the same political speech, read the same literature, scan the same editorial, or see the same film, they all encounter the same values, ideals, and expectancies given life there as if they were their own. Burke insisted that identity is "*not* individual," that we each identify ourselves with "all sorts of manifestations beyond [ourselves]," that "'identification' is hardly other than a name for the *function of sociality*."[23] His theory of form explains how that can be—how, in an encounter with that kind of composed experience, we can be "*acting-together*" in thought and feeling, living for a time the same "way of life,"[24] and how we can maybe take away from that the memory of an identity we share.

We want to come together with others. Even the most exuberant individualist cannot but advocate, "Be like me." Burke considered our shared sorrow over the fact that we can never come together fully. "My particular physical pleasures and pains are mine, not yours," he wrote, "and your particular physical pleasures and pains are yours, not mine. Though in our regional or national affiliations, and in our use of common language, we are members of groups, thus sharing in a *collective* identity, to a large extent our physical pleasures and pains are our private property." We live confined in separate bodies, seeking the sense of "identification" that is "compensatory to division."[25] However insistent we might be about our autonomy, there are times when this "physically inexorable kind of individualism" wears us down.[26] Any inkling of the opposite feels precious when it happens, even revelatory, as if it were "a report of something from outside the mind," a "communication with an ultimate, unitary ground."[27]

In consummation, separate identities dissolve into one, losing the differences that divide them in a felt experience of profound unity. Burke used "consummation" without explaining the term thoroughly, but he offered enough explanation here and there for us to be able to get at what he meant. If aesthetic form is a kind of journey that takes someone through a sequence of questions and answers that must be accommodated by new understanding along the way, then consummation is the culmination of that journey, arrival at a destination where in our interactions no adjustment is needed for us to understand each other. Burke's metaphor for that journey is an "Upward Way" that leads from alienation, separation and conflict to, ultimately, "unification, promise, freedom."[28] The obvious referent of the term "consummation" is sexual, of course—an allusion Burke almost certainly had in mind when he chose the term. In that kind of consummation, minds and bodies are bound together as one by their very differences, in an experience so fully shared that it seems as if there were no separation of people at all. But that is only momentary, and then we are decidedly separate again. We can remember that moment, though, and let our memories perpetuate the bond after its physical enactment is past. As a state of being, consummation is an ideal. But as an occasional glimpse, a momentary experience, and as a memory that maintains an aspiration, it is real—real enough to keep us wanting to work toward it.

The Example of Jazz

Four days after the concert, the music of the Jazz at Lincoln Center Orchestra is on my mind and I'm nodding my head in the rhythm we shared. That night, a full house of people moved together as the band made and then fulfilled its sequence of formal "promises," as Burke would say—though, as jazz must, with a few surprises. The music made and kept lots of promises that night, not only rhythmic but also melodic and harmonic, and certainly emotional, leaving a thousand people with the same smile. In the audience we felt at once energized and calmed by, as Burke would have described it, this "regularity of . . . design [that] establishes conditions of response in the body."[29] That language is too clinical, though. Let's try this: Jazz music is made by distinct individuals who invent and adapt their own musical expressions in improvised exchanges that, whether obviously or subtly, follow Burke's definition of form, which we can simplify in jazz terms as call and response. Consider the live rhythms so prominent in most jazz, and how they summon you to participate. They work on your body and mind as the old knuckle-knock does: *shave and a haircut* calls both body and mind to complete the pattern you expect with *two bits*. Most everyone who hears the pattern can't help but collaborate in completing it.

Jazz is more complicated than that, of course, and more satisfying. It's made of patterns both complex and flexible that let people interweave their own voices. But that "shave and haircut" interaction does demonstrate the capacity of *form*, in Burke's sense of that term, to bind individuals in a common project, in that the summons to participate can feel pleasantly compelling. Jazz is made of many such forms at once: not only rhythmic patterns and harmonic structures, but also conventions, traditions, and familiar phrases that allow an audience to join, even if silently, with the collective voice. Individuals participate in their own ways, at least interacting with, if not collaborating in, the making of a shared experience. Performers do that, as we know. Listeners can do it as well with, for lack of a better term, a vicarious sort of immediacy. In the audience we respond not only to what is happening in the music, but also to what is happening to the musicians, identifying with them. We feel satisfaction with them as their musical promises are fulfilled, and are surprised with them when something in their own or others' music comes unexpected and makes the music whole and coherent. We watch and listen as musicians who might agree only on the most general musical and emotional forms play together in their own separate ways, bound as they are by a commitment to follow those forms through to a coherent collective statement. To watch and listen to this is both startling and reassuring, as mind and body bear witness together to the fact that uncommon order and beauty can come from insistent individualists doing the work of getting along.

This concert of the Jazz at Lincoln Center Orchestra began with the rhythm section alone: the bassist, drummer, and pianist playing as a trio. Each musician started in his own mood, but eight bars in they were all out of themselves and locked together communicating a sound that was taking on a life of its own. My wife, Linda, stage-whispered in my ear, "They're an organism!" No one would say that of the church choir I sing in. There, individuals work to combine in a single voice that elides our differences, that provides our listeners with a living display of a unity in which individuality almost entirely disappears. That kind of unity is a powerful concept that can offer an uplifting respite from the contention and competition we must live with. And sometimes it can seem as though it would be a relief to live within such a thing. But we know that can't be realized outside of some sort of carefully controlled and rehearsed performance, and few of us would want to actually live that way. Listening to this rhythm section, we encountered a unity of an entirely different kind, one perhaps more possible and certainly more comforting. This was a unity of distinct individuals with different capacities and assignments, combined in selfless dedication to a common project. That's what organisms are made of. Watching these three musicians do that so eloquently, we found ourselves wondering if some practical version of that could ever be achieved outside the concert hall.

As the rhythm section proceeded along what was sounding to me like Burke's "Upward Way," their jazz energized and encouraged us in the audience with a promise to achieve it.[30] Bassist, drummer, and pianist moved rapidly through self-expression into communication and there, communicating, together began reaching out of themselves toward something that seemed to align with what Burke had in mind when he described "consummation."[31] We don't quite have words to describe it, but you might say it happened when the music they were making began to come not from separate selves but from three selves bound together by a common cause. You could see when it happened in their faces, as well as hear it in their music. To witness such a thing is hopeful. So we watched and listened to them, independent and interdependent both at once, playing as much in response to each other as to any personal muse—and occasionally, it seemed, to a muse that they shared.

Then the horns in the band came in, immediately settling together in the "pocket," as jazz musicians call it, that the rhythm section had made for them—a rhythmic and harmonic place maintained for them to improvise within. Each jazz tune must be composed and arranged, of course, but generally. Much of what you hear even in a big band is a product of the moment of performance. And when you hear it, the musicians are enacting a sort of unity quite different from that sought by my church choir. You might say that for the choir, unity is a precise point at which we all must converge, while for a jazz ensemble it is a space within which musicians gather to do their work. In the choir we try to sing the music correctly. For a jazz group, that concept of correctness doesn't make sense. Indeed, the goal in jazz is not so much to play the music as to play music *together*, and to stay together as the music develops through the process of performance. The rhythm section of the Jazz at Lincoln Center Orchestra set the stage for that, holding the music together as it was made, countering its inherent centrifugal force without setting its direction. They strove not to play jazz correctly, but to play it right.

To compose and arrange a jazz tune is to express an individual conception and voice that in performance becomes the raw material the people in a group use to make their own music. Each one takes it and turns it to self-expression yet again, but from deep within a commitment to this music that is shared with the others. So it becomes the purpose of every assertion of self to sustain the performance of the group. While my church choir requires subordination of one's individuality to a single voice, jazz requires the assertion of self in a collective voice. To hear and see that happen is also, if you let yourself notice, to confront what is a kind of summons to make of yourself—as what happens on a jazz bandstand demonstrates—something difficult and intensely rewarding: an individual deep in community. That phrase states the archetypal conflict that jazz, when played right, works continually to resolve before our eyes and ears. It's a summons to process rather than to achievement—not to a single performance, but to a shared way of life. And while that isn't at all easy, jazz shows us that it is possible.

The Reluctant Sextet

I was sitting in on a ten-day workshop designed to transition advanced jazz students into professional work, in which six prominent jazz performers were working intensively with promising young musicians from across the country. As I moved with the students through the rooms where the six were separately teaching history or technique or theories of jazz, I encountered with them an ongoing controversy that preoccupies many in jazz. On one side is the idea that jazz today is embedded in its history, and that performing it should be a project in innovative continuity. On the other is the idea that jazz should be doing now what it always has done: shed the constraints of tradition in experiments of discontinuity. Among the six faculty there, four taught their courses from middle spaces between those positions, while two took opposite sides. It wasn't as if this faculty ignored the difficulty of that controversy. Each addressed it frankly in class, and they discussed it together through the three weeks in plenary panels. They tried to keep the discussion conceptual, though, since the purpose of the workshop was to nurture open minds.

As the days passed, keeping that distance from the practicalities of the conflict became increasingly difficult for the students. For them, the workshop was a crucial moment in the development of their own identities as jazz musicians. Their teachers were well established. Because everyone knew who they were, these six could afford the distance of concepts. But not the students. Each had at hand the urgent matter of determining whom, professionally, to be and become. So, as the faculty explored these competing conceptions of the music in their separate classrooms, the students struggled increasingly with the conflicts between them. And that's the way it went until the last day, when these six teachers found themselves having to struggle as well, as they became a sextet and started preparing the concert that would culminate the workshop. Standing together with instruments in hand, they could no longer observe matters from a distance. They had to play jazz together.

So they met that last day after lunch to rehearse, and as soon as they started to talk about a playlist, the two horn players clashed. They were the ones on opposite sides of the controversy. The other four made up a rhythm section of piano, bass, drums, and guitar. One horn player wanted the ensemble to play from the rich jazz tradition that was essential for the students to know. The other wanted the group to play in ways that moved past that tradition, to offer an audience what might be the music's next phase. In any other setting these six would have been unlikely to combine as an ensemble, and their rehearsal didn't go well. They mostly debated, because at each attempt to play together, the tune broke down when the horn players couldn't help but begin to practice what they separately preached. After a while there wasn't much talking either. The rehearsal lasted barely an hour and broke up without a firm playlist.

That evening, the six teachers gathered again on a small stage in the club room of the hotel where the workshop was held. Their students filled the seats, a tense and anxious audience wondering where to steer a professional future. They had come to the workshop for answers, and at the end instead found themselves facing crucial and difficult questions about what music to play, about what jazz identity to embody. They were quiet as the bassist called a standard and started out, giving the others both key and tempo. The others followed according to convention:

playing together through the tune in harmonies that were increasingly improvised two or three times; then separating for solos on the tune's chord changes, taking turns as soloists and accompanists leading and following each other; then returning together in harmony to the tune again. That format is ubiquitous in small-group jazz, and when nothing unexpected happens it can be uninspiring. But on this night, things happened. As one horn pushed his solo his way, the other played things in accompaniment that pulled the soloist back into the quarrel, and that went on each time the solo roles were exchanged. Their assertions and answers, calls and responses, took on a raw and even contentious edge. The rhythm players worked hard at supporting and constraining them, urging each solo on but also pulling each soloist back from the edge of the ensemble's coherence, filling the chasm between them in the process. Piano, bass, guitar, and drum kit would pick up the music where a horn left it, and move it back step-by-step to the center, where the other horn could pick it up and then take it in the other direction. For the musicians, all this was exhausting; strenuous listening, sudden adaptation, and unhappy choices were required to keep the music alive.

The sextet struggled on for an hour in this way. You could see the strain in their faces. But the students were transfixed. They had learned much about jazz as a concept during the past ten days, but it wasn't until this performance that they began to comprehend this music as a mode of communication, of relationship, and as a way of life. They saw each man playing out of a strong sense of musical self while knowing that on that stage, and especially before that audience, their self-expression was only as good as what it could contribute to the music made by the group. For Burke, a "way of life" is the actions and interactions that express the values, ideals, and expectancies that constitute the identity of the individuals who find themselves sharing a situation of "acting-together"—of people in a predicament that demands of them the "common sensations, concepts, images, ideas, attitudes that make them *consubstantial*," at least for the duration of what they are called upon to do there.[32] What the students learned that night was that jazz is made in the practice of something like what Burke called "consubstantiality." It is made in relationships of an almost impossible sort, really, that enable the musicians who try to sustain them to work together, if not actually move the music, toward the ideal that he called consummation. It was not until the students watched these six strong individuals struggle to stay together that they understood that a jazz musician's identity is not a matter of musical style and ideology after all. It comes alive in the effort to make music with others on a stage before an audience, and in doing so with whoever else is present there. This is an effort that puts conflict in the service of music made together. Even in these two horn players, the students came to see a shared commitment that guided each player to engage the other, almost in spite of himself, in order to make the music. So the concert was a fitting end to an educational event designed to teach people not so much how to play jazz, but how "acting-together" is what enables them to *be* jazz musicians.[33]

The literature on jazz explores various controversies about dividing the music and musicians into enclaves. But that is a luxury of analysis and theory. A stage has no space for that. Musicians who might barely speak to each other offstage must play harmoniously together onstage. So they have to find ways to identify with each other—to acknowledge in each other a way of life that is an essential element of identity that they share. For Burke, it all boils down to a choice to connect or to separate. So, from deep in their differences, this reluctant sextet did what jazz music demands: they found ways to play through them together. They finished with the students on their feet cheering. The students cheered because the way forward was now much clearer to them. The music itself had demanded that their mentors provide them with that. So while divisions had shaped the sextet's rehearsal, the connections they made and the ways in which, however reluctantly, they identified themselves together shaped their performance. Jazz made it impossible for them not to interact constructively, because the music exists at the edge of incoherence and the mission of musicians is to keep it from going over that edge. Though some in the ensemble likely had little in common beyond that mission, it was enough.

The reluctant sextet left the stage as they had stepped upon it, irritable and frustrated. Maybe the tensions that sustained their performance kept them from recognizing its power. Or maybe they found whatever unity they had achieved to be too awkward or uncomfortable to celebrate. So they walked off unsatisfied, as the students cheered on, having witnessed what felt to them like some kind of redemption.

Virtuosos and Ensembles

The Jazz at Lincoln Center Orchestra concert we saw was not so strenuous as that workshop concert. Here, everyone was in the mood to celebrate, performers and audience alike. Soloists performed from a shared concept, collaborating in generous voices as each contributed fitting inventions. The JLCO is one of just a few big bands still operating on the model of Duke Ellington's and the others like it that began to fade away at mid-century. It is a repertory band, using its performances to introduce a broadening canon of American jazz, but also to support the development of new music that expands upon tradition and convention. We had last heard them in concert a couple of years before, playing music of Coltrane and Ornette Coleman. Their playlist on this night was mostly new work that incorporated Basque, flamenco, and Cuban elements into the band's more or less traditional sound. The music was challenging and completely engaging, played with infectious energy and satisfying precision. Any tensions the audience might have sensed in it were aesthetic rather than ideological. The band brought things together that challenged our capacity to understand what they were playing, but pleasantly, as we continued moving and smiling in time. At the end, this audience was also on its feet, hoping for an encore.

Wynton Marsalis came back onstage first, with the drummer, bassist, and pianist following. We quieted as they sat and laid down the spare foundation of a slow, throbbing blues, the taproot of American jazz. It took almost no time for us all to fall into that pocket. The blues is essential African America, descended directly from experiences of slavery and its long and sad aftermath. It always sounds familiar, because versions of its harmony and rhythm inflect so much of American popular music. The elements of a blues are few and simple: a blues tune is twelve measures long, played in 4/4 time. The lyrics of a four-bar phrase played twice repeat a question or bad situation, and call out for an answer or resolving response, which follows in a third four-bar phrase that answers and resolves what has come before. Even if the tune has no lyrics, we still know the story. Blues melody and harmony are simple, made from three chords. In terms of a musical scale, these chords are based on the *doh* (the root or tonic), the *fa* (the fourth), and the *sol* (the fifth) of a given key. All three are dominant seventh chords that represent scales with flatted sevenths, pushing back against the good cheer of the major key while not embracing the sorrow of the minor. Played in the key of F, the chords of a blues are F7 (the I chord), B♭7 (the IV chord), and C7 (the V chord). In a blues tune, their progression—the sequence of their changes, with each chord getting four beats—is

```
F7     F7     F7     F7
|////  |////  |////  |////|
B♭7    B♭7    F7     F7
|////  |////  |////  |////|
C7     B♭7    F7     F7
|////  |////  |////  |////|
```

A myriad of melodies can be made from these chords as they move through this sequence of changes.

Think of that mid-century standard, "Route 66," composed by Bobby Troup in 1946 and covered by performers ranging from Bing Crosby to Nat and Natalie Cole, Tom Petty and the Heartbreakers, the Rolling Stones, and Depeche Mode. "Route 66" is a classic blues in its melodic and harmonic structure, though *not* in its lyrics. But let's use the lyrics to remember again how it goes:

If you get a chance to motor west,
Travel my way; it's the highway, that's the best
Get your kicks, on Route 66.[34]

This particular melody is a minimalist one that follows the changes and the groove of the blues. But most versions don't express the emotion of the blues. There is too little at stake. The more substantial blues all tell the same hard story, retold countless times in its countless particulars for a century or more. You could say that the shape of its story resides in the music and its particulars in the lyrics; the two are bound together by an insistent rhythmic reminder that in all our sorrows, there is a kind of triumph in just continuing on. And by the naked statements of soloists, we come to know just how that continuing on can feel. The blues can get you feeling a little of that even if you haven't paid attention to the music before. To fully appreciate the blues is an acquired taste. But to feel the blues—it's hard not to. Follow that feeling and you begin to understand something about common human experience, especially if others with you are feeling it too. To feel the blues is to reach beyond reception of a musician's self-expression and communication. It is to feel something of what Burke called consubstantial: sharing with the band and those who listen that sense of "unification, promise, freedom" of "consummation."[35]

At bottom, the blues expresses an African American identity. We all work through rejection and sorrow, but for African Americans through the twentieth century and into the twenty-first, that work has itself been a way of life. The blues tells that story profoundly in its simplest lyric and musical forms. Trouble is stated in the first phrase and repeated in the second, and then the third statement answers the trouble, mostly by acknowledging it and getting on with life anyway. That form works on listeners rhetorically just as Kenneth Burke outlined in his theory of aesthetic form. In its lyrical terms, the first two lines of the blues state a problem, one for which we expect a solution to come. But the third and last line counters that expectation with the fact that the trouble will remain. It's the form of the music, not the message of the lyrics, that transforms the sorrow into hope. In the first two phrases we feel the energy of that sorrow in the music; and in the last phrase, where we expect to find resolution and the lyrics describe only resignation, that energy persists and even intensifies in its tonal and rhythmic expression, as musicians improvise on that predicament music of their own that makes you move along with them. You want to sing along with the blues, and dance. That's the civic work of the blues: it acknowledges the sorrows that people share, as well as the likelihood that those sorrows will continue, with music that keeps people confronting those sorrows together with the energy and hope that this companionship can bring.

An example is Robert Johnson's "Cross Road Blues." Born in Mississippi in 1911, Johnson was a founding father of the raw guitar and vocal style that became Delta blues. His music had such influence in its time that a legend developed about him selling his soul to the devil at a Mississippi crossroad one night in exchange for his uncanny ability to play a most penetrating blues. We can read the lyrics of "Cross Road Blues," as he recorded the song in 1937, as a reference to that legend or as an acknowledgment of the mundane and dangerous circumstance of a black man trying to hitch a ride at night at that time in that part of the South:

I went to the crossroad, fell down on my knees
I went to the crossroad, fell down on my knees
Asked the Lord above, "Have mercy, now, save poor Bob, if you please."

This is Johnson's acknowledgment of the fundamental vulnerability and alienation of a black man in the Jim Crow South, but also of something potential if not present in the experiences the rest of us share. This acknowledgment continues with further details in the song's second and third verses. The song's fourth and final verse does the same thing as the third line of each previous verse: with no denial of the depth of the trouble and pain, it points in a most minimal way toward the prospect that Bob might find his way through it.

You can run, you can run, tell my friend-boy Willie Brown
You can run, you can run, tell my friend-boy Willie Brown
Lord, that I'm standin' at the crossroad, babe, I believe I'm sinkin' down.[36]

It's hard to find hope in those words. But sung to the music, with its syncopated rhythm, the intensity of its feeling, and the reliability of its harmonic cycle, there is saving energy there, whether Bob's own or Willie Brown's. Whatever the lyrics might say, the propulsive energy of the blues that carries them along offers consolation and some hope. In melodies made from the blues, a relentless rhythm is lit up by the bare emotion of intense and inventive improvisation to suggest, though never state, a promise that things will change. In the meantime, Bob may be sinkin' down, but the way he's playing his guitar and singing about it makes you defy it all with him, with a tapping foot and a smile.

That tapping and that smile express what Burke called *"an attitude."* His late definition of *attitude* as "an ordered summation of emotional experience otherwise fragmentary, inarticulate, and unsimplified"[37] uses language that, overlaid on his theory of form, suggests that such a thing is communicated best aesthetically. It was not long after he had begun defining form as a pattern of experience that raises expectations and then provides response that meets or changes them that Burke augmented that theory using the term that names the rock bottom of the blues. "Alienation," he wrote, is a feeling that follows from the experience of "dispossession"—of being "deprived of the 'goods' which [one's] society has decreed as 'normal.'" When they feel it themselves, he continued, "people try to combat alienation by *immediacy*, such as the senses alone provide."[38] That's a good way to understand the attraction of the blues. The music and lyrics recount bad experiences that, contrary to what we expect of the stories people will tell us, simply stay bad. Deprived as they are of practical solution or resolution by their shared circumstances, people who make the blues share words and music designed to prompt the same immediate feeling in them all. We each have in our lives our own private particulars of what the blues describe, but when we can see in each other's eyes the same shape of experience, we feel we are comforted. In the blues, whatever the private sorrows we each must endure, alienation is no longer one of them. In that recognition, things get better.

That recognition filled the hall that night as the rhythm section of the JLCO started playing a hard-swinging blues for the band's encore. The piano, bass, and drums were leading us all along a path we could all recognize. It was as if the spare music made by the trio told us each our own story, but in a way that let us experience something like what Burke had encountered in *Run, Little Chillun!* that set the spectator "aquiver as he participate[d] in the vocal and mimetic exhilaration taking place before him."[39] There was no vocalist in the band that night, but each man made his instrument sing with the frank intimacy Burke had recognized in the singers he had heard: "the right . . . attitude."[40] The music we heard affected us as the music Burke heard had affected him. He encountered it as an "inchoate act" that, though still "incipient," had a "unifying force."[41] The music we heard left us, as Burke had been left, "dancing . . . an attitude,"[42] For Robert Johnson to *sing* that way about sinkin' down was to ensure that neither he nor his listeners would sink down all the way. Johnson's singing would move both his audience and himself a step or two back from despair as they recognized themselves sharing what amounted to the same experience, even dancing to it together.

The civic work of the blues would be to become, as Albert Murray put it, "a part of many people's equipment for living"—a phrase he took directly from Kenneth Burke, though Burke had not referred to the blues.[43] Burke described literature in particular and art in general as "equipment for living," to emphasize its capacity to help us comprehend how we can overcome alienation by "naming" together the situations we find ourselves sharing, and by developing from those names—from our understanding of those situations—attitudes that can get us through them.[44] Putting it another way, Burke said that art provides us "*strategies* for dealing with *situations*," noting that "another word for strategies might be *attitudes*."[45] In his own work, Murray applied that concept to the blues in ways that state quite clearly this rhetorical function: "Not only is its express purpose to make people feel good . . . but in the process of doing so it is actually expected to generate a disposition that is both elegantly playful and heroic in its nonchalance. . . ." That "disposition" is an attitude, and an attitude like that is an identity, really. It is "the direct opposite of resignation, retreat, or defeat,"[46] and "one of its most distinctive features . . . is its unique combination of spontaneity, improvisation, and control."[47] The "it" in Murray's sentence refers as readily to the identity the blues expresses as to the performance itself. So he wrote that the "disposition to persevere (based on a tragic, or better still, an epic sense of life)" is what "blues music at its best not only embodies but stylizes, extends, elaborates, and refines into art."[48] In effect, the blues provides people who are alienated—as most of us are in one way or another—with immediate, aesthetic experience that brings them together in an attitude that anticipates their cooperation. That is a civic matter.

James Baldwin captured much of this in "Sonny's Blues," his redemptive story of two brothers on the thin edge of hopelessness in 1950s Harlem, one striving joylessly to rise above a bad situation as the other sinks down into it. At the end of a grueling cycle of rescues and relapses, estrangements and reconciliations with all the attendant fear and shame, the elder brother—who is trying to hang onto a career as a math teacher—recounts his experience hearing the younger, Sonny, play piano in a jazz quartet for the first time since his release from a year or so of rehab. Seated in a dusky club, the elder brother watches as the leader, a bassist called Creole, gives Sonny his chance to lift himself and everyone else in the room after the band has been playing for a while, uninspired. Powerful in its entirety, the closing scene of the story culminates in this paragraph:

> Then Creole stepped forward to remind them that what they were playing was the blues. He hit something in all of them, he hit something in me, myself, and the music tightened and deepened, apprehension began to beat the air. Creole began to tell us what the blues were all about. They were not about anything very new. He and his boys up there were keeping it new, at the risk of ruin, destruction, madness, and death, in order to find new ways to make us listen. For, while the tale of how we suffer, and how we are delighted, and how we may triumph is never new, it always must be heard. There isn't any other tale to tell, it's the only light we've got in all this darkness.

A noisy club grows silent as the music combines separate lives. Alienation is at least latent in us all. We can't eliminate it, so we continually seek ways to deny it or work through it. Sonny's drug problem was his denial, while grim striving was his brother's work. Blues solos are both intimately personal and profoundly public, expressing for people together what one experiences alone. When these solos are embedded in a way of life that is marked by the mutual support the band enacts and displays, we are comforted. While it can be almost intolerable to listen to Robert Johnson alone with his guitar, we are comforted and cheered by B. B. King playing his while backed by his exuberant band. Playing the blues with others demonstrates that we are not alone with our sorrows and fears, and that makes it safe for us to acknowledge them.

So Baldwin describes the moment in this quartet's performance when the other three "all gathered around Sonny," playing together an "immense suggestion that Sonny speak for himself." They stayed close by as Sonny played his first solo in a long and hard time, close enough "every now and again" to say "amen." Baldwin gives us this image of what the older brother saw and heard:

> Sonny's fingers filled the air with life, his life. But that life contained so many others. And Sonny went all the way back, he really began with the spare, flat statement of the opening phrase of the song. Then he began to make it his. It was very beautiful because it wasn't hurried and it was no longer a lament. I seemed to hear with what burning he had made it his, with what burning we had yet to make it ours, how we could cease

lamenting. Freedom lurked around us and I understood, at last, that he could help us to be free if we would listen, that he would never be free until we did. Yet, there was no battle in his face now. I heard what he had gone through, and would continue to go through until he came to rest in earth.[49]

This is self-expression taken beyond communication to "consummation." The blues the JLCO played as an encore at the concert we saw was neither so urgent nor so intimate as this. Culminating a program of joyous jazz, played by accomplished and successful musicians to a full house of people who could afford the ticket, that blues was still music made by individuals who were expressing intimate experiences common to all of us. They were having more fun than Sonny, but they told the same kind of story. Linda and I had come to that concert with sorrows of our own that felt worthy of the blues. Our feelings were not desperate like Sonny's, and our desolation did not approach Robert Johnson's. But the need to feel that we weren't alone in sorrow, to find consolation in the fact that others shared something similar, was real. And our hope rose when the rhythm section began the blues. The bassist settled us down into a reliable quarter-note walk along the blues changes, and the pianist pushed us a step past where we had been as he colored the chord sequence we expected with the unexpected. And the drummer enveloped us all in a forward momentum that felt as safe as gravity—playing, as he told me later, "with intensity at a low volume," well prepared to "match the . . . mood" of each soloist" in order to offer them "affirmation and companionship" in the process of their performances.[50] We felt that for ourselves in his drumming. It made us ready to go where the blues would take us.

Then Marsalis's trumpet began with one note played three times, in time—the simplest melody it is possible to play over the changes of the first phrase of a twelve-bar blues. He played them long yet deep in a blues pulse. *Doh*-two-three-four, *doh*-two-three-four, *doh-ooh*-three-four, one-two-three-four. He repeated them. Then *sol*-two-three-four, *fa*-two-three-four, *doh*-two-three-four, *doh-ooh*-three-four. He changed notes when the chords changed, still playing each one long with implicit syncopated swing. In the second round he began to play out a melody line as the tenor player walked onstage having picked up from him that most basic blues phrase. The sax was asserting the rhythm more emphatically in those same single notes, and dropping an embellishment here and there to make them his own. Then two horns confronted each other and began a good-natured debate, trading blues phrases back and forth, each taking four bars, challenging, answering, and countering for a couple of choruses until the cycle came round again. And then Marsalis took off. The blues provides very good ground for improvisation, and his flowered quickly as he took it through the changes. He was pushing me to the edge. Just when I was losing track of where he was in the chord sequence I expected to follow, he would pull it all together and return to each chorus's expected conclusion. This was blues enacted: bursts of intense emotion sculpted into harmonic order with the precision of eighth, then sixteenth, then thirty-second notes that seem to spray away into meaninglessness and then find surprising ways home in the next measure or two. I didn't count the choruses Marsalis played before he handed the solo off again to the tenor player, who then told his own version of the same story. Marsalis was behind him now, his trumpet commenting, cheerfully mocking, encouraging, and pushing the sax further on, living the structure of the story with the tenor player as he narrated the details of his own alone. We all tell our stories alone because they are ours, because we need others to hear them and to tell us theirs back. Alienation evaporates in that exchange.[51]

In terms of rhetoric, this is compelling eloquence, and eloquence is of course the epitome of influence. Burke described it in the first extended presentation of his theory of aesthetic form: eloquence engages others in "a pronounced pattern of experience"[52] that "convert[s] life into its most thorough verbal equivalent."[53] That pattern of experience is a way of life that, thoroughly expressed, is made available to others who might make sense of their own experience within it. Art, then, as Burke still broadly defined it, is "the conversion, or transcendence, of emotion into eloquence," and so "a factor added to life."[54] An encounter with eloquence is, in the rhetorical history of the term, a shared experience, a public one. In Burke's description, it is a sort of civic communion that brings people together in a visceral understanding of important things shared. I listen to jazz for that.

Democratic Art

That art in America ought to be "thoroughly integrated with the national life," and that it should thus "represent, form, confirm, utilize, and project the national values, ideals, and expectancies," seemed necessary to Burke in a nation where those values, ideals, and expectancies were continually and contentiously contested. In a nation of professing individualists who must continually be enticed toward necessary cooperation, the efforts of persuasion alone are insufficient. People who try to reason with each other toward agreement without seeking ways to feel "consubstantial"—that theological term Burke used to add metaphysical charge to his concept of collective identity—can find their cooperation shaky and short-lived. Agreements on ideas alone may not be durable enough to sustain a nation so expansive and fractured as was Burke's throughout his lifetime. His work acknowledges that Americans inhabit a cultural democracy that keeps them in constant collision as they shop a tumultuous and unregulated marketplace of identities for values, ideals, and expectancies that ought to, or at least might, define them together. That the centrifugal energy of this marketplace never seems to lessen keeps Americans worried about themselves, individually and together—a worry that has kept both their art and their rhetoric engaged in civic work. As Ralph Ellison stated the dilemma, identity is "*the* American theme," yet "the nature of our society is such that we are prevented from knowing who we are."[55]

We can read Burke's work through the twentieth century as developing around this situation. You can find there a consistent appeal to his compatriots to attend to the intersections between a developing sense of personal identity and competing conceptions of a national identity as their first and foremost civic project.[56] On a patch of common ground cleared by what is for most a meager set of shared experiences, Americans pile conflicting claims regarding what they ought to want that leave them in pressing need of experiences more than descriptions. Art, in America at least, seems to work to address that need, enabling individuals to try on the values, ideals, and expectancies that the artists, at least, would have them share. The rhetorical effect of art is in the experience it offers of inhabiting an identity. If, as Burke insisted, "the individual's identity is formed by reference to his [or her] membership in a group,"[57] then the many groups that comprise a democracy leave individuals managing many identities.[58] So here is the American predicament: we seek in the morass of our interactions with others a shared "way of life," an "*acting-together*"[59] that identifies us. In those interactions we are all always enacting Burke's "basic principle . . . that all symbolism can be treated as the ritualistic naming and changing of identity."[60] And because he had found "the processes of change of identity . . . most clearly revealed by analyzing formal works of art and applying the results . . . to the 'informal art of living in general,'"[61] Burke would help us out by having us pay unrelenting critical attention to the "sensory imagery"—the aesthetic form of experience, really—that prompts each person who encounters them "to make himself [or herself] over in the image of the imagery."[62]

FOUR

Where Jazz Comes From

Our basic principle is our contention that all symbolism can be treated as the ritualistic naming and changing of identity.[1]

KENNETH BURKE

Burke is read mostly these days as an academic theorist rather than as a public intellectual whose fundamental concerns were civic. For most readers his work boils down to a set of fresh insights about ways in which communication made of exchanges of symbols affects identity and, so, attitude and action. But you can read his work also as a sustained attempt to teach his fellow Americans how to address their deep differences in ways that improve their capacity for cooperation, as if in response to what Ralph Ellison called the "combat" over an "ever more encompassing and acceptable definition of our corporate identity" that Burke saw his compatriots relentlessly engage.[2] The essay he published in 1967 in *The Nation* summarizes well the civic case he was making. Titled "The Responsibilities of National Greatness," it described what citizens ought to be doing when the "greatness" of the nation for which they shared responsibility, rather than something inherent, resides naturally in its capacity to do great good and great harm. In that year, when American streets were increasingly violent and US military action in Vietnam escalated to high-altitude blanket bombing, Burke was using this essay to explain to his fellow citizens that their primary civic responsibility was "meditating on our personal modes of identification with the great empire of which we are citizens," that the essential act of democratic citizenship was to pay unrelenting critical attention to the "marvels and mysteries of identification that come to an ultimate focus in that scarcely noticeable, workaday pronoun, 'we.'"[3]

Burke composed the essay in the spring of that year, probably in his small workroom at the top of the stairs in his rural New Jersey house. A visitor there can still see above the window by his desk the place on the unpainted drywall where he penciled the words *potius convincere quam conviciari / ad bellum purificandum*. Next to that window, still tacked to the wall, is the paper sign his wife Libby hand-lettered that reads "Welcome" and in smaller letters repeats the two Latin phrases.[4] The first phrase, translated as "better to prove than to reprove," raises expectations that, if they were realized, would fulfill the aspiration stated in the second, translated as "toward the purification of war"[5]—the phrase Burke used as epigraph for the book that began his most systematic explanation of his project, *A Grammar of Motives*. I don't know when he wrote on the drywall or when the little welcome sign went up, but I suspect that he looked up at both messages as he wrote "Responsibilities of National Greatness." Together, the two Latin phrases summarize the essence of Burke's civic project: to teach people how to render their conflicts productive rather than destructive. Understanding and encouraging this "competitive use of the cooperative"[6]—what Ralph Ellison more frankly called "antagonistic cooperation"[7]—is the project Burke pursued from his thirties, during the thirties in America, through the fractious twentieth century and almost to its end.

Ensemble jazz is not always harmonious. In late 1962 an enterprising producer managed to get Duke Ellington, Max Roach, and Charles Mingus into a studio for half a day to record a trio album that came out in early 1963 as *Money Jungle*. These three, who spanned two generations and multiple conceptions of jazz and had not worked together before, were by then all accomplished long-form composers as well as innovative instrumentalists. By all accounts, it was not a relaxed session. It interrupted each man in the midst of his own musical project addressing the intensifying racial conflict in America. All three seemed to have come in worn raw. Ellington was working on *My People*, his extended sequence of songs composed to mark the centennial of the Emancipation Proclamation the next summer. Roach had already composed and recorded *We Insist!*, his "Freedom Now Suite," to mark that centennial by directly acknowledging more recent movements to advance African American rights, and was bringing out an album that seemed something of a sequel, titled *It's Time*. Mingus, whose music was becoming as personal as it was political, had been addressing these issues directly for some time and would soon complete a long work expressing his own more intimate anguish, *The Black Saint and the Sinner Lady*. Mingus was pushing the limits of self-expression in the jazz form, and was now including segments of direct narration to sharpen his music's rhetorical point. (That's an element Terri Lyne Carrington would add years later to the remake of *Money Jungle* she recorded with Christian McBride and Gerald Clayton in 2013, *Money Jungle: Provocative in Blue*. This updated interpretation of the jagged original states more directly the anger that *Money Jungle* implied about things that really haven't changed much in fifty years.)

The *Money Jungle* album was made from new compositions that Ellington brought into the studio that day. Roach and Mingus had composed music for the session too, and were annoyed that only Ellington's was recorded. It went like this: For each tune, Ellington handed them a lead sheet that sketched only melody and basic harmony. Then, Roach recounted, Ellington "would give us a picture" of what the tune should express. Those pictures were not pleasant. Roach remembered that when Ellington handed them the sheet for what would become the album's title track, "Money Jungle," he said this:

> Think of a city like New York, and all the skyscrapers are tree trunks, but they are barely visible because of all the money flowing down the sides of the buildings like foliage. That's the money jungle. And crawling around on the streets are serpents who have their heads up; these are agents and people who have exploited artists. Play that along with the music.[8]

So that's what they did. Listen and you'll hear music made of fractious emotions around and between them. Ellington's piano starts out "Money Jungle" in block chords, dissonant and percussive. Roach's drumming lurches forward and then proceeds on its own momentum in what Ben Ratliff called "a pronounced lope rather than an evenly spread swing," keeping its distance from the others. Mingus sounds in the same mood as Ellington, though he is less subtle, stretching the strings of his bass to what sounds like a breaking point as he plays scratching strums and arhythmic eighth notes that are only occasionally interrupted by descents into the harmonics of expected bass-line support.

These three men seem to be improvising by provocation, antagonizing each other in order to make this tune. Their music is, as Ratliff described Ellington's playing, "mean."

Late 1962 was a tense time in America, and these three brought that tension into the studio. Ellington's image of a money jungle made vivid the frustrations they all must have felt as they contended with a jazz business in which white men kept most of the money from the music these black men exposed so much of themselves to make. This economy was but one subset of the demoralizing story of African America, and it prompted in Ellington a bitterness that, only once in a while, he would let others see. "There is hardly any money interest in the realm of art," he wrote in his autobiography, "and music will be here when money is gone. After people have destroyed all people everywhere, I see heaping mounds of money strewn over the earth, floating on and sinking into the sea."[9] Working with that kind of image through the session must have made them edgy, and though they admired each other, it was competition and personal vanity that made this music. According to Roach, Mingus stalked out at one point after calling Ellington a "has-been" and Roach a mere bebop drummer. "They had a lot of whiskey in there that day," Roach explained, "because it was a celebrated event."[10] So the music is made of differences and contention, of agitation and anger. It is eloquent in the straining way it barely holds together. The session is said to have disintegrated at the end, probably as the tune "Money Jungle" does. You hear how each man makes his separate way out of the trio and turns his instrument to noise. The result is one of the great recordings of a jazz piano trio, but these three refused to play together again.

To say that jazz makes conflict productive is not a bad way to describe how it works. That's what the jazz musicians who passed through Ralph Ellison's childhood hometown, Oklahoma City, seemed to him to have been doing. For these African-Americans who traveled from city to city in what in the American 1920s was still called the Southwest, "life could be harsh, loud and wrong if it wished," as Ellison wrote, "but they lived it fully, and when they expressed their attitude toward the world [in their music] it was with a fluid style that reduced the chaos of living to form."[11] Much of that chaos was made by the racial conflict so persistent throughout their nation. Yet Ellison saw in those musicians a calm sort of confidence that they could give their lives order and meaning, at least aesthetically if not politically, in spite of that. The jazz they made expressed an attitude that followed the trajectory of Burke's theory of form into aesthetic action, raising the expectations it then realized in music that brought performers and listeners together in a participating community.[12] The community is participatory because jazz is improvised, and improvisation, whether practiced or witnessed, has a way of developing in those who both play and listen what Burke called the "kinds of expectancy" that it fulfills and transforms as they follow its development into each moment, glimpsing together along the way "the principle of consummation"[13] that is always potential among people who are coming to understand themselves first and foremost as "participant[s] in a common situation."[14]

When Burke wrote that "personal identity comes to a focus in the complex of attitudes ('personal equations') that constitute the individual's orientation (sense of 'reality,' with corresponding sense of relationships),"[15] he approached the democratic assumption that individual attitudes and their consequent actions are guided and improved by cooperation. But his work goes on to take the next step, locating in cooperation itself the definitive enactment of the sort of democratic identity we ought to have. The practical problem, of course, is that though Americans expect to participate in a commonality they imagine as the compelling national identity they seek, they expect at the same time to be militant guardians of their own individual distinction. What that stalemate looks like in practice is what Ralph Ellison described in these terms: "Holding desperately to our familiar turf, we engage in that ceaseless contention whose uneasily accepted but unrejectable purpose is the projection of an ever more encompassing and acceptable definition of our corporate identity as Americans."[16]

What follows from this is alienation, the term Burke defined as a state of rejection of "the reigning symbols of authority"—or, I'll add, those that claim to reign—because you can't identify yourself in them.[17] If you find yourself absent from the image of an identity that claims to encompass you, you are alienated. That's the predicament of the "invisible man," the protagonist of the novel Ellison was trying to write in 1945 when he meditated on these things in a long letter to Kenneth Burke. "I, for instance, would like to write simply as an American," Ellison wrote, "or even better, a citizen of the world; but that is impossible just now because it is to dangle in the air of abstractions while the fire which alone illuminates those abstractions issues precisely from my being a Negro and in all the 'felt experience' which being a Negro American entails."[18] A few years later, *Invisible Man* would win the National Book Award on a critical consensus that its rendering of the felt experience of an African American captured as well an American experience that is also universal. That was despite the fact that, as Ellison told Burke in that letter, he couldn't help but write about the particular alienation of his own oppressed group.

Somehow the novel managed—and still manages—to provide diverse readers with an aesthetic experience of alienation with which they can all identify, and in that is a kind of "consummation," in Burke's sense of that term, that the National Book Award recognized. Burke's usual explanation of "consummation" involves, as he wrote, "'track[ing] down implications of a terminology' over and above the needs of either self-expression or communication,"[19] and so completing the three steps through which our interactions would ideally progress. Robert Wess helps here when he suggests that for Burke, "consummation" aligns not only with the idea of "culmination," but also with "entelechy"—the Aristotelian concept of realizing the potential that is inherent in an origin. Maybe that kind of realization, that completion of what ought to be, is what Burke meant by, in Wess's paraphrase, "tracking down the implications of a terminology that reach beyond its immediate pragmatic purpose.[20] Understood in that sense, consummation takes on the mystical inflection present in Burke's concept of "communion" as a moment of new recognition of "the interdependence of people through their common stake in both cooperative and symbolic networks."[21] There isn't much mystical in that language, but there is in a subsequent explanation where Burke links his use of the term with the communion that is a religious rite, one "that seeks to impress by picturesqueness, terror, or wound, the sense of a new identification"—a deep connection with others that transforms "the individual's identity."[22] This idea of communion adds considerable depth to his concept of "communication"—one that resonates with "consummation" and "consubstantiality" as well.

Civic Literature

What Ralph Ellison saw in the jazz musicians who passed through his town was a way of life, an identity in Burke's sense of the phrase, that he didn't see much of anywhere else. Everywhere else he saw Americans each "holding desperately to our familiar turf," living together but in a "ceaseless contention" about what "our corporate identity as Americans" should be. Alexis de Tocqueville saw that when the United States were not yet fifty years old, during his tour designed to help him learn from American practice "how to make liberty proceed out of that democratic state of society in which God has placed us."[23] But the sort of liberty he saw operating in America seemed hardly to support a society at all. Of the American democrats he met, Tocqueville concluded this:

> They owe nothing to any man, they expect nothing from any man; they acquire the habit of always considering themselves as standing alone, and they are apt to imagine that their whole destiny is in their hands. Thus, not only does democracy make every man forget his ancestors, but it hides his descendants and separates his contemporaries

from him; it throws him back forever upon himself alone and threatens in the end to confine him entirely within the solitude of his own heart.[24]

Identifying themselves in that way didn't seem to bother the Americans he met, but it bothered Tocqueville. A century or so later, it bothered Kenneth Burke as well. From what they could see around them, both had concluded that no one, and particularly no American, can really be autonomous. In a democratic culture, Burke wrote, "one's very "sense of reality is shaped largely not by our own immediate sensory experience, but by what others tell us." Given that, the liberty that so many want to use to separate themselves from others actually requires them to attend very carefully to what others say, not only to the concepts they convey but also to the ways that their words, images, and expressions "make us feel." We each tend to be vigilant regarding someone's attempt to assert to us a concept, to persuade, but the feelings that others find ways to lead us into we find harder to refute or resist, because that kind of change seems to come "from within."[25] A part of Burke's project was to explain that this is how art wields rhetorical power, with "art" understood as symbolic expression that communicates by the kind of experience his theory of form describes. Encountering that kind of experience, he said, people "saturate themselves with . . . changes of attitude imaginatively, personally." That power, like argument, is morally neutral, capable of influence for good or for bad. So, to put it bluntly, people need to be as wary of art as they are of argument. But in an individualistic culture where the default position is to resist any attempt to persuade, this means of influence can also be, in Burke's words, "a great virtue."[26] Still, we need to be careful.

For example, consider how the solitary heart that Tocqueville described saturated the American identity that was advanced by much of the literary work we now assign to the American Renaissance—mid-nineteenth-century writings that seem still to glow. Here is Ralph Waldo Emerson (after whom Ralph Waldo Ellison was named, by the way), writing to his fellow Americans not long after Tocqueville's tour: "Build therefore your own world. As fast as you conform your life to the pure idea in your mind, that will unfold its great proportions."[27] Here he is again, in similar mind: "Truly speaking, it is not instruction but provocation, that I receive from another soul."[28] And yet again: "Let me admonish you, first of all, to go alone; to refuse the good models, even those which are sacred in the imagination of men." For him, all this culminated in this conception of the ideal American: "Yourself a newborn bard of the Holy Ghost, cast behind you all conformity, and acquaint men at first hand with deity."[29] This was and remains high American art, treated through the twentieth century as secular scripture. Perhaps the only comfort available to those of us who share Tocqueville's and Burke's wariness of this attitude is in the fact that Emerson, though still often assigned, is probably not so often carefully read.

But that is small comfort because so many rougher and more simplistic images of that same ideal have been projected from the start in this nation's pervasive and accessible popular art. An example is the Western narrative that dominated the American culture of my childhood. In the midst of her sustained critique of the solitary identity in the image of which Westerns invite readers and viewers to imagine themselves, critic Jane Tompkins confessed that while she can readily articulate her "contempt and hatred for the Western hero, for his self-righteousness, for his silence, for his pathetic determination to be tough," when she reads or sees a good Western she still finds herself delighted by a visceral "desire to be the Western hero, with his squint and his silence and his swagger."

> I want to be up there in the saddle, looking down at the woman in homespun; I want to walk into the cool darkness of the saloon, order a whisky at the bar, feel its warmth in my throat, and hear the conversation come to a sudden halt. I want these things and I don't want them, because I have found in my own life, and through reading and watching Westerns, that the price for these experiences, or rather, for the power they represent, is too high.[30]

Tompkins's account of how Westerns exact that price demonstrates the kind of rhetorical effect that Kenneth Burke explained in his theory of form. Note how Tompkins's analysis brings to life Burke's description of how aesthetic form works: "Louis L'Amour says, in the first sentence of *Hondo* (1953), that the hero 'rolled the cigarette in his lips, liking the taste of the tobacco,' that he 'squint[ed] his eyes against the sun glare.' 'His buckskin shirt,' L'Amour says, 'seasoned by sun, rain and sweat smelled stale and old.'" Our response is to imagine ourselves experiencing these things. The feeling on the lips as a cigarette rolls, the aromatic bitterness of a bit of dried tobacco on the tip of the tongue, deafening light aching the eyes, the smell and scratch of the worn leather shirt—all become palpable and vivid in L'Amour's single sentence as we read it, animating it as we do with memories of our own bodily experience. What that does is call many and different readers to an experience of a single identity. Here is Tompkins again: "L'Amour puts you inside the hero's shirt, makes you taste what he tastes, feel what he feels. Most of the sensations the hero has are not pleasurable: he is hot, tired, dirty, and thirsty much of the time. His muscles ache. His pain is part of our pleasure. It guarantees that the sensations are real."[31] This is transformative experience. And it is problematical when the particular transformation is not a good thing.

What Jane Tompkins did in this study of the American Western is what Burke had in mind when he issued his call to Americans "to pause occasionally and ponder the bepuzzlements of 'identification' as they affect our sense of citizenship." And it's not unlikely that Tompkins did that at least partially in response to the daily news in the early 1990s as she was writing the book. Burke wrote "The Responsibilities of National Greatness" in response to what he was reading in the news in 1967, matters that merited the kind of critical attention and careful judgment that is required if people are to manage together the "notable risks and dangers which must be recognized if democracy is to function at its best."[32] Burke would have us learn to "look upon" that first sentence Tompkins reads from *Hondo* in the same way that we look upon the daily news: as prompts to attitude, with attitude understood as "an incipient form of action (in the pitting of some assumptions against others" that "leaves us with an implied code of conduct)" and that itself constitutes much of what becomes an identity.[33] It requires considerable effort for us to assess in every experience we encounter, however innocuous it might seem, which values, ideals, and expectancies it brings to life, and who they bind together as well as who they push away.[34] In America, because of the urgency of our search for "an ever more encompassing and acceptable definition of our corporate identity as Americans" that would bring order to our chaos and provide us with some peace, even aesthetic experience becomes civic rhetoric to the extent that it animates one version or another of what Ellison called "an ever more encompassing and acceptable definition of our corporate identity as Americans." But citizens should still proceed warily, reminding themselves constantly of what might be Burke's central understatement that "a rhetorical motive is often present where it is not usually recognized or thought to belong."[35]

Democratic Jazz

Walt Whitman may have bought Thoreau's resonant claim that "if a man does not keep pace with his companions, perhaps it is because he hears a different drummer"[36] before 1860, but by 1871 he knew that Thoreau's maxim was promoting an identity his nation could not afford. The Civil War had cost Whitman his faith in individualistic democracy. And in its aftermath, changed by his time in the besieged capital city and his work in the field hospitals on its outskirts, he wrote that long and moody essay, "Democratic Vistas," about prospects for an American democracy that were as ambiguous as Tocqueville's had been. As he put it there,

> the true nationality of the States, the genuine union, when we come to a mortal crisis, is, and is to be, after all, neither the written law, nor, (as is generally supposed), either self-interest, or common pecuniary or material objects—but the fervid and tremendous IDEA, melting everything else with resistless heat, and solving all lesser and definite distinctions in vast, indefinite, spiritual, emotional power.[37]

This statement acknowledges that the deliberate democratic project put in place at the nation's founding had failed. Whitman had once hoped that his fractious fellow citizens might yet find that common "IDEA" that would bind them together despite their differences. But six years after that devastating war, Whitman still hadn't seen even its traces. What had been Tocqueville's worry was now Whitman's conviction. The American habit of treating democracy as if it meant "individual liberty" alone had all but destroyed the nation's unifying project. "No current of her life," he was concluding, "as shown on the surfaces of what is authoritatively called her society, accepts or runs into social or esthetic democracy. But all the currents set squarely against it."[38]

So now Whitman was looking past politics for a "social, or esthetic democracy" that could save the nation. Only that, he believed, could offer Americans a definition and identity that would be both "acceptable" and "encompassing,"[39] one that would come to them not by proclamation but, in Burke's rich phrase, through "communication by the signs of consubstantiality."[40] Whitman looked now to "emotions, pride, love, spirituality" as the feelings Americans could be willing to share, and for a more durable constitution to "good theology, good art, or good literature."[41] But he confessed his anxiety that he wouldn't find it. "The fear of conflicting and irreconcilable interiors, and the lack of a common skeleton, knitting all close, continually haunts me," he wrote, and "nothing is plainer than the need, a long period to come, of a fusion of the States into the only reliable identity, a moral and artistic one."[42] Kenneth Burke would have concurred. The project of *e pluribus unum* can't be advanced by politics alone. For that, Whitman looked for some thoroughly American art of some sort and for the shared experiences it would provide, but without enthusiasm, because, as he put it, "America has yet morally and artistically originated nothing."[43] But Walt Whitman didn't live long enough to hear jazz.

To say jazz is a music of democracy is a statement both moral and aesthetic. Jazz is an art and democracy a morality, and how they connect depends on what "democracy" is understood to mean. If it means only that individuals are more or less equal and more or less free, they remain in the situation where Tocqueville found them: "[Happiness] perpetually retires from before them, yet without hiding itself from their sight, and in retiring draws them on," prompting "the strange melancholy that haunts inhabitants of democratic countries in the midst of abundance."[44] This, Tocqueville concluded, is the consequence of individualism, which he defined as that "mature and calm feeling, which disposes each member of the community to sever himself from the mass of his fellows" and "leaves society at large to itself."[45] That may sound good to many Americans, but it is precisely the opposite of what their nation needs. It needs a vibrant commonality, and a ready recognition that they depend for individual and collective happiness on each other, on interactions where "feelings and opinions are recruited, the heart is enlarged, and the human mind is developed only by the reciprocal influence of men upon one another." Based on what he found in America in the 1830s, Tocqueville concluded, "these influences are almost null in democratic countries."[46]

But soon after 1900 there was jazz in America, and over time it began to provide Americans with an aesthetic model for the very sort of identity they needed. That jazz is something of a civic project as well as an aesthetic one was acknowledged publicly in 1987 by the US Congress in a joint resolution that designated it "a rare and valuable national American treasure to which we should devote attention, support and resources to make certain it is preserved, understood and promulgated" as an "indigenous American . . . art form" that "makes evident to the world an outstanding model of individual expression and democratic cooperation." Jazz matters in America, the resolution continues, because it models "a unifying force" in "our diverse society, . . . finding its inspiration in the cultures and most personal experiences of the diverse peoples that constitute our Nation."[47]

A dozen years later, toward the end of the presidency that would conclude the twentieth century, Bill Clinton used his White House Millennium Initiative to promulgate that civic conception of jazz. As the general program announcement put it, "The theme of the White House millennium activities is 'Honor the Past—Imagine the Future.'" By doing so, "citizens" would "'give a gift to the future' that will strengthen our democracy, encourage citizen involvement and unleash the full creative potential of the American people as we chart our common future."[48] The centerpiece of the initiative was a series of performance programs titled "Millennium Evenings at the White House," hosted by the president in the East Room and broadcast on C-SPAN and online. The highlight occurred in the early autumn of 1998 when prominent jazz performers, historians, and educators joined the Clintons—as well as the president of the Czech Republic, Václav Havel, who was there on a state visit—to celebrate this American music. Titled "Jazz: An Expression of Democracy," the event was designed to explore ways in which this music fulfills that charge to "encourage citizen involvement and unleash the full creative potential of the American people as we chart our common future."

Clinton opened the program, suggesting that a new millennium is an occasion not only to think about "our commitment to the future" in new ways, but also to act upon that commitment in ways that would—and he quoted Thomas Paine—let us "begin the world over again." Jazz, said Clinton, shows us how we can do that as it creates on a stage a community that is designed to nurture the aspirations of individuals. By its very structure, jazz "poses challenges and seeks resolution" in the "coordinated efforts of the community as well as in the unique voice of the individual." To make jazz, individuals interact in a situation where "creativity and cooperation," individual freedom and collective solidarity, are rendered interdependent in the service of a common purpose.[49]

That's what democratic civic life can look like. But as Burke, Tocqueville, Whitman, Ellison, and certainly Clinton all knew, it's an ideal.[50] The reality looks something like the "fluid, pluralistic turbulence of the democratic process" Ellison described, which keeps individuals alienated and fearful, "clinging" to their "own familiar fragment of the democratic rock." There's irony here, as Ellison explained:

> The rock, the terrain upon which we struggle, is itself abstract, a terrain of ideas that, although man-made, exerts the compelling force of the ideal, of the sublime: ideas that draw their power from the Declaration of Independence, the Constitution, and the Bill of Rights. We stand, as we say, united in the name of these same principles that we ceaselessly contend, affirming our ideals even as we do them violence.[51]

As we try to "cooperate and communicate" while insisting on our individual rights first and foremost, that becomes the way in which we understand our often-stated aspirations to "unity-in-diversity," to "oneness-in-manyness." And it leaves us each "gazing out upon our fellows with a mixed attitude of fear, suspicion, and yearning"[52]—an apt description of the civic situation that Kenneth Burke tried throughout his work to address.

When Václav Havel rose to speak that night at the White House, he was prepared to respond to Clinton's ideal image with a more complicated reality. Havel could address the topic of jazz and democracy as a longtime fan of the music, who had lived through both the Nazi occupation of his country and then its Communist control—times when the music had been actively suppressed. Those regimes, Havel said, had "hated" jazz, and their policies forced "a lot of our Benny Goodmans [to play] in very secret, secret, secret cellars." The complaint against the music? Jazz "is free."[53] But, as the last president of Czechoslovakia and the first of the Czech Republic, who had to lead his people from Soviet to democrat in a very short time, Havel understood well the complexities of freedom. In an essay titled "Democracy's Forgotten Dimension," published at about the time Clinton began his second term, he had described problems inherent in the American concept that had, in his judgment, contributed to its failure to fill the void left in Eastern Europe by the fall of communism. The problem was that in America the universal values of "freedom, justice, and prosperity" were manifest in "ideas of democracy, human rights, civil society, and the free market" that themselves were enacted in

> moral relativism, materialism, the denial of any kind of spirituality, a proud disdain for everything suprapersonal, a profound crisis of authority and the resulting general decay, a frenzied consumerism, a lack of solidarity, the selfish cult of material success, the absence of faith in a higher order of things or simply in eternity, an expansionist mentality that holds in contempt everything that in any way resists the dreary standardization and rationalism of technical civilization.[54]

Here civic action is controlled by a conception of "freedom" that spins into the alienated self. And if Havel is right, then if Americans do find a model for democracy in jazz it is likely to be because what they think they hear in the music is individual expression unconstrained.

But musicians know well that in jazz, that freedom is never unconstrained and is always coupled with the unrelenting responsibility to others that is this music's moral other half. That's what Clinton, who used to play jazz, explained when he returned to the podium to respond to viewers' questions being submitted online. With the Jazz at Lincoln Center Orchestra on stage behind him, Clinton was asked by one viewer whether learning to play jazz when he was young had influenced his career choice of public service. His answer:

I had never thought about it before, but I think the answer is, my association with music and the discipline and long hours of preparation it took and the joy it brought, particularly when I got into jazz, had a lot in common with what I love about public service. It is about communication, it's about creativity, [and] cooperation.

"And like jazz," he added, "I don't think you can be really, really good at it unless you care about other people and have a good heart like these guys [behind me] do."[55]

What Clinton meant by a "good heart" may be what Havel considered "democracy's forgotten dimension." Saturated as it is with individualism, American democracy is met around the world with a resistance and resentment that might erode if this nation were, in Havel's words, to "rediscover and renew its own transcendental origins":

The relativization of all moral norms, the crisis of authority, the reduction of life to the pursuit of immediate material gain without regard for its general consequences—the very things Western democracy is most criticized for—do not originate in democracy but in that which modern man has lost: his transcendental anchor, and along with it the only genuine source of his responsibility and self-respect.

Jazz calls upon those who play it to practice an individualism made from that kind of responsibility and from the kind of self-respect that follows from acknowledging oneself bound with others in a commitment to direct each individual's unique capacities to a common purpose. At the White House that night, Presidents Clinton and Havel used jazz to explain that a good life cannot be lived entirely on one's own terms, though this nation's politics seems so often to deny that. Instead, they would have democrats be people whose communities are, in Havel's words, places "for quest and creation, for creative dialogue, for realizing the common will, and for responsibility." Short of that, the terrain of civic life would be an array of "mere battlegrounds for particular interests."[56]

Kenneth Burke's work prescribes attitudes and practices that would enable Americans in particular to make for themselves a way of life that is better than that—one that looks a lot like what jazz displays. Living that way is a demanding practice that requires individuals to listen well to each other and to respond, even in conflict, in ways that advance the common project. In a way, jazz is itself a practice of *ad bellum purificandum,* of war waged with an attitude of goodwill that is enacted by turning differences between people toward that project in the bright hope that something better for everyone will follow. The music can be encountered as a summons to a democratic practice that is, as Havel put it, "imbued with transcendence in the broadest sense of the word," which is "the respect of man for that which transcends him, without which he would not be and of which he is an integral part."[57] This suggests something else about jazz: that the music proceeds by making space in its performance for what can sometimes seem like a miracle. Perhaps jazz is the music of democracy not so much because it so well melds individual and group, freedom and order, though that is crucial, but because it does so through joint acts of faith. Jazz musicians play the music upon the belief that something beyond themselves will be manifest there—something that expresses, in William James's phrase, "immense elation and surrender, as the outlines of the confining selfhood melt down."[58]

Experiencing Community

All of that remained unrealized in America as the twenty-first century turned. The principle of individual liberty still dominated democratic values, and the nation remained an aggregate of individuals who competed for advantage while seeking occasional solace in the public myth of *e pluribus unum*. Perhaps we use myth to imagine that fully democratic kind of unity because we have so rarely experienced it. I have experienced *e pluribus unum* as an American only twice: through the three bright November days in 1963 that followed the Kennedy assassination and, much of my lifetime later, through a few bright days in the autumn of 2001 when we were all trying to make sense of what had happened on the morning of September 11. Except when things like that take us collectively by stunning surprise, the experience of being a distinct individual living in wholehearted concert with others is hard to come by, something that certainly limits this nation's capacity to realize the transcendent identity that it so persistently claims.

Most of the time, life in the United States seems more competitive than communal, but on a Friday in November 1963 and on a Tuesday in September 2001, that changed for awhile. After the young president was killed, Kenneth Burke responded in print with an anguished prediction that despite the intense unity Americans shared through the televised funeral days, "our country" would quickly "fall back wholly into its same trivial ways," what he described as "hagglings."[59] And that happened quite quickly. Burke was gone by 2001, but it wasn't long after we had all watched on television the loss of three thousand of our lives that the same sort of "hagglings" began yet again. But for most of us, I think, a memory persists of some comfort and reassurance, if not "elation and surrender," in the immediate aftermath of a traumatic national event as the "confining selfhood" that normally gives public life a hard edge seemed, for a little while, to "melt down."

As I walked out the door that bright Tuesday morning, I heard a report on the kitchen radio that a plane had crashed into the World Trade Center. I walked out to my car somehow imagining an accident involving a Cessna, and listened just to music through my short drive. But when I arrived at work I saw a crowd of my colleagues gathered around a twelve-inch screen in the department office, and joined them in time to see live the second plane explode into the South Tower. Within an hour classes had been canceled, and I had returned home to watch with my family as the towers fell and the Pentagon burned. That was the rest of our day: watching gritty and fiery footage, listening to news updates, and waiting for commentary that would make sense of it all and suggest what would come next. Classes resumed the next day under the blue quiet of an early autumn sky completely empty of contrails because only birds were allowed to fly. In classrooms and hallways people were quiet, even gentle with each other. Home again in the evening, Linda and I were still listening to the news coverage as we made dinner. Then, at 7:00 p.m., thirty-six hours after it had all begun, National Public Radio returned programming to its local affiliates. And on our local station, right on time, the nightly jazz program began.

There was a silent moment, and then a piano played a progression of two complex chords that sounded ambiguous in a place between major and minor. It was played as a very rhythmic phrase, the first a quick touch and the second sustained, the kind of phrase you would hear introducing a song in an African American church. Those gospel-tinged chords then moved ahead in some rhythmic and harmonic uncertainty; at least that's how it seemed to us. As with most everything else we'd seen and heard that day, we were searching those chords as we listened for a clear sense of where they were taking us. At first the rhythm was stiff and quiet, almost martial, in the left hand, as the right started to nudge it loose with hesitant fragments of improvised arpeggios inflected with the sound of the blues. The blues and gospel, of course, are the same music in different moods. We were hearing both moods at once here. Behind the piano we could also hear feet shuffling, a chair scraping, glasses clinking, a blur of conversation—what a jazz club sounds like before the music takes hold. And then it caught hold. The piano asserted a sequence of chord changes that seemed almost familiar. We couldn't identify where they were going, but we knew we were going somewhere. The rhythm of the changes became propulsive, syncopated, and we could hear the audience focus on the music and then join it with claps and an occasional shout. We had been half-listening until then, preoccupied, until suddenly recognition grabbed us. We stopped chopping and stirring when we recognized the melody in the pianist's right hand, a surprising one to hear that day, and as we spoke its name to each other the bassist and drummer picked up the piano, and us, with the momentum and purpose of a cross-country train. The music put the familiar words in our heads, swinging hard: "Glory, glory, hallelujah; glory, glory, hallelujah." We were smiling at each other, filled with our national dirge as an anthem of defiance and even celebration.

The trio played only the chorus, not the verses, of "The Battle Hymn of the Republic," playing it through multiple times. The pianist was improvising on the melody and changes with energy that brought to my mind an image of another performance I had seen, in which a concert grand bounced a temporary stage up and down in time. Another chorus, other improvisations, and then a tenor sax sang out to begin to culminate this makeover of the old "Battle Hymn" with a vibrant and elastic voice that we, at least, needed to speak for us then. This performance had been recorded long before September 11, 2001—but, broadcast across seven states on the exhausted evening of September 12, it gave us the first meaning of the events. The "Battle Hymn of the Republic" is about mortal threat to American community, about its fragility and the collective commitment required of those who would strengthen and preserve it. We found that night in this jubilant jazz a hope that Americans could now overcome that fragility and that threat together—that in this moment of common need, the insistent selfhood that confines us each would indeed melt down.[60]

I don't think it is the poetry of the "Battle Hymn" that makes it an iconic American song. Played without words on the radio on this depleted day, after thirty-six hours of broadcast talk that had made us fear and tremble, this music itself sounded to us like "the song above catastrophe."[61] In spite of all that had happened and all that might follow, in that moment we felt safe in our bond with the thousands of others we knew were at that moment listening with us. That feeling stayed with us after the song ended and another less timely jazz tune began. We turned back to making dinner, ready to move on. The "Battle Hymn of the Republic" didn't prompt that, but the jazz did. The radio program went on until midnight with few words from the usually talkative host. That night he just played jazz.[62]

Sometimes it seems that Americans find what Ellison called that "more encompassing and acceptable definition of our corporate identity" only when they are under the same attack. We contend about American identity the rest of the time, claiming the version of it that expresses the image of our faction. But when circumstances demand, we can still transcend all that and combine in what Burke called "a different state."[63] It doesn't last, of course, but if we can recall its consolations clearly enough, after they are gone we might not contend with each other with quite so much conviction. That memory, along with the native need for connection that Tocqueville, Whitman, and Ellison described, may be enough to keep us together and, in that phrase from both Burke and jazz, "swinging along."[64]

Transcendence

The pianist Bill Evans once said, "Jazz is not a what, it is a how."[65] Though I doubt he had, it's as if he had read in *Counter-Statement* where Kenneth Burke described aesthetic form quite similarly. Burke located the form of a work of art in the structure of the experience it provides to the person who engages it, as Evans located jazz in the way it is made and heard. On that basis it wouldn't be hard to explain how jazz offers a representative anecdote of Burke's concept of art that turns it from an artifact into an experience that makes what it abstracts concrete.[66] One way to understand how Burke says form works is to think of it like the plot of a mystery novel. That plot carries the readers along through a linked sequence of what amounts to a series of learning experiences. An event prompts an expectation, and in the next event that expectation is answered. When that answer is surprising, the reader must adjust assumptions and even attitudes toward author and characters, thus learning something new. This "kind of 'learning' that goes with an audience's engrossed participation in the successive disclosures of a plot," Burke suggested, "may be more directly explainable as a sympathetic delight in the perfect unfolding of a form, with its 'natural' order of attitudes." That's true in a mystery story: the "delight" is not in its ending, but in the process of getting there. The unfolding of aesthetic form is not always a matter of plot, and the lessons that follow from it can't always be articulated. But the process "engrosses" us, in Burke's words, in the way that a slow-motion film of "the gradual bursting of a blossom" does. Watching, we "participate" in a process that enables "us as onlookers to unfold with it," something that "can be more accurately explained in terms of action than in terms of knowledge"[67]—in the terms of "how" rather than "what." This sort of "engrossed participation" is what Burke was talking about when he used the phrase "swinging along." In that phrase, Kenneth Burke meets Duke Ellington, whose definition of "swinging" boiled down to the experience of "my pulse and your pulse . . . together."[68]

This concept of participation takes us back to Plato's design for dialogue, which for Burke was a touchstone. "Platonic dialogue," Burke wrote, "is not formed simply by breaking an idea into its component parts and taking them up in one-two-three order" as objects of knowledge. That's Aristotelian. Rather, it engages participants in "a process of transformation whereby the position at the end transcends the position at the start." For Aristotle, dialogue is epistemological, about knowing, while for Plato it is ontological, about being. Participants in this Platonic interaction change their minds about things but do so organically, so that, as Burke put it, "the position at the start can eventually be seen in terms of the new motivation."[69] What the person "knows" changes, but that is not nearly as important as the change of attitude that occurs through the process. Attitudes, you'll remember, are the material of which identity is made. Bill Evans said jazz is not a "what" but a "how." For Burke, "how" is a matter of changing attitudes."[70]

The "how" of jazz is enactment of an attitude to be shared by those who would play the music, and even by those who would listen to it well. That "how" is enacted in a willingness to confront tensions and conflicts together and then transcend them by finding ways to expand the boundaries of identity, individual and collective. That willingness—another word for attitude—follows from a realization that together people can accomplish what lies well beyond the capacity of any one of them, a realization that itself allows some space for miracles. Burke located that realization in a moment when, borrowing terms from someone else's study of Plato, "Myth 'bursts in upon the Dialogue with a revelation of something new and strange,'" something that moves things "from the order of Reason to the order of Imagination."[71] Our attitudes, as Burke uses that term, imagine ourselves interacting with others. Burke calls upon us to adopt attitudes that imagine us as being on the way to transcending an explanation, an argument, or a discussion. This interruption of reasoned dialogue by an aesthetic moment of "resonantly imaginative and poetic synthesis"[72] is not necessarily a good thing. It can be powerful deception. But when Linda and I needed it, that night of September 12, the interruption gave us a few moments of "communion" that blessed us—an almost mystical "perfect communication" that sustained us just then and enabled us to go on.[73]

Burke's term "consummation" gets at that. His use of the term suggests something different from his definition about the playing out of things in all their implications. Over time, the structure of his own intellectual autobiography—from "self-expression" through "communication" and toward "consummation"[74]—became the model he used to describe the ideal progression of productive communication, with the product being a "consummation" that participants experience as a "different state."[75] The most detailed description he provided of that experience has the distinct shape of a great jazz performance:

> At the beginning there is a kind of dispersion, scatteredness, conflict among the terms; then the terms . . . are subjected to progressive ideological criticism by the give-and-take of controversy; this is an "Upward Way" moving towards some "higher" principle of unity; once this principle is found, a whole ladder of steps is seen to descend from it; thus, reversing his direction, the dialectician [or, the musician] can next take a "Downward Way" that brings him back into the realm of dispersal, or diaspora, where he began; but on reentering, he brings with him the unitary principle he has discovered en route, and the hierarchical design he saw implicit in that principle; accordingly, applying the new mode of interpretation to his original problem, he now has the problem "placed" in terms of the transcendent, unitary, hierarchizing principle—and thus, instead of being merely scattered, the problematical element has become "structured," seen as part of a comprehensive context; thus, while it is still there, it is there "with a difference," and that difference makes all the difference.[76]

This is transcendence as Burke meant the term, an almost mystical move to the "different state." It is a different state of attitude and, so, of identity. And Burke's more familiar description of transcendence describes that as well: "Encountering some division, we retreat to a level of terms that allow for some kind of merger (as 'near' and 'far' are merged in the concept of 'distance'); then we return to the division, now seeing it as pervaded by the spirit of the 'One' we have found in our retreat."[77] But I like better his description of that same process in musical terms. He said that an arpeggio can transform a dissonant note that would otherwise destroy the chord into an unexpected interval that freshens the sound of the sequence. Perhaps people who are wary of the ideas of unity and community assume that both work in the way we play a piano chord—we select notes from those available in the scale that will be harmonious when played all at once. But communities aren't like that, especially democratic ones. They cannot ensure harmony at each count. Applied to people, the playing of chords is a perfectionist project that has little to do with daily reality. Unlike the vertical order of harmony that chords demand, our lives take on the horizontal order of arpeggio that moves forward like jazz does, improvising musical lines in the keeping of time. If someone plays a wrong note, someone else can next play one that makes it sound right, turning dissonance into a new melody. That requires a different way of understanding ourselves in relation to those around us. We don't have to live together vertically, in harmonious agreement. We can live together in time, sharing horizontal experiences of questioning and answering, anticipation and surprise, learning and change. The difference between chords and arpeggios is not in the notes we play. It's in how we play them.[78]

That's what Linda and I learned at suppertime that September 12 as we listened for not quite nine minutes to the "Battle Hymn" played as we had never heard it played before. We'd heard the song all our lives, but this time it was different and more useful, bringing order and direction to the chaos that had begun the morning before. So we followed the lead of the musicians who played it, and found our hope in their example that we could move forward together with energy and good cheer. Since then we've sought out live jazz performances to remind us of that, of the attitudes we need to have. In every performance of jazz you can witness each musician's uncertainty about what might come next. But you witness as well the commitment they share to play through it anyway. On September 12 we stopped our cooking and then our worry to swing along with that. Though the sites were still burning, the air in New York and Washington was still acrid and ugly, and people were still lost in the rubble, that jazzed version of "The Battle Hymn of the Republic" left us in a "different state"[79]—the one that, as Burke said, transcends "dispersion, scatteredness, [and] conflict" long enough to enable a glimpse of "some 'higher' principle of unity."[80] We still didn't know where the events of the day ought to take us. Perhaps the right speech could have told us, but that speech didn't come. But jazz had "burst in"[81] with a joyous image of proceeding anyway, and that felt like enough for us.

FIVE

What Jazz Does

We could say that there are certain "democratic situations," and that there can be democratic *nations* only so long as these democratic *situations* exist.[1]

KENNETH BURKE

For Kenneth Burke, our attitudes and actions are both enabled and limited by our situations. In his political phrasing, just as there are "situations favorable to dictatorship, or requiring dictatorship," so there are situations in which democratic life is possible.[2] So in that 1942 essay where he wrote that the nation's rapid military buildup was making American life not so democratic, Burke asked "whether a nation could possibly continue with democratic *acts* in a non-democratic *scene*."[3] "Scene" is Burke's term for a particular enabling and limiting situation in which we find ourselves interacting with others, the element of his pentad that most constrains the other four aspects of motivation—agent, act, agency, and purpose—as he described the system in *A Grammar of Motives*. There he described how scene—"situation," in the sense he used that term in the epigraph above—is "at the very centre of motivational assumptions," where it shapes not only actions but also identities among those who act.[4] So what sort of scene is a democratic situation?

American answers to that question tend to recall what many readers think Tocqueville is saying if they ignore the ambivalence that gives his *Democracy in America* its coherence. But factor in that ambivalence, and you find a shadow falling across every sunny hope for democratic life, and in each bright perspective on the American nation a nervous glance in the direction of despair. Tocqueville affirmed equality and freedom as the values that structure American civic life, but he also wished that the new nation would embrace organized religion to "purify its morals" and "mold its actions," and that it would find ways to choose leaders whose "knowledge of statecraft" would be sufficient to counter the people's "blind instincts." In fact, Tocqueville's reading of that democratic situation led him to conclude that to be able to govern themselves, Americans must ultimately "be guided" from without.[5] What seeps out of his description of this attempt at equalitarian democracy is the conclusion that a fixed framework of hierarchy remains necessary, that the equality and freedom that almost all the Americans he met considered democracy's dominant characteristic were not sufficient to sustain the civic project. It is as if Tocqueville understood democracy in America to be operating in the same way many Americans misunderstand jazz, as music made with a loose sort of order that, as Stephen Frederick Schneck develops the comparison, is "playfully constructed, improvised according to the desires of the players and the perceived intentions of the crowd, constituted in the naïve enjoyment of its technique and hearing." By that description, neither democracy nor jazz is a reliable or a serious project, because the assumption underlying that formulation is that the individuals involved share an "indisposition" to "discipline themselves to a higher order."[6] Indeed, Tocqueville came away from America with the impression that "nothing is more repugnant to the human mind in an age of equality than the idea of subjection to forms,"[7] an attitude reflected in reference to jazz in the notion that "good music cannot be trusted to emerge from ad hoc improvisation by serendipitous players."[8]

That conclusion misses the point of both democracy and the music, of course. Jazz demands that performers share a commitment to subject their own equality and freedom quite consciously to the project they share with the group. The democratic situation that encompasses them when they make this music renders them accountable to each other. Indeed, this kind of commitment seems also native to a democratic situation, because it is necessary to give palpable order to a looming disorder. So, as Schneck puts it in his comparison of jazz and democracy, jazz "[grows] from the techniques of the players as it is improvised *for* the circumstances of its playing."[9] They draw upon resources of their shared situation to express and to communicate what they are learning as they work within it. So we see again that there is more to freedom than Tocqueville's Americans, as well as most Americans of the present day, might think. "Freedom [is] not just being free from interference," writes political theorist Bernard Crick; "it [is] *acting freely* for the public good or the general interest.[10] That's how we ought to think of it. Individuals who consider themselves free, adds Eddie Glaude Jr., ought to "hold one another accountable and responsible in light of an understanding that democracy is a way of life and not merely a set of procedures."[11]

A way of life, as Burke said, constitutes an identity. A democratic way of life constitutes individuals as, among other things, citizens who join with others in sustaining civic life. Civic life is generally understood as the scene where politics is practiced, but if personal commitments to *e pluribus unum*, as well as its rigorous interpersonal practice, are not integral to that scene, the politics will not be democratic. We tend to read the Constitution as addressing us collectively rather than personally, but we ought also to read it the other way. Jazz music first addresses us each individually and immediately, as a work of art, by Burke's definition, must. Even if we sit in an audience of thousands the music invites each of us individually to experience for ourselves, intimately, what amounts to a particular musical way of life enacted. If we are paying attention we can learn more expansive lessons about what a democratic way of life requires of us, as well as the kinds of blessings that can follow from it.

For Kenneth Burke, a democratic situation is one configuration of the universal rhetorical situation into which all are born. We live in rhetorical situations that, by his definition, engage individuals in perpetual decisions and actions regarding "congregation and segregation"—with whom and with what to identify ourselves, and who and what we ought to keep at a distance.[12] His work focuses on the problems and promises of the democratic configuration of this rhetorical situation, addressing, as he puts it, the "bewilderingly interwoven nodus of elements, both symbolic and nonsymbolic," that constitute a particular moment's version of the ongoing problem of "the one and the many,"[13] of *e pluribus unum*. In a democratic situation, the decisions people make and the actions they take are exposed to the judgment of others who can hold them accountable for effects and consequences. At stake in such judgments are matters of identification and separation, of choices to align with or reject some idea or person or group: some identity, the essential rhetorical project in which everyone is engaged. For Aristotle, rhetoric involves influencing others or being influenced by them with an "ought" presented for acceptance or rejection. For Burke, the decision to accept or reject involves not only a proposition but also an assertion of the person one ought to be become.[14] Democratic situations are full of such "oughts" to be confronted and embraced or rejected. More accurately, they are to be struggled with as we try to decide which potential elements of ourselves—individually or collectively or both—to embrace and deny in a process that determines over and over again whom we understand ourselves to be.

Burke suggested that we make more of those decisions than we think. Each time we experience an "ought" placed before us, often wordlessly and even undiscernibly, and imagine ourselves enacting it, we calculate at some level of awareness its benefits and losses. So he proposed that we consider any symbolic structure that lets people try out an "ought" in that way to be rhetorical. The rhetoric might be conceptual, and take the form of some sort of argument; or it might be experiential as it flows over us, like an encounter with art. Jazz is that latter sort of rhetoric. And it is an art more participatory than most as it invites those who listen to the music into the process of its making, to share at just one small remove the way of life, the "*acting-together*," that making the music itself makes, to share with the musicians some of the "common sensations, concepts, images, ideas, attitudes that make them," as they make the music, "*consubstantial*."[15] The aesthetic sort of rhetorical experience Burke described in his theory of form demonstrates that "there is no chance of our keeping apart the meanings of persuasion, identification ("consubstantiality) and communication (the nature of rhetoric as 'addressed')."[16] Jazz is a display of "the showing forth of appearances with persuasive designs or consequences,"[17] an "*acting-together*" that can transform people, at the very least, for the duration of the music. It renders musicians profoundly interdependent as they try to sustain on the fly their unity with the materials of their diversity. And it makes those who watch and listen witnesses of that process, at the very least, if not participants who move with the performers a bit more than vicariously through the music being made.

The rhetorical power of this music resides in the experience that movement provides—an experience most intense for the musicians, of course, but available as well to attentive listeners. We experience jazz as a process of adaptation and change in response to sequences of the unexpected in each moment the unexpected unfolds.[18] If you don't like being supple like that as you listen to music, you probably don't like to listen to jazz. Improvised as it is, jazz music is made of the unexpected. It doesn't come together as a whole until it ends. People who want to stay with that kind of music must be willing to let themselves go where it takes them. They let their bodies move along with it, they listen well, staying alert for prompts from others that suggest how to situate themselves next throughout the performance. Here's what that's like for performers, from bassist Cecil McBee:

> We are all individuals. . . . When we approach the stage . . . we are collectivized there. . . . I mean history is about to take place, right? When . . . the band begins to play, history is going to take place. This energy proceeds to that area and it says, "All right, I'm here, I will direct you and guide you. You as an individual must realize that I am here. You cannot control me; you can't come up here and say, 'Well, I'm gonna play this,'" unless you're reading. . . . You can't go there and intellectually realize that you're going to play certain things. You're not going to play what you practiced. . . . Something else is going to happen . . . so the individual himself must make contact with that and get out of the way.[19]

McBee describes here individuals changing themselves in the process of playing together. That's how a democratic sort of individual transformation works. When jazz is played well, the reach of that transformation extends deep into the audience, where individuals can share a soloist's tension as she anticipates her next improvised phrase, and then feel with her the satisfaction and sometimes surprise that follow from what she plays.

To suggest that democracy fully realized ought to be something like that is to note how far civic life in America still has to go. Yet the ideal of coming together in ways that transcend self and advance the group has been around in America for a long time. Tocqueville picked it up when he proclaimed that "the only way opinions and ideas can be renewed, hearts enlarged, and the human mind developed is through the reciprocal influence of [individuals] upon each other."[20] Whitman expressed it when he wrote that "democracy is only of use there that it may pass on and come to its flower and fruits in manners, in the highest forms of interaction . . . in all public and private life."[21] Jazz displays what both those statements imply: that democracy is secondarily a political structure and that it is primarily an identity, a way of life, a way of being together, in which individuals constantly counterbalance their freedom "from interference" with their responsibility to act "*freely* for the . . . general interest."[22]

When Burke suggested that we understand art not as artifact but as experience—as, in his words, "a *way* of experiencing"[23] that invites us to "make ourselves over in the image of the imagery"[24]—he described an effect that he once called "incantatory,"[25] a term that jazz writers have used recently to describe the music of pianist Vijay Iyer, who in liner notes for his 2012 trio album *Accelerando* described quite precisely what that might mean: "Music is action. The sound of bodies in motion. When we hear a rhythm, we imagine the act that gave rise to it. Some call it neural mirroring, or empathy. Music and dance are linked in this way: bodies listening to bodies. If music has ever moved you then you already know."[26] We can read "neural mirroring" here as a clinical phrase for the kind of "identification" that is, for Burke, the outcome of successful rhetorical exchange. Whatever you call it, music has the capacity to summon us out of ourselves and transform who we understand ourselves to be. As philosopher Mark Johnson puts it, good music "captures us, carries us along on a sensuous, rhythmic tonal adventure, and then deposits us, changed, in a different place from where we started."[27]

That is how art does the civic work of binding divided and divisive people together. The bond may be momentary and only partial, but if the art is successful it is sufficient for the shared task at hand. Using the language of Johnson's description of how music works on us, you could say, in terms that align with Burke's theory of form, that art works by "present[ing] the flow of human experience, feeling, and thinking in concrete, embodied forms"[28] that can leave people changed. Jazz does that by bringing sustained intensity to the very way in which people in democratic situations must live their lives: improvising a shared way of life together as their changing situation demands. It calls people to participate, musicians to contribute their voices, and audiences to contribute theirs as well, even if that means just tapping or nodding or swaying with the music in time. Indeed, if you are in a jazz audience and don't move with the music you can feel distinctly separate, like a sort of dissenter. But jazz can also reach us in ways that summon us to action, often of an explicitly civic sort. Iyer writes in his liner notes that jazz "is best shared in context"—in the context, he suggests, of civic problems: "Today's context sounds like acceleration: rising inequality, populist revolution, economic crisis, climate change, Moore's law, global connectivity."[29] So he introduces his *Accelerando* as definitely not an album of smiling swing. Rather, its rhythmic and harmonic patterns are designed to prompt, at the very least, acknowledgment of and reflection on the deeply problematical human context that is the situation we currently share, the scene in which we must act together.

Advocacy Jazz

When Kenneth Burke worried about the ways in which Americans were using the term "we," it was because he wanted them to consider more carefully what national attitudes and consequent actions they were claiming as their own when they used that term.[30] Yet even in that worry he might have taken some comfort in the fact that their insistent use of the term suggests that they still value the possibility of community. Like Whitman, Burke longed for American community. He rarely confessed that longing directly, but you can read it between the lines throughout his work. He was explicit about it at least twice, in two letters he wrote in the thirties to the same correspondent, stating in his usual indirect way that his "interests" in both theory and cultural criticism "are, as always, a concern for the reversal of splintering rather than for its intensification."[31] That was early in his career, and I have seen nothing in what he wrote after that to suggest that those interests ever changed. If that is wishful thinking, it is a way of wishful thinking that is necessary among people who would sustain a democratic situation. Perhaps Burke stated this aspiration directly so rarely because he knew it would be tagged as naive.

But he was not naive. All his life, and even through the day of his death,[32] Burke followed closely the contentious political news of each day as he persisted in his project of trying to explain how the contenders could, if they chose, understand themselves capable of coming together. In that explanation is a rationale and method for a kind of civic interaction that would counter a practice of American civic life that makes the "manipulation of men's beliefs for political ends" its "most characteristic concern."[33] The stakes were too high for him to tolerate that. He understood that we make our lives individually and collectively from decisions about whom and what to embrace and from whom or what to separate ourselves. That is our inescapable rhetorical situation. "Put identification and division ambiguously together," Burke proclaimed, "so that you cannot know for certain just where one ends and the other begins, and you have the characteristic invitation to rhetoric."[34] Democratic situations are a subset of that predicament in which the invitation is always urgent and much depends on how people handle the influences that nudge them in one or another way. Perhaps it is because he lived when and where that democratic situation was pervasive that Burke tried to describe how these nudges work on us more expansively than Aristotle did.[35]

Burke called Aristotle's concept of persuasion rhetoric "as *addressed*."[36] Here the attempt to persuade, to influence, is immediately intentional and even sometimes aggressive. But Burke's revisionist definition of rhetoric as "a symbolic means of inducing cooperation in beings that by nature respond to symbols,"[37] as well as an engagement in the "ways of identification that contribute variously to social cohesion,"[38] expands the category to encompass music and the other arts that do their rhetorical work indirectly by picking people up imaginatively and carrying them to a new place. That is Burke's theory of form in action. It is how "formal patterns . . . readily awaken an attitude of collaborative expectancy in us." And this may be his most precise example of that:

> Imagine a passage [of language] built about a set of oppositions (*"we* do *this*, but *they* on the other hand do *that; we* stay here, but *they* go *there*; *we* look *up*, but *they* looked *down*," etc.). Once you grasp the trend of the form, it invites participation, regardless of the subject matter. Formally, you will find yourself swinging along with the succession of antitheses, even though you may not agree with the proposition that is being presented in this form. Or it may even be an opponent's proposition which you resent—yet for the duration of the statement itself you might "help him out" to the extent of yielding to the formal development, surrendering to the symmetry as such. Of course, the more violent your original resistance to the proposition, the weaker will be your degree of "surrender" by "collaborating" with the form. But in cases where a decision is still to be reached, a yielding to the form prepares for assent to the matter identified with it.[39]

That assent occurs as "shifts of attitude" that seem and feel as if they are coming "from within." It is one thing to analyze and then choose an attitude or action to adopt in response to a statement or argument, and quite another to encounter a story or a song so "saturated" with attitude that by engaging it you find yourself moving in its direction.[40] Because jazz can do that, it has been commandeered to act as advocacy rhetoric, particularly when the issues to be addressed are problems so deeply rooted that reason alone is not likely to prompt anyone to change. People often label problems like these "things we can't talk about," yet these things still hold American identity hostage. Three of those are race, freedom, and religion in America.

Race

Jazz was being invented at the same time, in 1903, that W. E. B. DuBois proclaimed that "the problem of the twentieth century is the problem of the color-line."[41] He turned out to be correct, and the situation he named is what provided both resources and limits that guided the development of this music. Because jazz first came to life among African Americans and continues with a strong connection to that identity, it has always, sooner or later, turned American attention to the problem of race.

One thing that jazz sometimes does is display what America might look like if that problem were solved. The music developed using instruments, harmonies, rhythms, and habits of expression from all sides of that color line: from Africa and African America; from Europe via immigrants, from Native and Latin America, and from an American high and popular culture that were predominantly white and in which Jews were prominent. While there is plenty of racism in the history of jazz, it's worth noting that those who made the music were mixing the races almost from the start, particularly in the informal jam sessions where musicians were, socially as well as musically, the most equal and free. It took quite a while longer for audiences in America to accept an integrated group playing on stage, though outside the United States that was rarely a problem. So jazz, this music first made by people playing their way through a racist situation, can suggest that the problem of race may not be insurmountable.[42] For Albert Murray and Ralph Ellison, for example, one way to address that problem positively would be for everyone to understand that in America, "all blacks are part white, and all whites are part black." And something like that seems to be understood in jazz. Indeed, jazz can model how what Ellison called "the problem of defining the American experience as we create it"[43] could take more constructive shape.

Much of that is implied in what this music does. Played well, it displays what a democratic culture ought to look like. But sometimes that display alone is not sufficient. Sometimes it is necessary for jazz to become a mode of rhetoric "as addressed," confronting people directly and coming at them from without to call upon them to change. So jazz has been used to call people out on racism, to challenge racist policies and practices, to compete with it in contests of politics and philosophy. Billie Holiday sang "Strange Fruit" to white audiences both on stage and on record—an intense and graphic song that confronted them with the reality of the lynching that in the 1950s was still being allowed past the law. Louis Armstrong faced those audiences regularly in elegant dress, with confident carriage and the capacity to sing and play with a humanity more expressive and, in its own way, more refined than anything they might have encountered before. And in case they might have missed his point, Armstrong often put it all on the table by performing for them "Why Am I So Black and Blue."

And there was Duke Ellington. It was early in 1943 when the Ellington Orchestra finally made it to Carnegie Hall and sold out the house. The publicity promised a major event, "Duke Ellington's first symphony," which he had titled *Black, Brown, and Beige* and described as a three-movement "parallel to the history of the American Negro." The term "parallel" referred to how the music tells the same story in "tones" as the narrative presented in the song lyrics and speech. In 1943 America was deep in wartime and in urgent need of unity. Yet its citizens were decisively segregated by race both on the battlefield and in the manufacturing cities that were producing the war materiel, and the problem of race was only intensifying. It was as if all of that coalesced in Carnegie Hall that January evening as Ellington explained to an audience that was itself "black, brown, and beige" that this musical performance would be about being black in America. Eleanor Roosevelt was there to hear it. So were Frank Sinatra, Leopold Stokowski, and Count Basie. All of them came to witness Ellington taking on in his music the American problem of race.

Ellington had been working on what became *Black, Brown, and Beige* for some time. Elements of it had been developing a dozen years before, when in an interview he described the exploration of African American experience as his general musical project. "The music of my race is something more than the 'American idiom,'" he had explained. "It is the result of our transplantation to American soil, and was our reaction in the plantation days to the tyranny we endured. What we could not say openly we expressed in music, and what we know as "jazz" is something more than just dance music."[44] The jazz idiom he was using, he said, was "forged from the very white heat of our sorrows."[45] He had gone on to describe the "rhapsody" he was then working on, composed in "the syncopated idiom" in an attempt to express all of that. It was, he said, his own primary project: "I am putting all I have learned into it in the hope that I shall have achieved something really worth while in the literature of music, [and] that an authentic record of my race *written by a member of it* shall be placed on record."[46] This was the beginning of *Black, Brown, and Beige*.

By 1941, Ellington was collaborating with a handful of others on what he was calling a "musical revue" intended, frankly, "to correct the race situation in the USA through a form of theatrical propaganda." This Los Angeles production, titled *Jump for Joy*, was billed as more entertainment than art, yet it became "bitingly satirical" each time it brought up problems of race.[47] Ellington later folded some of the music from that production into what he would perform that winter night in 1943 as *Black, Brown, and Beige*, a composition that, as one critic put it, "proudly delineated the black contribution to American history."[48] The Carnegie Hall concert lasted a little over two hours, with *Black, Brown, and Beige* filling forty-five minutes in the middle between bookend sets of popular Ellington tunes. The first movement was "Black." In the liner notes for the recording of that concert, Leonard Feather wrote that it "sets the tone for the entire piece." "Black" recounts the phase of African America when life was divided between slavery and faith, between the work song and the music of church. The next movement, "Brown," represents a subsequent phase that portrayed, in Feather's words, "black participation in America's military struggles" from the Civil War on, something that was on every mind in the hall that night. The third was "Beige," expressing ways of African American life from the 1920s on that developed a rich culture in the face of relentless racism.[49] Ellington had also prepared a narrative "script" to parallel the music by addressing the audience directly with the issues the music implied. But he used little of the script that night. He seems to have concluded in the moment of the performance that it was not a time for controversy. So he turned this music toward the cause of unity by concluding *Black, Brown, and Beige* with this statement to the audience: "We find the black, brown, and beige right in there for the red, white, and blue."[50]

In the 1950s and 1960s, Ellington was routinely accused of stepping back from the march against racism and toward what was called civil rights. His answer to that was always the same: that his music challenged American racism by affirming his people. But he hadn't been satisfied with the way *Jump for Joy* had done that. One review reflected the general response when it summarized that show almost innocuously as "the story of the Negro people, [tracing] the history of this great nation from its beginning here through chattel slavery, reconstruction, to the present."[51] *Jump for Joy* had its moments of sarcastic critique of racism in America, but to stay alive the show had to make that story entertaining for white audiences. Ellington had said at the time that he was finding it hard "to give an American audience entertainment without compromising the dignity of the Negro people." That problem prompted the more serious work that became *Black, Brown, and Beige*. It told the story, in his description, of "the Negro American as he is today, what he wants, what he's got, what he's tried to get and didn't, how he is going to get it."[52] So *Black, Brown, and Beige* told that story at Carnegie Hall that night in 1943, but it did so gently. It was not until twenty years later that Ellington was angry enough to transform some of this music into the substance, if not the form, of a protest march.

He did that in *My People*, another "musical revue," this one written for the "Century of Negro Progress Exposition" held in Chicago late in the summer of 1963 to commemorate the first century of the Emancipation Proclamation. *My People* was performed there every day for three weeks with the coherence and intensity of serious theater. The show combined new compositions with some Ellington had written for

Black, Brown, and Beige and before, to distill African American experience down to a sound he made by interweaving spirituals and the blues. A small version of Ellington's band, augmented by a gospel choir, combined to tell that story each day. And at a point in the program where the music transitioned from sacred to secular, Ellington called for a spoken monologue he had composed, and that he voiced himself in the studio recording. The monologue takes the form of a poem in its substance and rhythm, and was to be delivered, according to the script's explicit direction, "loud . . . driving home every point with tremendous force." In its performance each line sounded a summons to performers and audience alike. The recorded version, with Ellington himself as narrator and the whole Ellington band playing behind him, begins:

My people. My people—singin'—dancin'—prayin'—thinkin'—about freedom.
Workin'—buildin' America into the most powerful nation in the world
Corn—sugar—indigo—iron—coal—steel—the railroad—you name it.
The foundation of the United States rests on the sweat of my people.
And in addition to workin' and sweatin,' don't forget that my people fought and died in every war.

This is Ellington reminding Americans in 1963 of the same essential fact he had asserted in different terms in 1943: that "every enemy of the USA has had to face my people on the front lines." With that established, the monologue can then turn to the intimate sorrows that follow. Back from war come decorated heroes—"glamorous" heroes, he said, who attract "other men's women." Ellington then proclaims, "And right after that came the blues." What follows is a collection of blues songs that set men's and women's separate sorrows in a delightfully frank dialogue—something good blues can do better than most anything else.

Then there's a second transition introduced by a virtuoso display of Ellingtonian jazz titled "Jungle Triangle #2." This is music in full African American instrumentai voice that recalls the rambunctious sound of the Cotton Club but then ends in a more modern sequence of subdued dissonant chords that in turn set up a pointed song titled "King Fit the Battle of Alabam." Ellington composed this song in response to television images he had seen that year of the fire hoses, clubs, and attack dogs that Birmingham police used on the demonstrators led by Martin Luther King Jr. He and his orchestra had been playing the song at jazz festivals throughout that summer, and each time he had spoken its uncompromised lyrics himself. With the conviction of a deep jazz groove, this song names names and tells the truth.

Martin—Luther—King fit the battle of Bam—Bam—Bam—
King fit the battle of Bam
And the bull [police commissioner Bull Connor] got nasty—ghastly—nasty
King fit the battle of Alabam—Birmingham—Alabam
And the bull got nasty—ghastly—nasty
Bull turned the hoses on the church people—church people—church people
Bull turned the hoses on the church people—church people—church people
And the water came splashing—dashing—crashing.

Little babies fit the battle of police dogs—po-lice
And the dogs came growling—howling—growling
And the dog looked the baby right square in the eye . . .
The baby looked the dog right back in the eye and didn't cry
And when the dog saw the baby wasn't afraid
He turned to his Uncle Bull and said
That baby acts like he don't give a damn
Are you sure we're still in Alabam?[53]

At the time Ellington was preparing "My People" for recording, a friend of his learned that Dr. King was also in Chicago and quickly arranged for them to meet. Ellington got the unexpected call in his hotel room and grabbed his jacket, and when he met King on the street he stepped forward and embraced him. Then Ellington took him to the studio where the band was rehearsing, and they played "King Fit the Battle of Alabam" for him. King wept when he heard it.[54]

After "King Fit the Battle of Alabam" comes another instrumental display of Ellington jazz, and then "My People" concludes with "What Color is Virtue, What Color is Love?" This song is performed without introduction in the recording, but written into the script for live performance is a child walking alone onto the stage to offer the audience a parable about green people and purple people who fight each other to the death and find in the aftermath that their blood was all the same color of red. Recalling what would follow that in the performance, Ellington said, "We had Joya Sherrill come out and say, 'We finally got on to the subject and we're sorry. We tried to hold it back as long as we could so we're going to discuss color now.' And then we had her sing 'What Color is Virtue, What Color is Love?'" That ended the show, leaving each audience with that question in mind. "If you answer the question," Ellington once explained, "it says everything you want to say."

Ellington would claim that "*My People* is definitely not political."[55] Maybe he made that claim because he considered it art and not argument. And most of the time he avoided political confrontation, assuming that his music could work on people, as Burke had put it, from within. But when he found it necessary, he did turn his music toward direct rhetorical work, and direct rhetorical work often *is* political. Others in jazz did that during those years. Charles Mingus, one of Ellington's trio mates for *Money Jungle,* composed and performed his "Fables of Faubus" to protest the order by Arkansas Governor Orval E. Faubus in 1957 that sent troops to stop the integration of Little Rock High School. The other trio mate, Max Roach, recorded *We Insist!,* the "Freedom Now Suite," for the same 1963 centennial of the Emancipation Proclamation at which Ellington presented *My People*. John Coltrane, who recorded a remarkable album with Ellington in that same difficult year, also composed and performed "Alabama" in 1963 to mark the anguish surrounding the loss of four little girls when the Klan bombed the Sixteenth Street Baptist Church in Birmingham. The free jazz that was emerging at the time was itself made of bitter complaint about racism in America. But there was also through those Cold War years the overtly rhetorical project of the US State Department that sent American jazz musicians, black and white, into adversary and developing nations. The political purpose of those tours was to counter accusations of American racism by presenting jazz as an example of racial tolerance in the nation that would be continually chiding them about human rights. These were clearly instances of what Burke could have called rhetoric-as-addressed.

Freedom

In his autobiography *Music is My Mistress,* Ellington wrote, "The fascination of jazz as a music lies in the performer's freedom of expression, so that the listener is always asking himself, 'Where do we go from here?' "[56] This is Kenneth Burke's rhetorical concept of aesthetic form at work. That question, "Where do we go from here?," is what keeps a listener (or a reader or a viewer) engaged with the art. To explore the phrasing of that question is to see why. To ask "Where do *we* go from here?" is to begin the process of "identifying" with the artist and the art. To ask "*Where* do we go from here?" is to anticipate the new "state of mind" that follows from the aesthetic experience—the substance of an identity changed in "*preparation* for an act."[57] To ask "Where do we *go* from here?" is to acknowledge that we are going somewhere, that progress is necessary if we are to make things whole. Ellington's observation that jazz makes us ask that question points toward the way this music can affect us. Listening to jazz, we identify first with what looks like the unfettered self-expression of soloists, but then with the inklings their solos offer of the safety and support they feel as contributors to the shared purpose and project that unifies the ensemble. By contrast, Americans have learned to ask in any encounter with each other, "Where do *I* go from here?" and to expect the answer, "To freedom, of course." In terms of music, we might have in mind the kind of freedom that jazz soloists seem to display. But a little inquiry into what playing a solo requires will readily change that "I" to "we," as an initial idea of freedom is complicated by what we learn about a soloist's relationship with the ensemble.

People readily say that jazz sounds like freedom. The music began by defying convention. Then it defied all sorts of cultural norms, expressing such exotic and "exuberant individualism" that people reacted with both shock and some envy. But those who paid attention to the music, particularly those who played it, soon realized that it is how the individual freedom works in the collaborative context of the group that makes the music so good. Early jazz sounded to many, as rock music later would, like a music of cultural rejection and rebellion.[58] But even people with conventional taste would listen to it now and then because they wanted to leave the nineteenth century behind and, after two centuries of searching, find their own cultural voice. It was just then that recording and radio were making jazz readily accessible enough for many Americans, as well as people well beyond America, to develop a taste for it. One of the first foreign places where it found a foothold was a rapidly changing Russia. It later lost traction under Stalin, but found it again during the Cold War as the Voice of America began broadcasting jazz music on shortwave radio throughout the Soviet bloc. At that same time the US State Department started sending American jazz musicians, including many African Americans, on what amounted to propaganda tours to Russia and other Soviet republics and satellites, as well as to developing nations elsewhere. The music was immensely popular everywhere they took it, worrying one post–World War II authoritarian government after another not only because of the kind of freedom it exemplified but also because of its tendency to absorb, adapt, and "swing" to its own purposes whatever nationalist musical heritage a regime might want to use to root its rule in history and shape the citizenry as it needed.

So in Germany during the 1930s, the Nazis heard in jazz a direct challenge. They rejected it as the expression of inferior people who would corrupt their Aryan culture. But they rejected it also, they said, because they heard in the music a celebration of "criminals," "rootless pacifism," "bloodless intellectuality," "armchair communism," and all the other "rot of a decaying society."[59] Then, in the heat of World War II, jazz became a weapon used against them as the Allies broadcast their own narratives about the war deep into Germany, baited with this inherently hopeful-sounding music.[60] The United States later institutionalized this use of broadcast jazz as a Cold War weapon of choice aimed at the attitudes of people living behind the "Iron Curtain." While in America people simply listened to jazz, among people living in these other countries the music was positively treasured. That is evident in the memories that the Polish consul general in Chicago in 2000, Zygmunt Matynia, shared in his introduction to a jazz concert featuring Polish musicians. "Jazz existed in Poland before World War II," Matynia said, but during the Cold War "it was underground—it was considered the enemy's music . . . so it was forbidden." What that underground looked like was clusters of people with shortwave radio listening to a program broadcast on the Voice of America titled *Music USA*. Willis Conover created that program and hosted it from 1955 to 1996. It always began with Duke Ellington's theme song, "Take the 'A' Train," followed by Conover's mellow voice introducing yet another narrated evening of American jazz. Conover, who knew the music and the musicians well, not only explained the music but brought in its major artists for regular interviews, and the stories those artists told provided listeners with an education not only in jazz, but also in what it felt like to live, for a little while, what they imagined to be an American life. Conover explained jazz in simple and slow-spoken English so vivid that listeners who hardly understood the words could still imagine themselves in what seemed to them to be quintessentially American scenes. "Through this we got much information about jazz," remembered Matynia. "We were listening. Poles were always looking for freedom and liberty. And jazz is freedom."[61]

It's hard to know precisely what sort of freedom they heard in Conover's programs—the simplistic sort that amounts to individual "spontaneity" or the complicated collective kind that involves "discipline, rhythm, [and] the nuanced musical conversations entailed in improvisation."[62] But we know something of what Conover intended. He almost never discussed things like freedom conceptually on the air, believing that "jazz is its own propaganda" and operating on the assumption that by listening to jazz well, people would come to understand and value the kind of freedom that individuals can practice in democratic situations.[63] But off the air, addressing Americans who couldn't access the VOA programs, Conover would talk conceptually about jazz, though not for long, Once, for example, after stating that jazz was "structurally parallel to the American political system," he described "American freedom" this way: "The musicians agree on tempo, key and chord structure but beyond this everyone is free to express himself." He would also embed this concept of freedom in what he said to explain the rhetorical work of *Music USA*: "This is jazz. And this is America. That's what gives this music validity. It's a musical reflection of the ways things happen in America. We're not apt to recognize this over here, but people in other countries can feel this element of freedom. They love jazz because they love freedom."[64]

That's the message that Conover and his employer were sending through *Music USA*. And by all accounts, Willis Conover came to be seen by those who listened to his program as "an emblem of America, democracy and liberty."[65] He likely assumed that this perception alone had the potential to change the attitudes of people of those populations toward the United States. And in 2007, little more than a decade after his last program, some major academic programs in communication and diplomacy, as well as the Voice of America organization, which is overseen by the State Department, convened in Washington to honor him. The event, titled "Jazz: Voices of Freedom, Voice of America Tribute Concert," was introduced by the undersecretary of state for public diplomacy and public affairs in this way:

> On the surface, it seemed as if [Conover] was just broadcasting music, but the effect was quite subversive—as he explained, jazz conveyed the very spirit of democracy because it demonstrated the wide range of individual freedom within mutually agreed boundaries. As he put it, "The musicians agree on the key, the harmonic changes, the tempo, and the duration of the piece. Within those guidelines, they are free to play what they want. And when people in other countries hear that quality in the music, it stimulates a need for the same freedom in the conduct of their lives.[66]

That's what motivated the State Department to send famous American jazz musicians abroad on performing tours during the late 1950s and early 1960s, along with the unstated motive of countering the spreading awareness that the United States still practiced institutionalized discrimination against African Americans. Jazz music had been available on record in most of these other countries since the 1920s, and local musicians had developed their own practices of jazz with an enthusiasm for the music that often exceeded that of Americans. Along with the reach of Willis Conover's radio program, this ensured that performances on these tours attracted large audiences. But it also brought out local musicians for the Americans to jam with and befriend. That story is told by Penny Von Eschen in *Satchmo Blows Up the World: Jazz Ambassadors Play the Cold War*, a book that is as much a study of an aesthetic rhetoric as it is of a cultural history. Essentially, and in Von Eschen's precise terms, the State Department seems to have concluded that for purposes of propaganda, "jazz was more valuable than didactic programming."[67] In the meantime, the American musicians themselves were enriching their capacity to play jazz as an American music in a way that was becoming global in its elements and practice.

The jazz performances the State Department brought to these countries were, like the Conover broadcasts, ostensibly apolitical. But the superstructure that surrounded them—the social events, the publicity, even the selection of people to be in the audience—was as strategic and partisan as the most sophisticated argument. The rhetorical project here was to display individual freedom in harmonious action. The message, just short of explicit, was that people in these countries where such freedom was suppressed should demand it. The job of the African American musicians, particularly, was to exercise that freedom eloquently on stage, demonstrating in the process that the United States was indeed the land of the free despite reports otherwise.[68] But in musical terms, that sort of freedom was constrained on these tours and even contested. One of those contests went public during the first State Department–sponsored tour to the Soviet Union in 1962. The band was an integrated all-star ensemble led by Benny Goodman. But things didn't go well. Musicians who usually did not play with Goodman resisted the extent of his control over the music and his insistence that the musicians play from his scores. The audiences were as unhappy as the musicians were, hearing Goodman's orchestrated compositions from the 1930s when they had expected to hear the people they had followed on radio and record play improvised, cutting-edge jazz. At the same time, African Americans in the band were becoming increasingly agitated about the state of things at home. Von Eschen notes that this was a bad time for conflicts, aesthetic or otherwise, to surface among Americans in Russia. The two nations were just weeks away from a lethal standoff over missiles in Cuba that was itself was rooted in geopolitical questions about what sort of freedom should be allowed.[69]

This was the first State Department concert tour to the Soviet Union, but other tours had been going to Eastern Europe and into the Third World for a few years, and some veterans of those "freedom tours"[70] were drawing on that experience to address directly and publicly the question of American freedom at home. In the late 1950s pianist Dave Brubeck and his wife Iola, with inspiration and assistance from Louis Armstrong, composed a sort of musical revue they called *The Real Ambassadors* to confront the hypocrisy inherent in such state-sponsored displays of freedom as well as redirect attention to the more complex and important concepts of freedom to be learned from jazz as they informed what was going on in America. Their score and script combined to suggest that by exploring the kind of freedom jazz requires, in the context of the fact that their nation was still keeping that freedom from African Americans, the musicians who performed on those tours displayed a commitment to democracy much more complete than that of their government. Most of them were realistic enough to understand that their music was preaching an ideal rather than an American reality. But for them it wasn't America they were preaching anyway. It was the music itself that best enacted the democratic essentials they valued most. You can hear that in an abbreviated "concert version" of *The Real Ambassadors* recorded in late 1961. At the Monterey Jazz Festival in September 1962, just days before the Cuban missile crisis, Armstrong, Brubeck, Carmen McRae, the vocal trio Lambert, Hendricks & Ross, and members of the Armstrong and Brubeck bands performed a unrecorded full version of *The Real Ambassadors* to counter what the State Department was using jazz to tell the world.

A story synopsis of *The Real Ambassadors* typed by Iola Brubeck begins with Armstrong and his band making an unscheduled stop at a European island nation while on one of those State Department tours. They stop there because they have read that the local Communists, who have been bringing "spectacular exhibitions" in from the Soviet Union to entertain the citizens, are likely to win the upcoming election. Immediately upon its arrival, the Armstrong band begins to perform, and that performance undermines the Communists so thoroughly that the ruling "Free-Democrats" ask Armstrong and his band to stay on until after the election the next day. The country's king even offers his throne to Armstrong until then, "in order to win the people solidly behind the Free-Democrats." As the story develops, Armstrong's jazz not only wins the election but begins to suggest the shape of a "world peace movement"[71] that would move ahead in the way that Burke said aesthetic form works. In developing this narrative, *The Real Ambassadors* presents some hard-swinging jazz with lyrics like this:

The State Department has discovered jazz
It reaches folks like nothing ever has.

Then with a sharper edge, like this:

When all our neighbors call us vermin
We send out Woody Herman.

And then, with a sneer, this version of what the State Department had told them before embarking on those tours:

Remember who you are and what you represent
Always be a credit to your Government,
Remember who you are and what you represent
Never face a problem, always circumvent.

The title of this musical narrative, *The Real Ambassadors*, refers to a place in the plot where a credentialed State Department representative arrives on the island soon after Armstrong does, and the people who have assumed that Armstrong was the official US representative must now determine which of the two is the "real ambassador." But the whole show addresses the more pressing question of identity: who and what an ambassador for America ought to be. Despite the diplomat's credentials, the people choose Armstrong and, in a song titled "The Real Ambassador," Louis claims that identity:

Who's the real ambassador?
Certain facts we can't ignore
In my humble way I'm the USA
Though I represent the government
The government don't represent some policies I'm for.
Oh we learned to be concerned about the constitutionality
In our nation segregation isn't a legality
Soon our only differences will be in personality
That's what I stand for!
Who's the real ambassador, yes, the real ambassador?[72]

The Brubecks' synopsis describes Armstrong reflecting here on "how his concept"—his sense of his own identity—"has grown since he was King—how he began as a symbol of jazz and a representative of the [American] Negro, then grew to become a U.S. representative abroad, but [now has learned] that he, as all men, was something more." Now he represents "the great human race." Then, hearing "village priests crossing the square below his window" chanting "God made man in his own image and in the image of God made he him,"[73] Armstrong's sense of self advances one more step. The song he sings then, represented here by its first and last verses, aims well beyond any critique of the Department of State:

They say I look like God!
Could God be black? My God!
If all are made in the image of Thee,
Could thou perchance a Zebra be?
Can it be?
No, not He.

When will that great day come?
When everyone is One.
And there will be no more misery
When God tells man he's really free.
Really free . . .
Really free . . .[74]

Of course, the phrase "really free" addresses the racial struggle that was—and still is—ongoing in America. As jazz music offered the world images of American freedom up to and through the Cold War, it was also being used to question the ways in which freedom was being limited at home. And many of the musicians sent to embody that freedom abroad were losing patience at home. These included the usually genial Armstrong and even the elegantly apolitical Ellington. In 1957 a young reporter had asked Armstrong what he thought about President Eisenhower's failure to intervene when Governor Faubus defied the *Brown vs. Board of Education* decision and refused to allow nine black children into Central High School in Little Rock. For print, Armstrong said that Eisenhower had "no guts" and described Faubus as "an uneducated plowboy." But these phrases were negotiated later with the reporter. His actual response was unprintable. What did make it into print was his response to a question about taking another government-sponsored tour. "The way they are treating my people in the South, the government can go to hell," the quote read. "When the people over there ask me what's wrong with my country, what am I supposed to say?"[75] Similarly, Ellington was reaching a point where reliance on his music and gracious demeanor to "[highlight] the patriotism of black Americans and their centrality in the United States and American culture"[76] was no longer enough. On a tour up the East Coast during the early months of 1960, when segregated businesses were being challenged with sit-ins, Ellington played at Johns Hopkins University and afterward joined a group of students who had been trying to get service in a popular restaurant near campus that barred blacks. With his tour bus parked conspicuously on the street right in front, he and the students entered the restaurant only to be told by the owner that it was closing early. They turned and left, but slowly, allowing time for plenty of pictures that hit newspapers throughout the country the next day. The restaurant was out of business within a week.[77]

Ellington, Armstrong, and others in American jazz had assumed that this music could instruct Americans, and most everyone else for that matter, in a democratic way of life. But a new phase of jazz that soon followed challenged even that. Perhaps it is because he is not an American that Nicholas Gebhardt can see how this "tendency to reduce the world of human experience either to jazz or improvisation is deeply ideological in itself."[78] For one thing, that ideology involves an assimilationist conception of America that people may want to resist.[79] Assimilation in an American democratic culture mandates an individual identity that consents to voluntary constraints upon the self on the assumption that such consent is indeed a civic virtue, regardless of its reach. In its conventional origin narrative, jazz is assimilationist, combining elements of the varieties of music that were available in America at the turn of the twentieth century. For one thing, however, that kind of assimilation is quite different from the civic sort that would support democratic self-government. For another, the work of making jazz that we might idealize is always embedded in a capitalist economy wherein every element of freedom must have a price.

"Free jazz" reacted to these complications. An aesthetic and political project both at once, free jazz was initially associated with the Black Arts movement that resisted assimilation in all of the arts. That resistance proceeded through aesthetic assertion of a "Black" identity as a political act. For example, here is Gebhardt's rendering of Amiri Baraka's political aesthetic for jazz: "It is not the jazz *act* that is radical; rather, it is the jazz *form* that is radical *in its very impossibility*. The jazz act, in this sense, is never radical enough."[80] That form that enables expressions of freedom, he suggests, points the way toward expressions so unconstrained that they can leave form behind. Ron Karenga boiled it down into a formulation that refers to Black Arts in general: "Our art is both form and feeling but more feeling than form." Either way, free jazz enables individuals to express themselves with absolute individual freedom and directs them toward that. That's the theory. In its practice, collaborators and audiences must constrain that freedom for music to be made at all, though they do so in ways not nearly as limiting as in the conventional jazz to which this music reacts. Still, Karenga keeps reminding us, "Our creative motif must be revolution; all art that does not discuss or contribute to revolutionary change is invalid. That is why the 'blues' are invalid, they teach resignation, in a word, acceptance of reality—and we have come to change reality." Upon that principle, free jazz looks toward an individualism absolutely realized.[81]

In the words of one self-identified free jazz musician, Thomas Chapin, "The Free players were the first jazz musicians . . . to focus almost exclusively on a furtherance of the music's creative possibilities, and at the expense of being understood by a lay audience." By "creative possibilities," Chapin means its "expressive properties—and consequent de-emphasis on its harmonic and rhythmic customs." In practice, it was "free-form improvisation" that proceeded simultaneously within an ensemble. So Chapin describes the music of saxophonist Ornette Coleman this way: "Liberated from the need to [follow a cycle of chord changes to give structure to the tune], Coleman's creative choices were unencumbered by the exigencies of functional harmony," and that freed him to make the transition "from an adherence to a predetermined structure to the spontaneous interchange of ideas among the players." Chapin describes this music of simultaneous improvisation as producing a sound that "was raw and asymmetrical: intelligent, to be sure, but almost totally at the service of emotion and physicality"—emotion and physicality that are inherently individual. To the uneducated ear, free jazz sounds formless. But its sound does follow a form that produces one of the three rhetorical effects that, for Jacques Attali, music can be used to prompt: "to make people *forget* the general violence" of the world, "to make people *believe* in the harmony of the world," and, "by mass-producing a deafening, syncretic kind of music, [and] censoring all other human noises . . . to *silence*." All three uses make music "a tool of power."[82]

That third use may best describe the rhetorical effect of free jazz. Especially when seen *and* heard, free jazz confronts an audience, as T. J. Anderson puts it, with "the physicality of the musician" in an embodied "attitude" that makes the music a way in which one defies conformity and creates new ways of presenting oneself to the world."[83] So you get an ensemble with a drummer working at high velocity in no stable groove, melodies that continue to develop indefinitely in what sounds like indeterminate form rather than cycling back after twelve or thirty-two bars, and no set or cyclical chord structure to bring the music round again to recognizable repeating phrases and set up expectations for endings. The musicians play with an introspective intensity that makes them seem to be performing in parallel rather than together. Yet when done well, this kind of simultaneous improvisation provides audiences with an aesthetic experience that does become coherent in the intensity of their common effort to make music that almost disintegrates, but not quite. On the one hand, the effort of self-expression seems so intense that each musician's resources must turn inward in order to continue. On the other, they must remain intensely aware of each other if they are to meld together in a kind of free-form spontaneity that we thought could only occur individually. For Baraka, this is music made of struggle, of individuals struggling together at the same time. The sound is of separate people playing all at once—of, as Archie Shepp put it, "what's goin' on" for each one. "What's goin' on" for them all includes, among other things, their persistent awareness that the jazz language they use comes from slave music played on slaveholders' instruments. It is still a music of community, but of a severely damaged sort.[84] Out of all that comes a sound in free jazz that can be as exciting as it is unsettling.

What is called free jazz, or the avant-garde, runs a spectrum from Ornette Coleman's white plastic saxophone and Cecil Taylor's abstract piano to John Coltrane's late-period tenor and soprano, all of which took this new jazz music past the political toward the spiritual. Coltrane finally did get to a place where he could claim what Kenneth Burke called "the complete autonomy of art"—set apart from inheritance of tradition, from the calls and counters of others, even from the expectations of audiences. For Burke such a claim would be clearly problematical: "Complete freedom to develop one's means of communication ends as an impairment of communicability."[85] So he would always turn self-expression toward communication in order to save us from ourselves. But in free jazz, self-expression seems the best means to communicative ends. As the singer Abbey Lincoln put it, "All art must be propaganda; all art must have an attitude; and all art must reflect the times you live in."[86] And all of that must be expressed individually. Free jazz does that. Embedded in political reaction, what it communicates is almost all attitude. Emerging in the 1960s and 1970s, when many Americans were considering the prevailing notions of freedom to be no longer viable,[87] free jazz was an aesthetic expression of that predicament. People whose civic experience in America seems to them to be made of unresolved dissonances could find themselves in this music and feel precisely what the musicians were trying to say.

Spirit

"When we talk about the avant-garde," said saxophonist Archie Shepp, "a lot of it was inspired by John Coltrane, as far as I'm concerned. . . . What I'm suggesting is that Trane gave [those musicians playing free jazz] a sort of credibility by synthesizing their ideas, making it swing, and adding to it spirituality." Jazz musicians talk often about their music in spiritual terms, though like the rest of us they can use those terms to mean different things. For some the "spiritual" is religious, and for others it is not. For some it is profoundly personal, and for others it is inherently interpersonal or even mystically collective. But in jazz those differences don't need to matter very much, perhaps because it's hard to use music alone to promulgate dogma—particularly music that is primarily individual self-expression. Still, music is felt experience, and whatever particular experience one is trying to express, those to whom it is expressed must connect it to the experiences of their own that the music seems to suggest. So Coltrane, whose playing became increasingly personal, was working through the early1960s to make his self-expression align with what others would have experienced. Hearing him do that, Shepp said, "was like being in church," as Coltrane "raised [jazz] from the secular to an area of serious *religious* world music."[88] That category identifies what Coltrane was trying to create: music that could reach out from jazz and from his own biblical perspective toward a concept of the divine so expansive and generous that many people, and eventually all people, could find their own spirituality within it. He believed that would require of him—as his wife, the pianist Alice Coltrane, put it—"the entire experience of the expressive self."[89]

The mature Coltrane was explicit about that project in the liner notes he wrote for what most consider his spiritual masterpiece, *A Love Supreme*. This was clearly, for him, an act of testifying:

> ALL PRAISE BE TO GOD TO WHOM ALL PRAISE IS DUE.
>
> Let us pursue Him in the righteous path. Yes it is true; "seek and ye shall find." Only through Him can we know the most wondrous bequeathal.
>
> During the year 1957, I experienced, by the grace of God, a spiritual awakening which was to lead me to a richer, fuller, more productive life. At that time, in gratitude, I humbly asked to be given the means and privilege to make others happy through music. I feel this has been granted through his grace. ALL PRAISE TO GOD.

That "wondrous bequeathal" is this: "HIS WAY IS IN LOVE, THROUGH WHICH WE ALL ARE. IT IS TRULY—A LOVE SUPREME—."[90] Two years earlier, Coltrane had explained this conversationally in an interview:

> Overall, I think the main thing a musician would like to do is to give a picture to the listener of the many wonderful things he knows of and senses in the universe. That's what music is to me—it's just another way of saying this is a big, beautiful universe we live in, that's been given to us, and here's an example of just how magnificent and encompassing it is. That's what I would like to do. I think that's one of the greatest things you can do in life, and we all try to do it in some way.[91]

Most jazz musicians don't play with, or at least don't name, such explicit rhetorical intent.

Some do, though. When veteran pianist Mary Lou Williams became a Catholic in her mid-forties, she quit playing jazz altogether to devote herself to charitable work. She had been at the center of the African American jazz community in New York, opening her apartment and her piano through the 1940s to younger musicians, like Thelonious Monk and Dizzy Gillespie, who were developing their own versions of the form. Three years of "running thrift shops and helping musicians who were struggling with drug addiction," along with the urging of friends, left her believing that she could serve God best through jazz after all. Like Coltrane, Williams had come to understand her ability to compose and play music as a gift from God, so now she focused her attention on making sacred music from jazz and other African-American idioms. One of her compositions, and perhaps her best known spiritual work, *Black Christ of the Andes*, presents a cycle of songs that celebrate St. Martin de Porres, a seventeenth-century lay brother of the Dominican Order, a humble black man who worked with the poor and became "patron saint of interracial justice and of social workers."[92]

More recently, jazz pianist Eric Reed has described his own similar sense of calling:

> My music is influenced by a spiritual foundation (specifically, God's spirit, in this case), which encourages me to remain focused on the reason I was born with the gift he gave me—to praise Him. In addition, I share that love and desire with the audience, with the hope that they can be reeled into my spiritual space, to be entertained and blessed by the experience.

With Coltrane and Mary Lou Williams, this kind of spiritual motive has committed Reed to new musical directions: in his case, connecting gospel music with jazz. That effort has, as he puts it, "ignited a brushfire that sweeps through my bones," a good statement of the feeling his music would suggest. Whatever musical form that feeling might take, Reed acknowledges that "the vibration in the music of an individual genuinely connected to his faith cannot be ignored—even if you don't identify with his spiritual philosophy." For him, as for many others, "there is music for music's sake and then there is music that encompasses a deeper purpose."[93]

That "vibration" may be what we recognize as the sort of "spirit" that jazz music and other art forms can communicate. It is profoundly personal, because in art there may be no spirituality possible apart from the person expressing it, but in that person it does become available to others. Archie Shepp said something like that about John Coltrane: "The things he expressed were appreciated by us all, because he lived that way. That's who he was."[94] In jazz the meaning of that vibration is made in two moments of profound recognition. The first is more recognizable, the more you understand jazz: as Jim Merod puts it, "its one-hundred-year history of performance, inscription, recording, and songful execution is deeply spiritual," a spirituality that takes form "in an attitude of faith in life."[95] That attitude is the sort of spirituality John Dewey had in mind when he called Americans to embrace a "faith in the continual disclosing of truth through directed cooperative endeavor," one he considered to be "more religious in quality than is any faith in a completed revelation."[96] If we replace "religious" with "spiritual" in these statements and let what Dewey says define that term, we can begin to see why musicians can consider the making of jazz to be a spiritual as well as an aesthetic act.

Jazz can prompt our recognition of something worthy of, in a word, our reverence. This is philosopher Paul Woodruff's term for a kind of humility that is civic, in the sense of being individual and collective both at once—an individual attitude that has collective effect. To explain this idea, Woodruff uses music: not jazz, but a string quartet. A quartet plays well when the four individuals join willingly in their shared project by subordinating themselves to music they can only make together. They display that commitment in what is almost a rite that requires them to act their designated parts. They make their music by performing those parts together, "largely without ego," as he puts it, in a "clearly defined hierarchy." At moments in that process and afterward, they can share a "feeling of inarticulate awe" in the face of what they have done together.[97] That "awe," writes Woodruff, "is the most reverent of feelings. You feel, when you are in awe, that you are human, that your mind is dwarfed by what it confronts, that you cannot capture it in a set of beliefs, and that you had best keep your mouth closed and your mind open while awaiting further disclosure."[98] Such a feeling might even be intensified in jazz. As the members of a jazz ensemble subordinate themselves to a common project, they must give *it*—not give *up*—their most emphatic individualism, submitting not to a script but to a process of collaborative invention that requires the assertion of each separate self. When they succeed, they are changed. What they have done can seem to happen as if by grace. For jazz pianist Keith Jarrett, music like this can only be made from a special "place" that he considers "the only state from which to make music of any value to you or anyone else." To be in this "different state," in Burke's phrase, is "a gift." Says Jarrett, "I would never have been able to invent it. *I consider it a sacred thing.*"[99]

What transforms the worldly work of jazz into something like that is the attitude of "reverence," in Woodruff's sense of that term, that this music can and perhaps should evoke. Such "reverence," says Woodruff, "must stand in awe of something. . . . Something that reminds us of human limitations. . . . Something that satisfies at least one of the following conditions: it cannot be changed or controlled by human means, is not fully understood by human experts, was not created by human beings, and is transcendent. Such beliefs are the least you must have in order to be reverent."

Reverence is not spirituality, but spirituality is what reverence lets us feel.[100] When the jazz is good, it may well be the performers' reverence for what is happening that lets them make it so. Perhaps reverence is also what enables them to know when their audiences understand what they have mustered the courage to say, as well as what allows those audiences to find what has been said in their own experience, even experience they did not know they had. Coltrane talked about the first part of this idea, saying: "My music is the spiritual expression of what I am—my faith, my knowledge, my being. . . . I'd like to point out to people the divine in a musical language that transcends words. I want to speak to their souls."[101] Jazz writer Dan Morgenstern, remembering listening to Coltrane play live, described the second part: "'The intensity that was generated was absolutely unbelievable. I can still *feel* it, and it was unlike any other feeling within the music we call jazz. . . . It carried you away. If you let yourself be carried by it, it was an absolutely ecstatic feeling.'"[102] That was what Coltrane was after, and he understood how it can happen in terms that are consistent with Kenneth Burke's concept of the structure of aesthetic experience, of aesthetic form. When you listen well, Coltrane said, "you can get a feeling of expectancy and fulfillment in a solo, and an artist of ability may lead you down paths in music where many things can happen."[103] These are experiences intimately shared. But "sharing" is a weak word for what happens. This is how we *identify* with, even *inhabit* for a moment, someone else's experience of what Coltrane called, "my faith, my knowledge, my being." Perhaps this is what Burke meant by, "communion," by "consummation."

A recent essay on Mary Lou Williams describes the identity she tried to express in her music as a "communal" sort of individualism rather than the conventional "isolating" sort—one that takes her listeners along as she explores "the tragedies, triumphs, and spiritual longings of human life." What enables them to come along is that she animates the form of her music with the living attitude it would carry them into. That makes the process of "open[ing] *her* soul to the listener, offering spiritual friendship," rather than making the music itself, her primary aesthetic act—and it makes her spiritual goal "*interpersonal*, not communion with the divine."[104] That last distinction assumes a definition of the divine that would have it reside apart from us rather than within us. But sacred jazz often addresses something that can reside in both places at once. Certainly the divine is beyond human reach; yet it can engage us in ways that let us glimpse for just a moment what might be there. Sharing such moments is rare in everyday life, but a little less rare in jazz.

The Jazz Situation

In *The Real Ambassadors* there's an exuberant song titled "King for a Day" that has Armstrong's trombone player, Trummy Young, asking him the essential political question, "If you're king for a day, how'd you go about havin' your way?" Armstrong's answer is propelled by a cheerful drummer behind him: "If my every wish was my command I'd go and form a swingin' band with all the leaders from every land." Then, he continues, "The first thing I'd do is call a basement session." Trummy Young interrupts, "Oh Pops, you mean a summit conference." But Armstrong corrects him, speaking rather than singing now, "Man, I don't mean a UN kind of session, I mean a *jam* session." Then he sings this scenario: "They would fall right in a swingin' groove and all the isms gonna move. Relationships is bound to improve." Still the skeptic, Young sings back to him the other essential political question: "How can they all agree on one melody, won't each man call his own tune? They will want the song they've played all along. You're expecting too much too soon." But Armstrong rejects that, on his conviction that jazz gets people to "move": "Don't you mind I'll swing this deal," he sings, adding that "it's the only session of its kind where harmony you're sure to find."[105]

A democratic situation encompasses people who consider themselves each equal and free and who know that they must find ways to get along well enough to work together. In a rhetorical situation—by Kenneth Burke's conception—they find those ways through influence and change toward the end of being able to identify something of the self in the other. The process is fraught with tension, of course, if not contention. An attempt at influence prompts a choice, and changing entails the risk of losing something. In jazz, though, those tensions become creative as potential contention is transformed into an adventure in collaboration that prompts us to change as the music we make lets "us feel such shifts of attitude not merely from without but from within." There is harmony in that because, as Burke continued, "we are best able to exercise our sympathies by seeing [our] differences *from within*" in ways that allow us to experience in advance the changes we might make "imaginatively, personally."[106] In a jazz situation that task is the same as in a rhetorical situation: choosing to identify with one person instead of another, to embrace this idea and abandon that one. But in jazz we are all working together toward the same end, and that offers us some respite from the conflict that is inherent in every democratic situation.

Jazz and Kenneth Burke both propose a way of life that shows us how getting along in democratic situations is not a lost cause. Both acknowledge choices about "congregation" and "segregation" as the instruments we use to improvise our lives and celebrate our separate individualities as a happy necessity, cheering us on in their exercise. But both jazz and Burke also refuse to grant inherently equal value to the alternative aspirations of congregation and segregation. With constant critical awareness, they both advance the project of congregation whatever tensions it encompasses. They don't provide the two options equal time, probably because combining with people is so much more difficult than separating from them, and because we are not nearly so good at it. Throughout his work Burke looked toward and would lead us toward something like what he called "communion," though he used a few other terms to denote that ideal as well. He defined communion twice in *The Rhetoric of Religion* as a perfect correspondence "between the symbolized and the symbol,"[107] and once as a "perfect communication" through which individuals come together in what he calls " 'Love.' "[108] Once, in a letter, he tried to explain what he meant using some terms from formal religious practice:

We have a communion merging the individual with the group. Or one may say that "the religious man thinks only of himself." Or . . . I believe that one may say, "dialectically," both of these at once. And in all three there would be much justice, though I should tend to put most store by the third. At least, in the acts of communion there is conversion, transubstantiation—and there must be some isolated individual center that is undergoing this process, however intensely the reference is to participation in the group.[109]

That statement describes precisely how a performance of jazz can affect those who play the music as well as those who listen, though to different degrees.

Perhaps no jazz is so rhetorical in that way as Duke Ellington's three *Sacred Concerts*. The first was written and performed in 1965, the second in 1968, and the last in 1973—years that saw Ellington's music becoming more explicit about matters of race, freedom, and spirituality all at once. Harvey G. Cohen locates the *Sacred Concerts* in Ellington's ongoing effort to reinterpret "the complicated history of blacks and religion in America,"[110] an ongoing interpretative project with clear rhetorical designs upon his audience. This is rhetoric that would work by "reach[ing] people emotionally," by presenting people with something of the composer's own spiritual experience in musical form rather than by preaching it. By this time Ellington seems to have understood thoroughly what Burke observed about art in general and music in particular:[111] that people use it to act "on themselves and one another."[112]

Each of Ellington's three *Sacred Concerts* was performed in a different church. The music is rich and joyous, breaking with church-music traditions with upbeat drum-kit grooves and bluesy saxophone solos, and even a tap dancer's demonstration of what the biblical David might have felt as he danced before the Lord. When Ellington first performed these concerts, many complained about those elements, and not just because they pushed the conventional limits. It was also, as he once told a reporter frankly, because most Americans see in jazz something of the kind of man you wouldn't want your daughter to go out with,[113] the kind you would never see in church. Some of that impression was, no doubt—and perhaps still is—because to white people jazz can sound vaguely "black." But for most, the honest vitality of Ellington's sacred music overcame all that. For him the *Sacred Concerts* were "a prayerful contemplation of the love and beauty of God," and for others, as Janna Tull Steed puts it, they presented touching "evidence of an encounter between Ellington and the One whom he honored in them."[114] Like Coltrane, Ellington was coming to consider himself a messenger and this music his message. So each of the *Sacred Concerts* expressed Ellington's generous sort of spirituality as performed by those who joined him to give it voice. Steed describes these performances as a "magnificently human example of one striving to transcend [the] conflicts" that every one of us must face "while simultaneously giving himself to the world." It's a practical kind of spirituality, she wrote, that "could reveal God to us, and us to ourselves."[115]

Ellington's *Second Sacred Concert* took up the topic of freedom in this practical spiritual context in a song, "It's Freedom," in which the composer included, as he had done in songs about such things before, his own brief narration. This was in 1968, a bad year for the nation. It brought the assassinations of Martin Luther King and Robert Kennedy, confrontations between young people and police on college campuses and city parks, and then a contentious election that degenerated in violence and dismay. And in 1968 Ellington was still mourning his dear friend and collaborator Billy Strayhorn who had died young just months before. The *Second Sacred Concert* was performed early in that year, but seems now almost a response to the events that would follow in its calls upon Americans to reconceive freedom less as a matter of individual rights and more as "a way of treating people with love and respect."[116] So to prepare for the song's final verse, with a choir singing behind him, Ellington faced his audience and proclaimed the kind of freedom which Strayhorn had taught him that we all ought to seek: "Freedom from hate unconditionally; freedom from self-pity; freedom of fear from doing something that would help someone more than it does him; and freedom from the kind of pride that could make a man feel that he was better than his brother."[117] These are not freedoms of the separating sort. They are freedoms to connect. Rather than have us be wary, they would have us care for each other. Ellington would proclaim these four freedoms again just a year later at the White House as he was awarded the Presidential Medal of Freedom by Richard Nixon, perhaps to redefine the meaning of the award by turning on its head what most Americans think being free means. Freedom is a matter of *we* as much as it is a matter for *me*.

Jazz takes us to the place where *me* and *we* meet. There, individualism and separatism on the one hand and connection and community on the other are both good and necessary. How they interact depends on what is called for in the situation, and that makes the vigorous exercise of personal judgment essential if people are to progress both separately and together. But that progress must occur in the context of, in Kenneth Burke's terms, the "attempt of the divided to overcome division" that is the ongoing process of "identification" in which each of us is necessarily engaged.[118] This is the primary act of personal as well as civic life through which we each try to approach *e pluribus unum*. The perspective on all this that jazz music can provide may be enough to get people working together toward a way of life that is good for *we* and *me* both. One way to measure the quality of a jazz performance is to see how people come away from the music feeling about themselves and others together. Do they feel better about *we*? That's a good measure of life together in general: if people get along in ways that help them care better for both themselves and each other, their shared way of life is working.

SIX

How Jazz Works

Who would not call all men to him—though he felt compelled to dismiss them when they came, communion residing solely in the summons.[1]
KENNETH BURKE

That sentence culminates a moment of hope in *Towards a Better Life,* Burke's otherwise discouraging 1931 novel about profound selfishness. It's a brief moment, dimmed by ready acknowledgement that because consciousness can't reach beyond the boundary of the body, we can never get out of ourselves. But that bit of hope does affirm the effort of continuing to try. In the terms of the novel's title, it's that effort that seems to constitute "a better life"—a phrase that, as Burke used it here, aligns with descriptions of what he called the "good life" that thread through his work. In his *Permanence and Change,* written at about the same time, "the good life" involves interacting with others as a "*participant*" rather than from a "competitive aspect."[2] And in *Attitudes toward History,* written soon after, Burke defined "the good life" quite concisely as "a project for 'getting along with people.'"[3]

The idea that the good life follows from interacting with others as coequal participants, rather than as competitors striving separately for dominance, envisions a "social structure" in which the common project is "pyramidal" as people work toward the end of some sort of agreement even if it remains out of reach. Some of that work proceeds through persuasion, though that method readily ignites the competitive. But getting along requires more than that. It requires people to understand themselves to be engaged in a common project not so much for the sake of that project itself as to infuse their character with what Burke called "the cohesive motives" inherent "in the thought of oneself as a participant in it."[4] This is a matter of identity rather than strategy.

By that description, the protagonist in *Towards a Better Life*, John Neal, renders himself incapable of getting along. That is evident even in the structure of the novel as a series of his monologues, as well as in the misadventures that follow from his manipulation of others, and which shape its plot. Through most of the story, John Neal is entirely self-absorbed. But there is something in the New England countryside that sometimes can reach a self-centered young man and turn his gaze outward if it catches him in the moment of vulnerability that brings him meditating along its paths. It got to the young Jonathan Edwards that way and, in the next century, to Ralph Waldo Emerson, encompassing them suddenly with vivid awareness of things greater than themselves. In Burke's narrative it seems to have touched John Neal, at least for a moment. Walking alone at dusk in contemplation of his current clashes with those whose lives he has been trying to control, he is suddenly immersed in the sensations of the place to which he has until that moment been oblivious. Here is Neal's description of that moment:

> Vigorous young frogs chirp, doubtless enchantingly, in the swampy portions of the meadows. The trees fringing the crest of the hill show no evidence of wind. And distantly, against the seething of my pipe, I catch a bell, shaken by the cropping of one cow, but announcing the herd. The night patiently descends, with a coexistence of sound and silence that is the quality of expectation, and thus of twilight.

Emerson and Edwards read redemption in sensations like that. Edwards found himself accepted by God, and Emerson found divinity within. What John Neal finds, at least for a moment, is a sense of an identity very different from his own. Neal has gone walking to wonder how he might justify the damage he has caused and will continue to cause those who love him. "Can one be said to have misused a woman's gentleness who has always thought of it with gratitude?" he asks himself. Hasn't he, after all, accepted that gentleness "with gratitude, applying it for the very preservation of his life, and even serving by his praise to make her more gentle?" It is as if he is on the way to concluding that in his very selfishness will be his redemption. Indeed, he wonders whether he might somehow have been already "purified by excess, [his] virtue remaining in the sterile ash left from the conflagration."[5]

But then that "Nature" where Emerson said "all mean egotism vanishes"[6] breaks through, and Neal momentarily understands everything anew:

> There is peace in the sequence of changes fittingly ordered: vegetation is at peace in marching with the season; and there is peace in slowly adding to the structure of our understanding. With each life the rising of a new certitude, the physical blossoming of hesitancy, the unanswerable dogmatism of growth. Who would not call all men to him—though he felt compelled to dismiss them when they came, communion residing solely in the summons.[7]

For the duration of this moment, John Neal can understand himself as a "participant" in a life larger than his own, able to describe that participation in this brief inner monologue that offers in concise terms a method for getting along: Stop striving for dominance and submit to "the sequence of changes fittingly ordered" that is inherent in each situation you share. Do that by practicing "new certitude" and "hesitancy," conviction and humility, both at once while adapting all along to the "unanswerable dogmatism of growth" that you learn along with others as you go. Express and enact that growth to others in ways that "summon" them to their own. And find your hope in that—maybe not in coming together, but at least in sharing with very different others your intent and your effort to do so.

Thirty-five years after *Towards a Better* Life, Burke returned to John Neal's brief epiphany in order to sharpen a major point that he had tried to make through his work. He used this language in a talk at Drew Theological Seminary in 1966 that he titled "A Theory of Terms" and would publish in revision the next year as "A Theory of Terminology." Talk and essay both were about the blessings and perils that language can bring to the project of getting along. Both concluded hopefully by recounting what he seemed to have considered the best blessing that language makes available to us: "How happy each one of us is whenever he chances to say something, even if it be but a single sentence, that someone else agrees with."[8] How to approach that is what Burke's work is about. "I never think of 'communication' without thinking of its ultimate perfection, named in such words as 'community' and 'communion,'"[9] he would write a few years later. So we might think of "a better life," "a good life," in the same way—as the "perfection," the completion, the fulfillment of our ongoing interactions with others. That perfection is not found in the achievement of perfect agreement. But it comes into view in the incremental changes those interactions enable us to make to ourselves, however routine and even mundane they might seem. Someone agrees to see the world our way, giving us companionship and, so, confidence and even courage as we continue along the path of our developing plan. Or someone rejects what we say, setting up for us a chance to reflect and to change. Unless we blithely ignore the rejection in response, we can see the world differently and adapt our direction, or we can see what we saw before even more clearly and with greater commitment, and separate ourselves further from the critic's alternative. Either way, as John Neal glimpses, there is a kind of "peace" that follows from participation in such a "sequence of changes" that, following from our efforts to find a fit for ourselves in situations shared with others, give clearer shape and direction to our experience. In that participation itself comes a "summons" to us toward a better life.

After Burke, the young music critic, had come away unexpectedly moved from that musical play *Run, Little Chillun!*, he recounted the experience in his published review. He had been moved, he wrote, by a scene that

> so combined the planned and the spontaneous as to offer the fullest opportunity for the workings of those hypnotic processes by which the cast, like migrating birds, could fall into a unity, and this unity in turn could absorb the spectators, precisely as one might, in observing the birds' movements, veer and deploy with them.[10]

This describes the effect of an encounter with aesthetic form as he had theorized it in *Counter-Statement*—one that had culminated for him, as he wrote there, when "a 'communion' took place." Burke had experienced a kind of communion each time the cast managed to reach beyond "the professional aspects of performance" in their words, movement, and song to perform as if doing so were a "calling."[11] Such a sense of calling involves two kinds of "summons." There is the summons of the call itself, which those who feel it must answer. And there is the summons they must present to others in order to answer that call.

Music encompasses both kinds of summons. It summons us to submit ourselves to an ordered sequence of experiences that would change how the world just now feels, as each element of that sequence presents what Burke considered the essential human choice: to connect and combine with something or someone or to separate. This is what happens as we follow a progression of chords from harmony into dissonance. Do we reject that dissonance because it isn't what we expect the music to be? Or do we go along with it on the chance that doing so will change our understanding of music when we hear an unexpected sort of harmony play itself out? And music can confront us with changes that matter more than that. When the sacred music Duke Ellington's orchestra performed in cathedrals slips into backbeats and blue notes, you are confronted with a choice—actually, with a sequence of linked increments of this choice: Do I accept this as reverent, as the sound of worship, or not? If you choose not to accept, you leave the music and go on your separate way. But if you want to stay, you must learn to change what you understand worship to sound like—indeed, what you understand worship to be. Integral with that understanding, of course, is how you understand your relationship with the divine. If you choose to let the music help you through changes in that understanding, you answer Ellington's summons. You don't come to understand it as Ellington does, necessarily. But you and Ellington do move along the same way: a movement that is itself a sort of summons for others to follow.

Not long ago, Loren Schoenberg and Jonathan Batiste came to my campus for an event we called "Jazz and the Art of Civic Life." Both are accomplished jazz musicians involved in the educational work of the National Jazz Museum in Harlem. Loren is a veteran tenor saxophone player and bandleader, with a comprehensive understanding of the music and its history. Jonathan is a young pianist from New Orleans who is already prominent among the newest generation of jazz musicians. The purpose of the event was to invite, if not summon, people who are neither musicians nor even fans to consider jazz as a productive parable for a better life that individualists can make for themselves together. The visit culminated in what Loren called an "informance"—a sort of annotated jazz performance using music, explanation, and discussion to explore what we all can learn from this music about getting along.

The large lecture room was full when I arrived. I was surprised to see two students, one with a drum kit and another with a bass, set up by the upright piano down front. We had not expected them, but jazz musicians seem always to know when and where someone needs a band. Our only plan was to have Loren and Jonathan begin the event by starting to play, now joined by drummer and bassist, without introduction. So they began. Student chatter stopped as Loren's tenor filled the room and Jonathan's piano answered. They started out on a tune the students would readily recognize and then eased them along into an exchange of increasingly abstracted improvisations. They called and responded, mimicked, and reinvented each other's riffs, quoted and counterquoted different tunes. Their eyes locked, their faces showing alternately effort, pleasure, and surprise as they listened hard to each other, challenged and delighted each other, with the students sharing in it all. Now Loren started walking up and down the aisles as he played, taking his horn into the seats. After a chorus or two, Jonathan did the same, leaving the piano for his harmonabord—a harmonica horn with a piano-like keyboard, also called a melodica. Soon Loren was in one aisle and Jonathan in the other, with the students between them. As they played together across the audience, a student slipped out of his seat and made his way down to the empty piano bench to take over the chord changes. Now backed by a complete rhythm section, Loren and Jon played on in simultaneous duel and duet. They ended the tune with everyone in the room smiling, some with considerable surprise—all this having happened without a word being spoken.

So now I introduced the musicians and began a discussion with the audience on how they might think about what they had just seen and heard, and how it could prompt them to rethink what they believed about cooperation and competition, individuality and community, unity and diversity—about "getting along." The students were ready with smart observations, insights, and questions that soon led Loren and Jon into a crash course in jazz: on listening, improvisation and individual expression, call and response, harmony and rhythm. They talked, then played, and then talked again, blending explanation and demonstration with a few choruses from jazz standards along the way. The discussion moved toward less talk and more music as the students caught on, and toward the end music alone was doing the teaching.

We were winding the event down when someone signaled from the back that the pizza we had promised for the end of the hour had not arrived. This was when Loren stepped forward, swinging his sax into a rollicking version of "Somewhere over the Rainbow." Everyone grinned as the rhythm section kicked in. Loren played the melody through two or three times, elaborating more each time, and then Jonathan started answering on the harmonabord, resuming their eloquent display of what Kenneth Burke would have called "the competitive use of the cooperative."[12] The students were delighted. This hour at the end of a long class day had been a respite for them, and going overtime seemed to be welcome. They were of the generation whom college had promised to provide with a better life, but now that they were *in* college, in the aftermath of the Great Recession, that promise was on hold. To them a good life was looking to be hard to come by: the path leading to it both hard to find and overcrowded. They were worrying about grades and about student loans, about competing for seats in their classes, finding places in internships, and getting job interviews. Competition, they were learning, is lonely and full of risk. But during this hour they had witnessed competition in a more encouraging form. These two jazz musicians had displayed a "cooperative competition,"[13] as Burke would say it, that had "added to the structure of [the students'] understanding" of those matters that reached well beyond the realm of music and jazz. On that basis they could begin to envision another way of life, another attitude toward their present and future, really, that involved "swinging along." Soon this performance would end and they would return to the rest of their day in what Burke called the "Scramble,"[14] but they would return having been summoned to something that promised to be better.

Loren and Jon were trading improvised choruses of "Somewhere over the Rainbow" now, each in turn reinventing the melody to challenge the other's capacity to follow it, then falling back into the song's familiar form just as listeners needed its reassurance. The students were basking in the cycles of tension and release, and the momentum of the exchange was still building when a gesture from the back of the room told us that the pizza was ready. So Loren's tenor turned mellow, the rhythm section followed, and Jonathan let Loren take the last solo. His saxophone sang softly through the tune in its simplest form, this time with a tenderness that made many eyes in the room begin to shine. Then, at the coda, he let the horn hang from his neck strap as he lifted his arms in summons and sang:

If happy little bluebirds fly
Beyond the rainbow,
Why, oh why, can't I?

By the end of the first line, everyone in the room was singing with him. In the second, we all seemed joined in the plea that, with Dorothy, we might each find a good landing some day. In the third, we felt together our common longing for a comfort we knew we couldn't quite have. A few voices broke in that moment as, to use Burke's words, "a 'communion' took place."[15] Then the song ended; then there was stillness, and then there was applause and the chatter began.

Feeling Form

Jazz affects us most when can we see and hear it both at once. On recordings we hear traces of what making the music entails, but to see and hear it happen lets us understand what the music requires of those who play it. On recordings we hear the musician's mastery of their instruments and the music—their virtuosity—but being there, we can see what it takes for a group of musicians to bring that together, and somehow it is as if we have joined them in that effort. Kenneth Burke's concept of form describes how art summons us to inhabit experiences that someone else has composed. We follow recorded jazz by attending to what a moment in the music leads us to expect, and then to what the next moment does to that expectation. But that takes deliberate concentration. Present at the music's creation, we can't help but attend to it; we are enveloped by it, finding it almost impossible not to "surrender," and we allow the music to "take us somewhere outside of ourselves," in Daniel Levitin's description of what happens.[16] That's what most of us remember about a live encounter with music. Watching a band make jazz, we see the exertion of mind and body: how strenuous the composing, the arranging, and the expressing of self all at once in the moment can be. We see musicians smile when they are surprised by where the music takes them or when they are satisfied that things have gone well. And we see their smiles fade when things don't. Seeing and hearing it all, it's hard not to put ourselves in their place. It's hard to encounter live jazz without identifying with the musicians who are playing it. We smile when they smile, and tense up with them when it becomes clear that making the music is particularly hard. We dig deep into our own feelings as the musicians dig into theirs. The experience is powerful rhetoric because it is made of those feelings—and, as Levitin suggests, it is finally by emotion that we are motivated.[17]

In that observation, Levitin begins an explanation that can help us understand how Burke's theory of form works on us more precisely. "As a tool for activation of specific thoughts, music is not as good as language," Levitin writes. But "as a tool for arousing feelings and emotions, music is better than language" because it speaks with a vocabulary of "systematic violations of expectations."[18] That last phrase locates the moment of most potent effect in the confrontation between what one expects to happen and what actually does happen that is the rhetorical core of Burke's concept of aesthetic form. In his own descriptions of this concept, Burke was never so clear. Levitin continues with the same precision, noting that musicians affect us "by knowing what our expectations are and then very deliberately controlling when those expectations will be met and when they won't. The thrills, chills, and tears we experience from music are the result of having our expectations artfully manipulated." When people share that experience, they are affected in similar ways, and in that similarity resides the power of music to, in Levitin's words, "connect us to one another."[19]

I cite Levitin because his conclusions about music, drawn from brain science, explain so well the rhetorical effect Burke described in the theory of aesthetic form that he often used music to illustrate. Wrote Burke in *Counter-Statement*: "One reason why music can stand repetition so much more sturdily than correspondingly good prose is that music, of all the arts, is by its nature least suited to the psychology of information, and has remained closer to the psychology of form. . . . Every dissonant chord cries for its solution, and whether the musician resolves or refuses to resolve this dissonance into the chord which the body cries out for, he is dealing with human appetites.[20] By "appetites," Burke seemed to refer here to reflexive expectations that are, if not physiologically hardwired, at least culturally programmed. An example is a *cadence*. Whether harmonic or rhythmic, a cadence in Western music is a pattern that works like a narrative, directing the listener from its beginning to its closure. That familiar "shave-and-a-haircut" rhythmic cadence may not be hardwired in us, but it is certainly cultural firmware. Three or even two beats into the pattern we know and feel what is coming. And if the two resolving beats at the end don't come, we find that we have to provide them.

The II–V–I chordal cadence that is common in jazz music works on us that way. We ride through it on a sequence of expectations that is an imprint of our modern musical culture. You'll recognize it immediately if you just play the root notes of the three chords. On a keyboard, play D–G–C in sequence and you'll hear in this harmonic progression a familiar and conclusive story. Play D–G alone without that third note and you are left suspended, wondering what such an incomplete sound might mean. You can either judge it bad music or adjust your expectations and begin considering the possibility that good music has structures you haven't anticipated as you try to understand differently what that sequence of D–G is doing. Those are our choices in response to such a prompt to change.

In explanation of what amounts to music's rhetorical effect, Levitin points to Miles Davis, who structured his solos to hold listeners in that kind of suspension, in tension, before either fulfilling or "violating" their expectations.[21] Perhaps the best illustration I can think of is that version of the ballad "Autumn Leaves" Davis played with the Cannonball Adderley ensemble: the one that replaced the last note of the familiar first phrase with one that was entirely unexpected, making that tune tell a different story than the one listeners expect to hear.[22] If you know the song, you expect its familiar trajectory. And even if you don't know the song, "Autumn Leaves" follows the II–V–I progression that serves as a structure in most popular songs you have heard, leaving, as Oliver Sacks puts it, your "musical 'circuits' or networks . . . supersaturated, overcharged with that harmonic sequence."[23] So when Davis starts the melody of "Autumn Leaves," we remember other performances of the song that we have heard: Nat King Cole's classic vocal and Bill Evans's upbeat piano version are just two examples among many, many others. Even if we're hearing the melody for the first time, our cultural immersion in the II–V–I progression takes over. If we don't know how the tune sounds, we know how the chord changes should; when Davis goes to a note at the edge of the I chord we are left unsettled, wondering what this unexpected and almost uncomfortable ending of the phrase makes the tune mean.

For Sacks, "We humans are a musical species no less than a linguistic one." We share feelings with music and explain concepts with words, and understanding things requires something of both. Kenneth Burke acknowledged this when he expanded the conventional definition of "persuasion" to encompass what he called the "'semi-conscious,' 'unconscious,' 'class-conscious,' and 'autosuggestive' rhetorics" we encounter in our experiences of "'identification.'" He was not the only one to recognize them. As Sacks points out, William James had worried that we might not be able to manage such things so well. James once observed that "our higher aesthetic, moral, and intellectual life seems made of affections of this collateral and incidental sort which have entered the mind by the back stairs, as it were, or rather, have not entered the mind at all, but got surreptitiously born in the house."[24] For James it most certainly ought to be otherwise: "The way of 'experience' proper is the front door."[25] But Burke knew that this is not the way it is. Regardless of how we would like our influences to come, we are influenced and changed as often as not by experiences that, coming via that back door, "make us feel . . . shifts of attitude from within." The arts generally don't advocate change—at least not the kind of advocacy that knocks on the front door. Rather, they "saturate" us with what such a change feels like,[26] summoning us to "make ourselves over in the image of [their] imagery."[27]

The more alive that imagery, the stronger its summons. That's why it's one thing to hear jazz and something quite different to watch it happen. Watching it, we recognize that this music is made in the making of human relationships. That we all know intimately the ways of making and unmaking those relationships is the music's "back-door" power. Whatever we might be reading or seeing or listening to, it is the modes of relationship embedded in it that Burke would have us make our object of study. Watching a jazz pianist accompany others with sensitivity and still sound so eloquently like her*self* makes us smile, knowing from our own experience the difficulty of this kind of interpersonal work, and smiling because the fact that she can do it in music offers all of us hope that it can also be done in other settings. A cutting contest between a trumpet and saxophone that becomes so intense that the music comes apart for a time makes us cringe. That's because we also know what that kind of thing feels like; we've each made that kind of mistake before. Part of what entrances us in a performance by a jazz ensemble is what we are learning from it about ourselves with others. Part of what makes us want to walk out of the performance between tunes when an ensemble plays without voice, unity, or heart is how it reminds us of how often people refuse to reach beyond themselves. Seeing this, as Burke put it, we "see our own lives as a kind of rough first draft that lends itself at least somewhat to revision."[28] We are always looking for models to follow, or not follow, in each next step. That is why Burke would have us attend to the ways even music works upon us.

In *Art as Experience*, John Dewey defined "*an* experience" as the form and order we impose on what happens to us and around us in order to provide ourselves with a sense of "integration and fulfillment reached through ordered and organized movement." This is an "artistic structure" that "may be immediately felt."[29] By "immediately," Dewey meant individually, intimately. So in the category of "artistic structure," he would have included everything from a symphony to what we say to someone who asks what we did today. Both are compositions we use to make sense of things by moving ourselves as well as others through their meaningful changes. A symphony proceeds through its movements to become whole. A description of a day's events makes meaningful what is otherwise cluttered and even chaotic. When Burke said that "art is not *experience*, but *something added* to experience,"[30] coherence and meaning were the "something" that he meant. Art, defined in the broad sense he suggested in his theory of form, provides us with "a way of experiencing" that has coherence and meaning, an encounter that offers us, if not demands of us, adjustment and change.[31] That's what jazz does. That's how a performance like Loren Schoenberg's of "Somewhere Over the Rainbow" lifted listeners into an unexpected experience of an unaccustomed perspective on things that, at least for a moment, gave relief and comfort to their competitive souls. Perhaps, for some, it even started them down a path toward a better life. Like John Neal said, "There is peace in the sequence of changes fittingly ordered."

Ordering Change

In his epiphany moment, John Neal recognizes that the fitting order of change in the plant life around him is cyclical, "marching with the season." For us, Burke had him acknowledge, the fitting order of change is similar, proceeding by "slowly adding to the structure of our understanding" in a cycle of confidence and humility. So we begin in green "certitude," confident and vulnerable as a seedling. Then, like fickle spring weather, events come in a mix of encouragement, opposition, and complication that leaves us bruised and hesitant. Making it through that, we gather energy and capacity, like a plant in full summer that overwhelms a gardener with its "unanswerable dogmatism of growth." We know who we are now—knowledge, we realize, that only marks the start of the next cycle of change.[32]

Ultimately, though, we try, as Neal should have learned, to make these cycles sequentially progressive, since Burke described the order of this change as "entelechial, culminative, summational, paradigmatic"[33]—in a word, "hierarchic."[34] This is the process of change that proceeds by what he called the "Upward Way," the route by which Plato's kind of dialectic takes us through conflicts that prompt our revision and refinement along the way toward "some 'higher' principle of unity." Having glimpsed that principle, we can handle better the "Downward Way" back into the opposition and contradiction in which we live, because we are equipped with a perspective that lets us locate common ground to share what we hadn't been able to recognize before.[35] Essentially, this is the sort of form and order Burke finds in the aesthetic experience of "an arousing and fulfillment of desires,"[36] a "creation and gratification of needs."[37] When that experience itself is composed by someone else, we can't help but encounter the unexpected, and must decide how to adjust and whether to change. This can be a process in our individual progress that works the way a narrative does: by leading us incrementally toward a conclusion we haven't anticipated at the start, one that lets us understand things differently, and perhaps better, than we did earlier. The changes we make to get to that conclusion can be temporary and trivial, or lasting and profound. Perhaps it's the depth and durability of the changes it facilitates that measure the quality of a work of art. Stories are good when the "unfolding of a form" invites such "engrossed participation in the successive disclosures of a plot"[38] that you come away transformed.

Because we are not alone when all this occurs, because it must occur in the context of our interactions with others who are engaged at the same time in the same process, Burke called this practice "dialectical transcendence."[39] It is change and, hopefully, progress, that proceeds interactively rather than individually by, as James Zappen says, "mutually testing and correcting ideas with hope of producing better ideas than any one person alone could produce." Zappen continues:

> In a world filled with a cacophony of conflicting voices . . . transcendence offers not more persuasion ("You should believe me . . .") or even identification in its simple and limited sense ("because you and I are really very much alike") but a promise of larger unities—transcendences—that encompass individual and group differences ("You might agree with each other if you could see that each of your views is partial and incomplete without the others—and perhaps even at odds with itself).[40]

That seems to be the experience being described by Burke's theory of aesthetic form. What follows from it is not so much agreement as a sense of commonality and even community among those who share it. That is how art does rhetorical work. And it is how music is rhetorical. "In responding to a piece of music," Roger Scruton writes, "we are being led through a series of gestures which gain their significance from the intimation of community," of a common "life which grows and fulfills itself in tones." It "compels our feelings to move along with it, and so leads us to rehearse a feeling at which we would not otherwise arrive." To describe this feeling, Scruton uses a word that Burke liked to use when conditions could support it: "communion."[41]

Pianist Vijay Iyer recounts a conversation that made it to studio tape when John Coltrane and his band were recording the album *Giant Steps*. This was difficult music, even for Coltrane. As they were taking a break, the microphones caught Coltrane telling the others with some frustration that on the next take he'd try "just . . . makin' the *changes*," that he "ain't going be tellin' no *story*." Someone said in response, "Really, you make the changes, *that*'ll tell 'em a story." Another picked that up: "(The) changes *themselves* is *some* kind of story." What Iyer finds implicit in this exchange is the idea that what matters in jazz is not what you say, but what is required of a musician to say it and of listeners to hear it. The communication that counts in jazz then may well be, as Iyer puts it, the "collective activity that harmonizes individuals rather than a . . . mere transmission of literal, verbal meanings."[42] So while Coltrane says he won't try to *tell* a story in that next take, he will enact one. There will still be a compelling movement to carry those who listen beyond themselves, but this plotline will be what Iyer called "the moment to moment act of making the changes."[43] One writer notes that Coltrane's mature music always expressed his "abiding sense of search" for "the one single line," the "more lyrical" sound. That this kind of search can never conclude suggests that Coltrane might have found his fulfillment not so much in the search itself, but in the sharing of the searching. Listen for conclusion and closure, and you'll find that his late music makes little sense. But listen for "changes fittingly ordered" by a sequence of musical moments to which you must continually adjust, that require you to change expectation and judgment as you keep trying to understand, and you join him. Listen well and you find yourself part of a "quest" [44] that proceeds without expectation of a destination.

But that's much of what the fitting order of jazz music requires musicians to do. Take Branford and Wynton Marsalis, for example, playing a duet in front of the family band at a New Orleans concert that honored their father, the band's pianist. To introduce their tune, Wynton reminds the audience that brothers inevitably have their differences. So, he says, here's "Cain and Abel."[45] It is upbeat, with a simple and jagged melody that sounds something like fifties bebop made for horns. They play it through twice together, Wynton on trumpet and Branford on saxophone, sibling rivals weaving together harmony. Then they start to challenge each other, matching and countering, mocking and surprising, trading four-measure phrases and then just four-beat measures back and forth, fast and then faster. Then they settle into longer exchanges, improvising whole choruses each. At first Branford follows Wynton, echoing and rearranging, but then he starts sending back his own lines that change things. He takes his own choruses for a while, until Wynton raises his trumpet again and shoots back. So it goes as the music gathers momentum and intensity until you hear the audience cheering them as they hand the tune off to the band to bring it to an end. Their point is clear. Their brotherhood is found not in common sound but in the depth of their common commitment to a musical order that makes them push each other into change.

Sheila Jordan and Harvie S play their duets to a different point. Jordan sings as Charlie Parker played his horn (he was her musical mentor), and Harvie S works his bass like a song. In this duo, the bassist does far more than accompany the singer. His sound is full partner with her singing—sometimes supporting, sometimes leading off—and sometimes his bass finds ways to sing along. In the terms of dialogue and dialectical exchange, the Marsalis brothers were rigorously symmetrical in their duets, counterparts who were sometimes adversaries, equals in what Kenneth Burke would have recognized as "cooperative competition,"[46] where two voices assert themselves separately and clash at conflict points, accommodating each other enough to keep the music going. By contrast, Sheila Jordan and Harvie S proceed in obvious mutual support. When they perform Duke Ellington's "It Don't Mean a Thing,"[47] their dialogue is asymmetrical—they meet in the music in interdependent rather than parallel roles. Most of the time, Jordan chooses the tunes they play and the keys they play them in: keys she can sing well. Harvie S fills each song out, managing to prompt, push, and follow her all at once in harmony, tempo, and feel.[48] His bass not only keeps time and outlines the changes; it also gives voice to places of potential in the melody for Jordan's improvising to explore. They are not two virtuosos in contest; they are two virtuosos combining. The Marsalis brothers each assert their own identity, each giving his own a sharper point through the process of playing together; meanwhile Sheila Jordan and Harvie S each move persistently through the music toward expression of an identity they are coming to share.

There is another kind of dialogue in jazz as well: one that brings old and new, as well as jazz and not-jazz, into productive dialogue. Duke Ellington's recordings with John Coltrane, and with Charles Mingus and Max Roach—all musicians a generation younger than himself—are an example of that. So is the veteran sax and flute player Charles Lloyd's collaboration with the young pianist Jason Moran, whose own work puts him in dialogue with Theolonious Monk and even Brahms. In her first album, the emerging singer Cecile McLoren Salvant connects directly with Fats Waller and Bessie Smith, as well as with Sarah Vaughan and Abbey Lincoln, with a band behind her that crosses almost three generations. *Cover Art*, an album made by eight rising jazz musicians collaborating as the NEXT Collective, remakes songs from recent rock, rap, and radio music as fresh and elegant jazz. These recordings document artists finding ways to align across boundaries, the kind of dialectic that has since classical rhetoric marked moments when people combine in their differences to make something together that advances upon what they had to work with before.

In the conventional concept, dialectic involves the sort of "purely verbal manipulations" that, as James Zappen put it, have a way of "leaving competing voices in jangling relations with one another."[49] For Kenneth Burke, though, dialectic is a project in harmony as, in Zappen's description, it "encompass[es] a diversity of individual voices in larger unities that preserve, but transcend, any one of them."[50] It can render cooperation competitive by directing the conflict of individualistic identities toward the same end, as in the Marsalis brothers' exciting performance of "Cain and Abel," or it can enable individuals to combine in a collective identity made resonant and rich by a moving blend of their separate gifts, as do Sheila Jordan and Harvie S. In either case, it is the developing identities of the individual musicians that provide the material they use to make jazz. So however it combines the individual and collective, jazz has the capacity to present what Burke called a "mythic image" of what people might become together. At its best, jazz—to borrow a phrase from Burke—"figure[s] a motive that transcends reason,"[51] that displays in ways well beyond words what the rhetorical achievement of "inducing cooperation" can achieve.[52] In an extended essay, Vijay Iyer describes something similar, using terms that return to what Burke considered rhetoric's primary project: the changing of identifications.

> The experience of listening to music that we know to be improvised differs significantly from listening knowingly to composed music. A main source of drama in improvised music is the visceral fact of the shared sense of time: the sense that the improviser is working, creating, generating musical material at the same time in which we are co-performing as listeners.

So when we witness musicians improvising, we can't help but be right there with them, sharing at least some elements of their experience. Listening well to good jazz does indeed feel like "co-performing": our expectations rise with those of the musicians, and are met or frustrated at the same moments as theirs. For Iyer, this is an instance of empathy. And the word "empathy" may be a good analogue for Burke's "identification." Iyer writes,

> In improvised music empathy extends beyond the concept of the physical body to an awareness of the performers' coincident physical and mental exertion, of their "in-the-moment" process of creative activity and interactivity. Listening to Coltrane on "Giant Steps," one cannot help but agree with his colleague, who suggested that the breath-taking reality of Coltrane improvising and creating his way through this maze tells quite an awesome story indeed, one that at the very least elicits our empathy.

The outcome, writes this thoughtful musician who likely has never read Burke, is expression of "a holistic musical personality, or *attitude*"[53]—what Burke called identity.

An experience of "co-performing" is a powerful prompt to change.

The young Burke described how that prompt works in the explanation of aesthetic form he developed in *Counter-Statement.* But the mature description he offered in his talk about terms and the essay that eventually followed, "A Theory of Terminology," makes the effect he was trying to describe seem less abstract, more immediate. "An encounter with art is itself a performance," he wrote in that essay; a sheet of music and a page of poetry are both "instructions for performance" to those who read them. While a painting completed won't "come to life for [us] unless [we] empathize with it,"[54] a sheet of music or page of poetry, when we read it, engages us as participants in an experience of empathy, of shared identity, with the one who composed it. That experience becomes present for us in the narrative order Burke found inherent in aesthetic form. But our engagement with jazz music that is improvised in the moment we encounter it is even more immediate. In that immediacy is a summons to let the experience take us wherever it goes.

Coming Together

People who overcome their separation and come together don't necessarily do good things. Burke pointed this out to his compatriots in his 1967 essay "Responsibilities of National Greatness." Before joining with others in support or rejection of anything, each one of us is responsible "to pause occasionally and ponder the bepuzzlements of 'identification' as they affect our sense of citizenship." These bepuzzlements are of two kinds. One is "the kind of corporate identity the individual citizen possesses by reason of his personal identification with the collective," a very self-conscious sort of identity. The other kind is almost unconscious, composed of the unnoticed identifications that are only implied by "other transactions" that must follow from one's role as what Burke called "an autonomous specialist." His memorable example, one he offered more than once, is "the shepherd, qua shepherd," who "acts for the good of the sheep" and yet cannot help but be "'identified' with a project that is raising the sheep for market."[55] That aspect of the identity shared by Americans in 1967, he said, "extends from men in combat to gamblers in war stocks."[56] Subjecting such things to our own careful scrutiny before claiming an identity was, Burke suggested there, an essential civic act.

That this kind of self-awareness is advocated throughout his work suggests that Burke could be characterized as a civic theorist of a critical rather than political sort. Asked in a 1970s interview whether his work was driven by a "utopian or humanitarian motive," Burke responded,

"You do have an idea of wanting things to be better, but on the other hand I think the longer you fool with things like that the more range you allow for the recognition that things can't be that way." So Burke readily acknowledged the practical constraints that contain such aspirations, but he still claimed them. While he didn't expect them to be realized, he still urged us on in the effort of trying. So in that interview he followed that last statement with this: "Actually, what you're talking about would be a variation on this thing I call consummation. To affect the world that way [making things better] would in that sense be the completion of my thinking. You always get into problems, though, when you put your theories into practice."[57] So despite the contention and deception he described in his essay about "national greatness" in *The Nation*, Burke could still write that "everywhere I go in this country I find, along with the squabbles that we all get into, a constant background of good fellowship." He concluded by reclaiming "the humanity of our people, the fountain of good will that keeps welling up anew" and summoned his fellow Americans, saying, "With this we *must* be identified."[58]

Burke's statements in that interview express what could be described as the kind of "world-weary melancholy and transcendental yearning" that Edward Strickland said he could hear in the last music John Coltrane made. Coltrane recorded his final album, *Expression*, at the about the same time that Burke was composing "Responsibilities of National Greatness," and when Strickland described Coltrane at this difficult time as striving for a "consummation," he might well have been describing Kenneth Burke's reach in his later years for a completion of things that remained beyond his reach. But in listening carefully to Coltrane's inconclusive last music, Strickland thought he found a sense of consummation not in Coltrane's conclusion but in his "abiding sense of search." He could hear Coltrane performing "the musical quest as its own fulfillment,"[59] seeking his peace not in achieving something but in the ongoing process of continuing to try. This is what Burke's beleaguered protagonist, John Neal, had found for a few moments in "the sequence of changes fittingly ordered," in "marching with the season," in "slowly adding to the structure of our understanding" as people found ways to combine in response to a shared "summons" to some kind of "communion."[60]

People might think Coltrane's late music makes no sense because it doesn't come to completion. That's why it seems incoherent. But just as Burke relocates art from the artifact to the experience of those who encounter it, Coltrane finds wholeness not in the music he makes but in his own unfailing commitment to the process of making it, to continuing the sequence of changes toward an end that remains still unknown. This music offers listeners not what they expect—the satisfaction of a familiar order that cycles from the familiar to the unfamiliar and back to the familiar again—but the vulnerability and risk of continuing to move ahead, step by step, with no end in sight. The order operating here is that of Burke's theory of form: a sequence of expectations and answers that, when the answers that come are unexpected, demand adaptation and change. Coltrane once tried to explain some of this when a jazz writer asked whether it concerned him that listeners were confused by his music. "I never even thought about whether or not they understand what I'm doing . . . ," he said. "The emotional reaction is all that matters—as long as there's some feeling of communication, it isn't necessary that it be understood."[61] Living with uncertainty and confusion as we do, this focus on sharing the experience of a process might be our most useful concept of consummation and communion. In another interview Coltrane said, "I think music is an instrument" that "can create the initial thought patterns that can change the thinking of people."[62] For him those patterns would communicate "higher ideals," with "brotherhood" as the highest one, but not in the form of concepts you could explain. "You can't ram philosophies down anybody's throat," Coltrane said; ". . . the music is enough!"[63]

So an experience of consummation, as Burke used the term, seems to be less about concepts of coming together than about experience of the process: what some of the most difficult music of John Coltrane would have us try to do. That focus on process may be the reason why Burke insisted on treating art not as object but as experience, and rhetoric as "semi-conscious," and even "unconscious," as readily as it is direct and deliberate. It may be why he maintained that "some such term as 'identification' rather than 'persuasion'" is necessary if we are to understand how "the dialectical element in the structure of social hierarchy itself can influence us." Influence is the current we swim in, which propels both our connection and our separation. Coming together with some, often at the cost of connection with others, is what we do, and to do it responsibly we must attend to "the cohesive motives implicit in the thought of oneself as a participant in" that process.[64] We can't combine with everything and everyone, but we can become "consubstantial" with some, sharing the experience of the elements of identity it creates. In that sharing, we change; and by continuing to share and change, we might even keep what unnecessarily separates us from others from standing unassailed for too long.

Burke used the term "consummation" most often as the third term in a three-term sequence that described not only the development of his own goals as a writer and critic of communication but also the developmental steps that individuals must move through to sustain cooperation. Whatever that term might seem to mean in different places in his published work, he defined it persistently as "the sheer 'tracking down of terministic possibilities' because one sees them, or thinks one does, implicit in a given terminology, and one cannot rest until such potentialities are actualized."[65] That actualization is, in his phrase, the "end of the line,"[66] completion of a kind we hardly ever achieve. So maybe in Burke's definition the term doesn't apply here. "Consummation . . . is what happens when an artist sits down and simply works something out on its own terms," Burke once told an interviewer. "And this whole principle of "going to the end of the line in art, of getting the kind of work which leaves a spell on you," amounts to that.[67] But that last statement, the one about art that "leaves a spell on you," suggests that Burke's definition of the term "consummation" *does* apply here. What art offers is, in his terms, a "mythic" experience that takes us beyond the reasoned reality we live in most of the time to the kind of experience his John Neal described. So in 1967 people could also read this from Burke:

> Are things disunited in "body"? Then unite them in "spirit." Would a nation extend its physical dominion? Let it talk of spreading its "ideals." Do you encounter contradictions? Call them 'balances.' Is an organization in disarray? Talk of its common *purpose*. Are there struggles over means? Celebrate agreement on ends. Sanction the troublously manifest, the incarnate, in terms of the ideally, perfectly invisible and intangible, the divine.[68]

Jazz does something like that. I hear it happen in the performance of "In a Sentimental Mood" that Coltrane and Duke Ellington recorded together in 1962.[69] It is the first track on a duet album that a producer brought them together to record. Both giants of jazz, of different generations and of competing if not conflicting sounds, they came together and recorded seven tracks. With Ellington trying to abstract his familiar jazz a bit, and Coltrane trying to render more lyrical his increasingly agitated sound, together that day they made the most elegant music. Their "In a Sentimental Mood" was a quartet performance. Backed by drummer and bass, Ellington and Coltrane played their own immediately identifiable lines in new ways, with Ellington's piano developing a harder edge as Coltrane's saxophone softened what on other gigs was tending toward a frenetic scream. Jazz historian Ted Gioia describes each of them in this session as "driven by a tough-as-nails commitment to his personal musical principles" but enacting that commitment in ways that demonstrated that "on occasion, demi-gods do consent to give and take."[70] In that give and take you hear mutual respect, a profound openness to change, and Ellington and Coltrane's relentless common effort to find in their differences ways to come together—to approach, perhaps, what both were seeking in their own work: some sort of communion.

I once thought this was an exceptional performance. But when I asked Marcus Roberts to point me toward recordings by his own trio where such a thing had happened, his response surprised me:

> I think the communion you speak of happens every time my groups play together. It's a requirement, since the give and take required to play jazz demands that we listen in order to know what spontaneous musical choice to make. Of course, there are more successful nights than others. . . . When the audience gets it, it does mean that the musicians have invested a lot of spiritual energy, and that the audience's response to that energy makes the intangibles that creativity thrives on even more available to the artists.[71]

So communion is what the best jazz musicians try for when they come together to make the music. But whatever they do is not enough to achieve it. The music they perform is not consummated, taken to the very end of the line (which of course is not a stopping place but a sustaining of a process), until those who watch and listen participate with them by "spontaneously willing its completion and perfection"—by, in Kenneth Burke's fortunate phrase, "swinging along."[72]

Making Our Way

We can't merge hearts and minds even if we want to, but we can use the experiences we can create and share with our symbols in ways that let us feel like we come together, at least for a moment or two. It turns out that we want to do this, living as we do contained within enclaves and factions. But in the exchange of questions and answers that followed the talk he gave in 1966 which became "A Theory of Terminology," Burke explained that, as he liked to say, "it's more complicated than that."[73] In our interactions we "mature one another, knock the edges off one another." That's how we combine and how we separate. These things we do, working to transcend our differences while at the same time using them to divide us from each other at the same time, "are just with us whether you like them or not," Burke told this audience. Such "congregation by separation" is the necessary way of coming together. It's a fact that is, as Burke put it, "bitter,"[74] showing us the dark side of community and communion. Burke considered World War II to be a compelling case of that dark side. "War" is the "ultimate disease of cooperation," he wrote in its aftermath, adding that "you will understand war much better if you think of it, not simply as strife come to a head, but rather as a disease, or perversion of communion."[75] The elation of any experience of communion achieved in war must collapse when you notice the cost.

Burke went on that day to remind his audience at Drew Theological Seminary of "the Scramble, the Wrangle of the Market Place, the flurries and flare-ups of the Human Barnyard, the Give and Take, the wavering line of pressure and counter-pressure, the Logomachy, the onus of ownership, the Wars of Nerves, the War," of the way we live.[76] It is what we are stuck with, he said, since the only connections we can make with each other are those we must make from unreliable concepts and terms. Still, life together in our communities, our civic life, must go on. So in consolation, perhaps, Burke offered his audience what he called "a parting sunshine thought." We must use these concepts and terms if we are to persist, individually and collectively, in our tedious and unstable progress towards a better life. But there are also other kinds of communication available that can offer us respite in those moments when we are reminded of what we are working toward. This is the point when Burke reminded his audience that working together toward communion is itself likely to be the kind of communion we seek. He suggested that the way to a better life might well be to remember the lesson into which John Neal, the thick-headed protagonist of his only novel, had stumbled. Burke quoted that lesson in conclusion: "Who would not call all men to him—though he felt compelled to dismiss them when they came, communion residing solely in the summons."[77] Consider jazz such a summons.

SEVEN

So What?

A complex social organization is maintained by a state of mind, and that state of mind is constructed out of art.[1]

KENNETH BURKE

A "myth," Kenneth Burke wrote, is a "narrative form," one that provides "a kind of 'existential definition'" for an "essence."[2] And an "essence," of course, is the core substance of identity.[3] Put another way, a myth explains what something is by telling its story. It is, then, "poetic" in both form and function."[4] So for Burke the term "poetic" refers more to a kind of effect than to a kind of text. It is more or less synonymous with "aesthetic," in his highly rhetorical sense of that term. Actually, he tended to use the term "poetic" as a synecdoche for aesthetic expression in general. Read with that in mind, his statement that "the poem *contains more than can be discussed in terms of Poetics alone*"[5] implies a primary insight of his work: that art, like argument, can change those who encounter it. Again, argument would persuade us to change our minds, but art would change our "state of mind." That's Burke's rhetorical aesthetic, his "counter-statement" to the assumption that what matters most in art is the artifact itself, apart from any practical work of influence. Burke's corrective locates art in the experience it provides for those who encounter it, an experience that unfolds as a narrative does. "We are put into a state of mind from which another state of mind can appropriately follow," he wrote.[6] By "state of mind," Burke usually meant "attitude,"[7] and by attitude he meant a shaping element of identity.[8]

Burke once told an interviewer, "Every time a situation changes enough, a new state of mind is required to deal with it." This statement was made in an explicitly civic context.[9] In the broader conceptual context of his book *A Rhetoric of Motives*, he stated something similar: that art prompts a "state of mind" that has us leaning forward in "an attitude of collaborative expectancy." It opens us to change. As the aesthetic experience proceeds, we move with the artist through a "fitting order" of attitudes and ideas that constitute what amounts to the identity the artifact would express and project. What makes that order "fitting" is the particular sequence of appropriate steps we are led by the process to expect. "For instance," Burke said, "imagine a passage built about a set of oppositions ('*we* do *this*, but *they* on the other hand do *that*; *we* stay *here*, but *they* go *there*; *we* look *up*, but *they* look *down*,' etc.). Once you grasp the trend of the form, it invites participation regardless of the subject matter." You participate regardless of whether you agree with the assumptions that support it or the conclusions to which it leads,[10] and that participation itself immerses you in concepts and feelings that otherwise you might have missed or ignored. The steps in that process comprise the plot of a story that culminates in an experience that includes something of a new sense of yourself.

That kind of ongoing process of individual change is precisely what life in a democratic culture requires. "Personal identity," Burke wrote, is something we must continually compose from the "complex of attitudes . . . that constitute the *individual's* sense of orientation," and our "'reality'" consists largely of "a corresponding sense of relationships."[11] It is in our social life that we must be both wary of influences and open to them as we align ourselves with others in an ongoing process of change. As a civic theorist, Burke worked long and hard to explain to his fellow citizens the many ways in which they were interdependent while, at the same time, putting them "on the lookout" for the many influences coming at them—rhetorically or aesthetically—and which they had to decide whether to reject or embrace.

Andrew Delbanco's project is similar. Delbanco is a scholar of the American national culture who marked the turn of the twenty-first century with a short book, *The Real American Dream*, which argued that the individualistic American Dream we have inherited needs rethinking, and that it offers no one at all "the good life." Delbanco believes, as Kenneth Burke did, that "the good life" is lived as a participant rather than as a competitor,[12] and like Burke he offers alternative stories that Americans can inhabit. So as the new century turned, Delbanco was urging his compatriots to locate themselves among citizens in a story that "leads somewhere and thereby helps us navigate through life," propelled by the "hope" that can follow from a common enterprise.[13] His point is that while people in the United States may have been enculturated to believe that we must each find our own separate way to happiness, there is inherent in the national culture an unfulfilled aspiration for the kind of community in which at least occasionally, as William James put it, "the outlines of confining selfhood melt down."[14] The miracle of jazz is the fact that it can combine those opposing desires in a single experience, making the melt happen in ways that sharpen selfhood. Participate in that process or even witness it being done well, and you can shift your state of mind away from constant wariness toward the expectation that people can, after all, get along.[15]

Finding Harmony

"So What" is the first track on *Kind of Blue*, the classic album Miles Davis recorded with five other musicians in the spring of 1959.[16] Some say that Davis took the title of the tune from his brother-in-law's response to his youthful announcement that he would leave his East St. Louis home to take his trumpet to New York. Others say that the phrase was Davis's own typical challenge to almost any decisive statement that someone might make to him.[17] Whatever the title's referent, "So What" and the tunes that followed on *Kind of Blue* issued a direct challenge to jazz as it was then being performed. Since World War II, jazz had become a small-ensemble music, the kind we often still hear made from turn-taking solos on the chord changes of simple and familiar tunes. The soloists joined together at both the beginning and the end of a tune to play it together, but they made the music between in sequences of solos that followed the same cyclical pattern of chord changes. Alternating the roles of soloist and accompanist, each musician improvised in response to the others in ways that let them play as much separately as together. This could make the jazz exciting as each musician found ways to fit into an ensemble's sound while still expressing a self that sounded coherent and distinct. In civic terms, this seems at least in principle to be a good model for democratic cooperation among individuals who are distinct and disparate and yet are deliberately prepared to assert themselves in the service of a common cause. That is the predominant pattern in most modern jazz, and it can produce great music. But it can also be limiting and even mechanical.

Kind of Blue challenged that. The sextet went into the studio on just two separate days to record new compositions that Davis had created but had not let them see or hear in advance of the session. Even as they began to record, this music was not written out nor even much rehearsed. Davis wanted to give them musical concepts and then have them play to find out where they would take them. Those initial explorations were what he wanted to capture on tape, and what eventually went on the record were these first takes. This was not a surprise to the rest of the band. They had anticipated something like that, knowing that it was how Davis was working these days. Davis thought that jazz too often sounded complacent, lacking the anxiety that would sharpen each improvised performance and freshen the music. With no prepared phrases to play over familiar changes, these musicians would each have to invent their way through a live musical dialogue to be performed without a net. This would require them to let themselves find a new state of mind as they played, in Burke's sense of that phrase—one that would enable each individual to reach deep and draw out of his experiences new feelings and phrases, making music in the collision of the concepts Davis had given them and their own separate gifts. In the album's liner notes, pianist Bill Evans explained it in this oblique way:

> There is a Japanese visual art in which the artist is forced to be spontaneous. He must paint on a thin stretched parchment with a special brush and black water paint in such a way that an unnatural or interrupted stroke will destroy the line or break through the parchment. Erasures or changes are impossible. These artists must practice a particular discipline, that of allowing the idea to express itself in communication with their hands in such a direct way that deliberation cannot interfere.

While "such pictures lack[ed the] complex composition and textures" that would come with more time, Evans continued, they displayed "something captured that escapes explanation." Such art proceeded on the principle that, as he put it, in the "direct deed is the most meaningful reflections."[18]

Whatever it was that Davis expected in "So What" and the rest of *Kind of Blue*, these six jazz musicians played this new music with a sensitivity, focus, and precision that suggested that they found much at stake in the work of "worrying their way through such unfamiliar territory."[19] They didn't know what to expect from the music, but they had played together enough to know what to expect from each other. So in the recording you hear them respond to each other in ways that display the most careful listening, ways that make space for each individual to do the kind of thing they all know he can do well. Listen for that kind of thing and it can sound as if the primary art the musicians are practicing is not music, but the art of getting along. Getting along is an art in Burke's sense of that term if it takes the progressive form he described: of individuals moving themselves through the "changes fittingly ordered" that can bring them together in purpose and project. The instrument of this art is not a piano or horn, but a capacity to adapt as circumstances demand so that separate purposes and single project can proceed together. As the sextet performs "So What" you can hear it solving musical problems to which the repertoire each individual brought to the studio didn't fully apply. That's because those problems were less about music than about *making* the music together.

"Every time a situation changes enough a new state of mind is required to deal with it," Kenneth Burke once told an interviewer.[20] By "state of mind," Burke usually meant "attitude," and by "attitude" he usually meant "incipient act."[21] But there was also something else, not unrelated, that he used the term "attitude" to mean: what he called "the characteristic responses of people in their forming and reforming of congregations."[22] Change is the form our lives take. When we confront what is unexpected, we must decide how to change in order to find a fit for ourselves in the situation. As Burke put it, in terms that recall Bill Evans's description of that Japanese art, "We might get the truest slant on ourselves by thinking of our lives as first drafts, as hastily organized essays that we never have a chance to revise."[23] What we hear in "So What" can sound something like that, as six individuals summon each other to combine in a state of mind that brings the music together. That may be why *Kind of Blue* sounds so eloquently developed, so deeply felt, and why it has spoken so powerfully to so many for so long.[24] As Burke wrote in reference to his theory of aesthetic form, "Eloquence is a frequency of Symbolic and formal effects," one that that "bring[s] up some picture, or summarize[s] some situation, or in some other way recommend[s] itself as an independent value." As such, it is a vibrant call to comprehend, as he put it, "means as ends."[25] In *Kind of Blue* those means that are ends are the musical processes of getting along.

In *Towards a Better Life*, Burke's John Neal surfaces from self-absorption just in time to grasp that there is peace to be found in submitting oneself to "the sequence of changes fittingly ordered."[26] Jazz musicians do that as they play the changes, improvising their way through a sequence of chords that gives stability, shape, and direction to the tune they play.

When musicians submit themselves to that order, their separate improvisations stay in harmony as each individual limits self-expression to notes that fit the chords through which they are all moving. What a musician can't do and still keep in harmony is play notes that don't fit into the scales that the chords played in each tune comprise. To do that would be dissonant. Musicians describe playing through changes this way as "vertical," meaning that in the moment that belongs to a particular chord (which may be a measure, just a single beat, or even a part of a beat), the options available for improvisation are the scale it signals—options that are open only until the chord changes. Individuals playing together fit themselves into the order of the music by "playing the changes" that way. Life is like that. But it is also, at times, like "So What?"

The musicians who made *Kind of Blue* were all masters at playing the changes. But that day in the studio, they faced something different. The music Miles Davis had brought in did prescribe chord changes, but they were very few—just two or three to each tune—and the sequence they followed wasn't rapid and cyclical like that of a twelve-bar blues or a thirty-two-bar popular song. With so few chords, there was no predictable pattern of changes to guide them in structuring their solos. That was because "So What" and most of the other tunes on *Kind of Blue* were structured not on chords but on scales. A chord implies a scale, of course—that vertical inventory of the notes available for improvisation in any moment of a jazz performance—and those notes are the only ones a chord can support (a minor chord supports the notes of a minor scale, and so on). What holds most jazz performances together is not the scales but the chord changes. Their order is set and you move through them fast. The problem, as the composer George Russell put it, is that musicians can't "sing [their] own song really, without having to meet the deadline of a particular chord."[27]

But "So What" isn't made that way. This music is horizontal. That is, instead of having to move simultaneously through the same sequence of chords, the musicians must each find a fit with the others using the open-ended resource of a few scales to play out their own songs. In the terms of music theory, this is modal music. A scale can be treated as a "mode" that invites improvisers to use everything it offers them, including notes that would be dissonant in a particular chord made from it, to sustain a linear statement without having to interrupt its melodic development to change chords with every one or two beats. There is more to modal music than that, but in general this is how Miles Davis, John

Coltrane, Cannonball Adderley, Bill Evans, Paul Chambers, and Jimmy Cobb were thinking about what they would be doing the day they prepared to record "So What."[28]

The difference between vertical and horizontal jazz is not so much the music's substance as its state of mind. Modal jazz lets musicians play out the potential of their own inventions over a chordal support that is minimal and thus flexible. Held together by a scale rather than by a lockstep sequence of chord changes, musicians can improvise longer, individually and together, exploring what they find they can say more thoroughly. This slows the music down in ways that lets individual musicians "invent and reinvent as long as necessary to tell a story," as Ashley Kahn puts it.[29] Aesthetic form still has a narrative shape, but now it proceeds without a set direction or conclusion. "After you initiate the solo, one phrase determines what the next is going to be," said drummer Max Roach. "From the first note that you hear, you are responding to what you've just played: you just said this on your instrument, and now that's a constant. What follows from that? And so on and so forth. And finally, let's wrap it up so that everybody understands that that's what you're doing."[30] As Vijay Iyer describes the process, an ensemble holds this music together with constant attention to what may be the most intensely collaborative work: that of "conveying a steady rhythmic momentum (swinging), displaying a strong and personal timbre, constructing original melodic phrases, and amassing these phrases into a compelling 'whole.'" There are no "top-down notions of overarching coherence." Rather, the musicians come together as their "bottom-up views of narrativity" combine in the order of "the shifting, multiple, continually reconstructed subjectivities of the improvisers."[31] Lacking the sturdy structure of composed chord changes, it seems as though this kind of improvised music would fly apart. What prevents that from happening, as you hear throughout *Kind of Blue*, is the distinct state of mind that follows from a profound awareness of each moment being shared by those who perform it.

Kenneth Burke at least twice advised us to find wisdom in our lives by playing our dissonances out as arpeggios rather than expecting things to make sense on the sort of order that is prescribed by a composition of chords. An arpeggio that is made from a particular scale can harmonize even if it includes notes that would be dissonant when played in a chord. So, he wrote,

> If you strike *do-mi-sol* simultaneously, you get a perfect concord. If you added *fa*, thus playing *do-mi-fa-sol*, you get a discord. But if you draw this discord out into an

arpeggio, by playing the four notes not simultaneously but in succession, they are not felt as discord. Rather, they are transformed into a melody, since the dissonant *fa* acts merely as a passing note.

This is Burke's musical model for a practice of what he liked to call "transcendence," a way of accommodating if not overcoming dissonance by acknowledging that things which seem out of place tend to change with time. He was suggesting that instead of rejecting dissonance or letting it stand, one should try "stretching" it "out into a narrative arpeggio, whereby a conflicting element can be introduced as a 'passing note,' hence not felt as discord."[32] In that sort of order could be found places of peace that were not apparent in the more demanding sound of what he called "a simultaneity."[33] This is another aspect of modal jazz that frees musicians to express themselves more thoroughly, to experiment more broadly with alternative ways to find places for themselves in a fitting order. So in "So What" we can hear, in John Szwed's elegant description, "John Coltrane's astringency on tenor . . . counterpoised to Cannonball Adderley's soulful alto, with Davis moderating between them as Bill Evans conjures up the still lake of sound on which they walk. Meanwhile, the rhythm team of Paul Chambers and Jimmy Cobb seem prepared to keep time until eternity."[34]

Learning a Civic Self

Being a good jazz musician requires more than technical mastery of music and its instruments. It requires, as Paul F. Berliner states it, "the creation of a unique improvisational voice within the jazz tradition," which must occur within the "mutual absorption and exchange of ideas" that is the very essence of playing together. In that social context of "dynamic interaction," individual expression "entwines with jazz's artistic tradition" in what Berliner calls a musician's "unique vision that accommodates change from within and without." This statement is as much about the development of identity as it is about art, with identity understood, like art, as not artifact but process—one that is embedded in ongoing "changes" of a sort entirely different from any order of chords. These are changes in experience and thus in attitude, in state of mind, that are sufficient to make the opposites of "shared community values and idiosyncratic musical perspectives" richly complementary.[35] In his description of the sound of an African-American church choir, T. J. Anderson III captures how improvised music lets this happen:

"Distinct individual voices can be heard among the collective, with various members singing in slightly different cadences, timbres, or keys" to acknowledge that "although the communal voice is crucial in order to convey the general quality and spirit of the music, it is also informed by the collection of individual voices in which every member has a 'story to tell or a song to sing.'"[36]

That very young Kenneth Burke who once confessed to "what enjoyment" it was at the piano "to tantalize oneself with dissonances and then resolve them" seemed to enjoy the movement from tension to peace and back to tension as much as any sound of resolution.[37] He would describe that kind of experience again a decade or so later, having witnessed in those who performed the play *Run Little Chillun!* "an attractive positive ability, exemplified with a conviction, a liquidness, a sense of aesthetic blossoming, and a gift of spontaneous organization which is capable . . . of actually setting the spectator aquiver as he participates in the vocal and mimetic exhilaration taking place before him."[38] This was "*acting-together*," another phrase Burke would align with "identity" and use to indicate its elements: "common sensations, concepts, images, ideas, attitudes that make [people] *consubstantial*."[39] These singers, "like migrating birds, could fall into a unity, and this unity in turn could absorb the spectators, precisely as one might, in observing the birds' movements, veer and deploy with them." Then, at another point, they could combine as separate voices with "almost an orchestral set of timbres" in diverse "departures [and] permissible variations" within a plot, as if each felt "'called' to do what one [was] in the act of doing." Having "'empathetically' participated" in that way of life for an hour or two, Burke did indeed leave the theater "aglow" and, thus, changed by the experience.[40]

For a long time people in jazz assumed that such things couldn't be taught, that gifted people were drawing upon something inherent inside themselves to play together in this way. And for decades they proceeded on that assumption. But in the 1950s some musicians, along with a few students and fans of jazz, decided that such things could be learned after all and started a school in that summer bastion of white privilege, the Berkshire Hills of western Massachusetts. New Yorkers Philip and Stephanie Barber had recently acquired an old estate in the town of Lenox, just down the road from Tanglewood, and turned it into a live music venue they called the Music Inn. Tanglewood was and remains today a premier summer venue for classical music; the Barbers intended the Music Inn to supplement it as a venue for jazz. They opened it in 1950 with a modest series of concerts. The performers they booked to play there also stayed there, and found this pastoral place conducive to the kind of conversations that as gigging musicians they were rarely able to have. After awhile, as these conversations among musicians started to include a jazz writer or two and began to draw crowds, the Barbers formalized the Jazz Round Table, a discussion series that soon included critics and the new jazz scholars as well as musicians. Even Leonard Bernstein would come over from Tanglewood on his off nights to join the discussion. The topics of the Round Table ranged across the terrain of jazz, from its connections with African music to its methods and practices of improvisation to the links between contemporary developments in jazz and its history. It was in these discussions that major figures from different jazz generations—Dizzy Gillespie and Eubie Blake, for example—got to know each other and, in the process, came to understand for the first time how they fit together in the music's development.[41] By the mid-1950s formal courses were offered, and out of those came the Lenox School of Jazz.

The Lenox School of Jazz developed its curriculum on a general pattern that jazz academies still follow. Every August at the Music Inn it offered a three-week residential program designed to provide student musicians of high school and college ages with formal instruction as well as informal mentoring from the most important jazz performers of the time. That mentoring came as the students played with those performers in the ensembles in which their teachers placed them. Pianist John Lewis of the Modern Jazz Quartet quickly became the intellectual leader of a faculty that through the years included people like Ray Brown, Dizzy Gillespie, Oscar Peterson, Max Roach, Dave Brubeck, George Russell, and the English professor who invented academic jazz scholarship, Marshall Stearns. The school soon overlapped with the Music Inn concert series, now staged in a building of its own on the grounds, called the Music Barn, and the musicians booked to play at the Music Barn often stayed on for an extra day or two to join the students and faculty in discussions and to jam with them. The curriculum included composition and arranging, large and small ensemble playing, and jazz history, as well at least two private lessons each week for each student from a faculty musician who did *not* play the same instrument—that to encourage them to find their own voices. Students were selected on the basis of their technical mastery of their instruments, and the school then immersed them in the experience of playing jazz.

Jule Foster, a producer, talent manager, and arts program executive, emerged as the designated dean of the school. On one occasion—in a panel discussion at the Berkshire Museum on music education held in 1958—he itemized the elements of the school's educational mission: to teach students "to read in jazz terms," to direct their experience playing with others toward "retain[ing] . . . individuality while becoming part of the ensemble," to help them understand "a functional use of theory" that freed them to improvise, and to enable them to understand in greater depth their own "capabilities." Those were the elements, Foster said. But at the Lenox School, "these four ideas [were] not presented in separate compartments." Rather, "they [were] taught as the means for developing specific ideas in specific works." Students learned and practiced all four ideas at once "through playing experience," particularly in "the improvisation at hand" that came to them as opportunities to express themselves.[42]

Two years earlier, at a round table on "the composer in jazz," composer and arranger Bill Russo had interrupted a discussion about that sort of self-expression in jazz to direct it into a more rhetorical realm of purpose that seems to have aligned with Kenneth Burke's own progression from self-expression to communication and beyond. "I guess it's an unpopular viewpoint," Russo said, "but I don't feel that the writer-artist of any sort should be . . . in the field because it pleases him or expresses his personality." He continued:

> The reason that I write music is that I am trying to make an art/object that will in some small way, perhaps, improve our life. . . . I want to do more than excite anger or create emotions. I'd like to make possible, perhaps, an easier way of living. . . . So what I'm implying is that not only does the artist reflect what is going on around him, but, generally, he attempts to impose a little order upon what is going on, if only in the sense of creating an ordered object that so represents one of the tendencies of man to get to something beyond himself . . . , better than himself, a direction which would perhaps achieve a better way of living.[43]

So What?

"An *individual*, in being proud of his accomplishments, may easily become an ass," Kenneth Burke was writing at about this time, but "things are happier when a *community* can be proud of its accomplishments."[44] This was the principle upon which the Lenox School of Jazz tried to operate. Jazz education is now highly developed on the model of enculturating individuals into the life of ensembles, but the Lenox School was the first structured attempt at doing that. In his own copy of Albert Murray's *The Omni-Americans*, Burke marked up considerably the pages on which Murray described the blues that lay at the roots of jazz as one of the "esthetic solutions" that African-American culture had found to the problem of the "ever-increasing standardization, regimentation, and conformity" that characterized American life." Those solutions all spun out from "an orientation to elastic individuality"; Burke enthusiastically underlined that last phrase.

"An orientation to elastic individuality" is a state of mind Murray attributed to African Americans.[45] Burke and Murray were interlocutors and friends, so when Murray wrote that phrase he was likely aware of the way in which Burke treated the term "orientation" as resonant not only with "state of mind" but with "attitude" and "identity."[46] And my reading of both Burke and jazz suggests that "elastic individuality" is good term for the kind of civic identity necessary for successful democratic life. A few pages away from that statement, Burke not only underlined but also marked in the margin another of Murray's claims: that "the solo instrumentalist turns disjunctures into continuities."[47] That phrase may describe the essential civic act.

Jazz shows us that it is individuals who must dignify democratic life. Albert Murray suggested something similar when he wrote that "when great Negro musicians like Armstrong, Basie, Ellington, Parker, play by ear, they do so not because they cannot read the score but rather because in the very process of mastering it they have found it inadequate for their purposes." That's much of what the sextet that recorded *Kind of Blue* had to do. "Nor should it be forgotten that they often find their own scores inadequate," Murray added, in a statement that expressed most of the rest of what they had to deal with. Burke both underlined and marked in the margin these two sentences as well.[48] Democratic life is itself an aesthetic act, made from nothing but hope and experience and given form in situations that keep calling on people to make judgments, adapt, and change. Jazz shows us that people answer that call not on the ground of ideology but through encounters with what Burke called myth. Burke used those two terms to make an essential distinction between two powerful modes of influence. Ideology gets at us through agreement; myth does it through experience. We can take or leave ideology, but when we encounter a living experience of another way of life, when we find ourselves cast in its story as if it were our own, we inhabit a myth and thus are liable to be transformed. [49]

The "very thought of oneself as a participant" in such a story, as Burke tried to explain, can overcome for a time the alienation that is always potential in every human life.[50] Burke had gotten at something like that very early in his career, in that first review as music critic for

The Dial. Before he started on the performance that was his topic, he used the review to explain music's rhetorical function. At a time when totalitarianism loomed abroad and depression was developing at home he wrote, "In dark and fetid places, there are the gnarled in body and mangled in mind. But the concert hall shall be the denial of these vices, shall prove that this same state of affairs has its pride and asseveration." That "asseveration" is the declaration of a better alternative, like a new doctrine. Despite how bad things might get, he wrote, "music, we had decided, would be the song above catastrophe." And "perhaps it would grow firmer and spread even to those dark and fetid regions," he ventured.[51] In the meantime, though, Burke would try to enlist people in the participatory project of sustaining the sort of hope he found inherent in every song. Langston Hughes wrote in the 1950s, years that exacerbated the inherited pain of the people he spoke for: "To me jazz is a montage of a dream deferred. A great big dream—yet to come—and always *yet*—to become ultimately and finally true."[52] Waiting for that dream, looking toward it, might have to be comforting and encouraging enough as, in Burke's words, a "communion" residing solely in the summons."[53]

Here's a last jazz story. In a winding canyon cut by the Colorado River through brittle layers of cream and coral sandstone, there is place where the river bends back on itself enough for a lodge and its lawns to occupy its bow. On the lawn near the river's edge one early evening was a large event tent, the kind with sides that could be rolled up, and which was broad and deep enough to shelter a small stage and 150 or so folding chairs set in rows. This was a concert venue of the Moab Music Festival. On this bright evening the concert was by the Marcus Roberts Trio, joined by banjoist Bela Fleck at the Utah stop of the tour this quartet had titled "Across the Imaginary Divide." Here jazz would meet bluegrass, bringing together two American musics that had much to divide them. When the concert began, the four musicians—three black and one white—let these musics roll across each other, calling out in one idiom and responding in the other, exchanging idioms, and gradually developing a hybrid sound in a new voice of both jazz and bluegrass. It was late in the day in August, monsoon time in the southern Utah desert. And as they were playing a joyous tune made from the two music's contrasts—it might have been "Petunia," as recorded on the tour CD[54]—wind suddenly blew down into the canyon. The sky went dark, thunder broke, and rain came hard. Some of the people who were seated on the lawn outside the tent got up and ran for their cars. Others crowded inside, unrolling the curtains and tying them down behind themselves as the rain turned sideways. The audience inside was doubled now, the chairs pushed together to make room for people standing. Those of us who had seats could not even stand up.

The tune "Petunia" first juxtaposes and then combines blues and bluegrass. Bela Fleck played a Scruggs-style banjo roll through the first chorus, with Jason Marsalis and Rodney Jordan keeping bluegrass time on drums and bass until, on a single beat, they dropped into a blues groove that Roberts picked up on the piano. Now the four were crossing back and forth between two musics, taking their turns and then trading. When Bela picked up Marcus's blues and Marcus began answering with the piano like a bluegrass banjo, we were still watching and listening but our hearts were not in it. The rain on the tent was so loud we could hardly hear the music even just three rows back; the tent fabric was popping in the wind as the posts and poles that held up the whole tent were twisting at their joints. People were looking up at the tent's aluminum frame, and then out at possible exit routes. But we were all so tangled together inside the tent that trying to get out would have been difficult if not dangerous. Then, as a bigger burst of wind that entirely drowned out the band looked as though it might bring the tent down, Marcus dug deep into the piano. Rodney and Jason, who had been watching the tent's roof shake as they played, looked to each other and to Marcus, and followed. Bela, who also had been looking up, turned to the trio and made his banjo take flight, touching down now on the one beat in four that makes in jazz and blues a hard swing. The musicians were summoning us back, demanding our participation as well as our attention. We had listened well to the music until the storm had come along, but now we became a part of it. We were shouting, clapping, and stomping together over the sounds and sights of the storm. And we kept that going until the storm passed over.

Then the wind dropped and the rain stopped as fast as both had come, and the music pulled back. Sitting in the middle, we began to untangle ourselves, as those who were standing around the edges rolled the curtains back up and moved chairs out onto the wet grass. As the sky cleared, the low sun reddened the cliffs and turned the brown river silver. Desert air, softened and chill, floated through the tent. We could shift our chairs back into rows and straighten our legs. In the worst of the storm we all had decided at once to trust ourselves to the music. We had found an unexpected peace in our moments of fear by swinging along—the best way I can think of to get along.

Notes

CHAPTER ONE

1. Kenneth Burke, *A Grammar of Motives* (Berkeley: University of California Press, 1969), 358.
2. Terry Eagleton, *The Meaning of Life: A Very Short Introduction* (New York: Oxford University Press, 2008), 84, 100.
3. Martin Williams, *The Jazz Tradition*, 2nd ed. (New York: Oxford University Press, 1993), 263.
4. Cited in Wynton Marsalis with Geoffrey C. Ward, *Moving To Higher Ground: How Jazz Can Change Your Life* (New York: Random House, 2009), 151.
5. As he begins his discussion of constitutions in *A Grammar of Motives*, Burke notes the focus of the primary American constitutional problem: "a *plurality* acting as a *unity*" that Americans encounter in the ubiquitous reminder, " '*e pluribus unum*' " (375).
6. Burke, *A Grammar of Motives*, 342.
7. Letter from Kenneth Burke to Jim Chesebro, September 24, 1987. Kenneth Burke Papers, Eberly Family Special Collections Library, Pennsylvania State University. Used by permission of the Kenneth Burke Literary Trust.
8. Burke, *A Grammar of Motives*, 362.
9. Letter from Kenneth Burke to Dutchie (Elspeth) Burke, February 21, 1989. Kenneth Burke Papers, Eberly Family Special Collections Library, Pennsylvania State University. Used by permission of the Kenneth Burke Literary Trust.
10. Kenneth Burke, "Art—and the First Rough Draft of Living," *Modern Age* 8, no. 2 (spring 1964): 158. Burke used versions of this image to summarize the aesthetic effect he explained in his theory of form. Ann George and Jack Selzer note its

source in common usage of the time in *Kenneth Burke in the 1930s* (Columbia: University of South Carolina Press, 2007), 59.

11. Letter from Kenneth Burke to Dutchie (Elspeth) Burke, February 21, 1989. Kenneth Burke Papers, Eberly Family Special Collections Library, Pennsylvania State University. Used by permission of the Kenneth Burke Literary Trust.
12. Kenneth Burke, *Counter-Statement* (Berkeley: University of California Press, 1968), 190.
13. Burke, *A Grammar of Motives*, 20.
14. Burke, *Counter-Statement*, 125,
15. Burke to Malcolm Cowley, May 1, 1916, in *The Selected Correspondence of Kenneth Burke and Malcolm Cowley, 1915–1981*, ed. Paul Jay (Berkeley: University of California Press, 1990), 24.
16. Burke, *Counter-Statement*, 41.
17. Kenneth Burke, "Rhetoric—Old and New," in *New Rhetorics,* ed. Martin Steinmann (New York: Scribner, 1967), 63.
18. Kenneth Burke, *The Philosophy of Literary Form: Studies in Symbolic Action* (Berkeley: University of California Press, 1973), 306.
19. Burke, *A Grammar of Motives*, 341.
20. Robert G. O'Meally, "Introduction: Jazz Shapes," in *Living with Music: Ralph Ellison's Jazz Writings*, ed. Robert G. O'Meally (New York: Modern Library, 2001), xi. Emphasis in original.
21. Burke, *A Grammar of Motives*, 323.
22. O'Meally, "Introduction: Jazz Shapes," xii–xiii.
23. Burke, *A Grammar of Motives*, 360, 362.
24. Burke, *A Grammar of Motives*, 323.
25. Ralph Ellison, "Living with Music," 227–36, in *The Collected Essays of Ralph Ellison,* ed. John F. Callahan (New York: Modern Library, 1995), 229.
26. A rich description of the full context of the relationship in which Ellison's letter to Burke was written is central to Bryan Crable's *Ralph Ellison and Kenneth Burke: At the Roots of the Racial Divide* (University of Virginia Press, 2011).
27. Garth Pauley, "Criticism in Context: Kenneth Burke's 'The Rhetoric of Hitler's Battle,'" *KB Journal* 6, no. 1 (fall 2009): n.p.
28. Quoted in Beth Eddy, *The Rites of Identity: The Religious Naturalism and Cultural Criticism of Kenneth Burke and Ralph Ellison* (Princeton, NJ: Princeton University Press, 2003). 108.
29. Ellison, "Living with Music," 228.
30. Burke, "Art—and the First Rough Draft of Living," 158.
31. Burke, *The Philosophy of Literary Form*, 227.
32. Burke, "Art—and the First Rough Draft of Living," 158–59.
33. Aristotle, *Politics*, trans. T.A. Sinclair (New York: Penguin, 1985), 462, 466.
34. Susanne Langer, *Feeling and Form: A Theory of Art* (New York: Scribner's, 1953), 126, 129.

35. Mark Johnson, *The Meaning of the Body: Aesthetics of Human Understanding* (Chicago: University of Chicago Press, 2007), 236.
36. Daniel J. Levitin, *This is Your Brain on Music: The Science of a Human Obsession* (New York: Dutton, 2006), 236–37.
37. Burke, *Philosophy of Literary Form*, 223–25.
38. Walt Whitman, "Democratic Vistas," 460–516, in *Leaves of Grass and Selected Prose*, ed. John Kouwenhoven (New York: Modern Library, 1950), 466.
39. Kenneth Burke, "Musical Chronicle," *The Dial* 9 (December 1928): 529.
40. Eagleton, Terry. *The Ideology of the Aesthetic* (Oxford: Blackwell, 1991), 25.
41. Ralph Ellison, "The Charlie Christian Story," 266–72, in *The Collected Essays of Ralph Ellison*, ed. John F. Callahan (New York: Modern Library, 1995), 269.
42. Marsalis and Ward, *Moving to Higher Ground*, xv.
43. Marsalis and Ward, *Moving to Higher Ground*, 12.
44. Gene Lees, "The Poet," in *Reading Jazz: A Gathering of Autobiography, Reportage, and Criticism from 1919 to Now*, ed. Robert Gottlieb (New York: Vintage, 1999), 426.
45. Duke Ellington, *Music is My Mistress* (New York: Doubleday, 1973), 465.
46. Marsalis and Ward, *Moving to Higher Ground*, 40–41.
47. Paul F. Berliner, *Thinking in Jazz: The Infinite Art of Improvisation* (Chicago: University of Chicago Press, 1994), 497.
48. Berliner, *Thinking in Jazz*, 503.
49. Nicholas Gebhardt, *Going for Jazz: Musical Practices and American Ideology* (Chicago: University of Chicago Press, 2001), 19.
50. Gebhardt, *Going for Jazz*, 129.
51. Ingrid Monson, *Saying Something: Jazz Improvisation and Interaction* (Chicago: University of Chicago Press, 1996), 26–27.
52. Monson, *Saying Something*, 66–67.
53. Monson, *Saying Something*, 215.
54. Gebhardt, *Going for Jazz*, 19.
55. John F. Callahan, "Introduction," in *The Collected Essays of Ralph Ellison*, ed. John F. Callahan (New York: The Modern Library, 1994), xx.
56. Ann Douglas, *Terrible Honesty: Mongrel Manhattan in the 1920s* (New York: Noonday, 1995), 3.
57. Douglas, *Terrible Honesty*, 116.
58. James first used the word "personate" in a study of spiritualism to name the medium's goal of expressing the identity of the one who is dead. William James, "Report on Mrs. Piper's Hodgson-Control," in *Collected Essays and Reviews* (New York: Longmans, Green and Co., 1920), 484–85.
59. T. J. Anderson III, *Notes to Make the Sound Come Right: Four Innovators of Jazz Poetry* (Fayetteville: University of Arkansas Press, 2004), 7.
60. Anderson, *Notes to Make the Sound Come Right*, 79.
61. Anderson uses the term to describe "a way in which one defies conformity and creates new ways of presenting oneself to the world" (7). Amiri Baraka

uses it in much the way as Burke does: "thought perfected at its most empirical, *i.e. as* attitude, or "*stance*" (152); that is, effectively, "incipient action" (*A Grammar of Motives*, 242).

62. Burke, *Permanence and Change: An Anatomy of Purpose*, 3rd ed. (Berkeley: University of California Press, 1984), 309.
63. Robert G. O'Meally, afterword to *The Book of Rhythms* by Langston Hughes (New York: Oxford University Press, 1995), 53.
64. Langston Hughes and Carl Van Vechten, *Remember Me to Harlem: The Letters of Langston Hughes and Carl Van Vechten*, ed. Emily Bernard (New York: Vintage, 2001), 278.
65. Langston Hughes, *The First Book of Jazz* (Hopewell, NJ: Ecco, 1982), 22.
66. Hughes, *The First Book of Jazz*, 5, 8.
67. Kenneth Burke, "Poetics and Communication," in *Perspectives in Education, Religion, and the Arts*, ed. Howard E. Keifer and Milton K. Munitz (Albany: State University of New York Press, 1970), 406.
68. Burke, *A Grammar of Motives*, 342.
69. Kenneth Burke, *Attitudes toward History*, 3rd ed. (Berkeley: University of California Press, 1984), 285.
70. Burke, *Attitudes toward History*, 210.
71. Kenneth Burke, "The Rhetorical Situation," in *Communication: Ethical and Moral Issues*, ed. Lee Thayer (Gordon and Breach Science, 1972), 263–75, 268.
72. Timothy W. Crucius, *Kenneth Burke and the Conversation after Philosophy* (Carbondale: Southern Illinois University Press, 1999), 37.
73. Dana Anderson, *Identity's Strategy: Rhetorical Selves in Conversation* (Columbia: University of South Carolina Press, 2007), 168.
74. Anderson, *Identity's Strategy*, 28, 168
75. Burke, *Counter-Statement*, 54.
76. Jack Selzer, *Kenneth Burke in Greenwich Village: Conversing with the Moderns, 1915–1931* (Madison: University of Wisconsin Press, 1996), 147.
77. Ann George and Jack Selzer, *Kenneth Burke in the 1930s* (Columbia: University of South Carolina Press, 2007), 60, 109.
78. Burke and Cowley, *Selected Correspondence*, 24–26.
79. Burke and Cowley, *Selected Correspondence*, 262.
80. Burke, *Counter-Statement*, 140–41.
81. Debra Hawhee, *Moving Bodies: Kenneth Burke on the Edges of Language* (Columbia: University of South Carolina Press, 2012), 25.
82. Jeffrey Carroll, "The Song Above Catastrophe: Kenneth Burke on Music," *KB Journal* 7, no. 2 (spring 2011), http://kbjournal.org/carroll. This article is a monograph that fills the entire issue. *KB Journal* is an online publication that does not paginate.
83. Burke, *Counter-Statement*, 36.
84. Burke, *Permanence and Change*, 74.
85. Burke, *The Philosophy of Literary Form*, 221.

86. Burke, *The Philosophy of Literary Form*, 227, 229.
87. Stanley Crouch, "Blues to Be Constitutional," in *Considering Genius: Writings on Jazz* (New York: Basic Books, 2006), 171.
88. Crouch, "Blues to Be Constitutional," 172.
89. Crouch, "Blues to Be Constitutional," 175.
90. Crouch, "Blues to Be Constitutional," 176
91. Kenneth Burke, "Responsibilities of National Greatness," *The Nation* 205 (July 17, 1967): 50.

CHAPTER TWO

1. Kenneth Burke, *A Rhetoric of Motives* (Berkeley: University of California Press, 1969), 58.
2. John Dewey, *Art as Experience* (New York: Perigee Books, 2005), 36.
3. Kenneth Burke, *Counter-Statement* (Berkeley: University of California Press, 1968), 77.
4. Bill Evans, *Conversations with Myself*, Polygram Records, 1997.
5. Loren Schoenberg, interview with the author, July 2011.
6. Marcus Roberts, interview with the author, February 2002.
7. Wynton Marsalis and Carl Vigeland. *Jazz in the Bittersweet Blues of Life* (New York: Da Capo Press, 2001), 72.
8. Wynton Marsalis, interview with the author, March 2000.
9. Natalie Cole, *Unforgettable*, Elektra/Wea, 1991.
10. Kenneth Burke, "The Rhetorical Situation," in *Communication: Ethical and Moral Issues*, ed. Lee Thayer (London: Gordon and Breach Science Publishers, 1973), 34.
11. Ralph Ellison, "The Little Man at Chehaw Station: The American Artist and His Audience," in *The Collected Essays of Ralph Ellison*, ed. John F. Callahan (New York: Modern Library, 1995), 492. See Bryan Crable, *Ralph Ellison and Kenneth Burke: At the Roots of the Racial Divide* (Charlottesville: University of Virginia Press, 2011),
12. Ellison, "The Little Man at Chehaw Station,": 500, 502–3.
13. Burke, A Rhetoric of Motives, 58.
14. Ellison, "The Little Man at Chehaw Station," 500, 502–3.
15. From that study came my book *Rhetorical Landscapes in America: Variations on a Theme from Kenneth Burke* (Columbia: University of South Carolina Press, 2004).
16. Cannonball Adderley, *Somethin' Else*, Blue Note, 1958.
17. John Dewey, *A Common Faith* (New Haven: Yale University Press, 1960), 26.
18. Kenneth Burke, "Responsibilities of National Greatness," *The Nation* 205 (July 17, 1967): 50.
19. Kenneth Burke, "Rhetoric and Poetics," in *Language as Symbolic Action: Essays on Life, Literature, and Method* (Berkeley: University of California Press, 1966), 305, 307.

20. Burke, *A Rhetoric of Motives*, 21.
21. Terry Eagleton, *The Meaning of Life: A Very Short Introduction* (New York: Oxford University Press, 2008), 90–91.
22. The 1928 review is titled "Musical Chronicle" and it appeared in the April 1928 issue of *The Dial*. The 1933 review is titled "The Negro's Pattern of Life" and it appeared in *The Saturday Review of Literature* in July of that year; it was subsequently republished in *The Philosophy of Literary Form: Studies in Symbolic Action*, 3rd ed. (Berkeley: University of California Press, 1973), 361–68.
23. Kenneth Burke, "Musical Chronicle," *The Dial* 84 (April 1928): 357–58.
24. Hall Johnson, *Thirty Spirituals Arranged for Voice and Piano* (New York: G. Schirmer, 1949), 5.
25. Burke, *The Philosophy of Literary Form*, 362.
26. Burke, *The Philosophy of Literary Form*, 365.
27. Burke, *The Philosophy of Literary Form*, 366–67.
28. Burke, *The Philosophy of Literary Form*, 365
29. Burke, *The Philosophy of Literary Form*, 365.
30. Jim Chapin to Tom Chapin, recounted in e-mail message to author, January 12, 2004.
31. Kenneth Burke, "Rhetoric—Old and New," in *New Rhetorics*, ed. Martin Steinmann (New York: Scribner, 1967), 59–76.
32. Kenneth Burke, "The Calling of the Tune," in *The Philosophy of Literary Form: Studies in Symbolic Action*, 3rd ed. (Berkeley: University of California Press, 1973), 223.
33. Burke, *Counter-Statement*, 31.
34. Burke, *Counter-Statement*, 143.
35. Burke, *Counter-Statement*, 152.
36. Burke, *Counter-Statement*, 154.
37. Burke, *A Rhetoric of Motives*, 21.
38. Burke, *The Philosophy of Literary Form*, 223.

CHAPTER THREE

1. Kenneth Burke, "The Calling of the Tune," in *The Philosophy of Literary Form: Studies in Symbolic Action*, 3rd ed. (Berkeley: University of California Press, 1973), 223.
2. Kenneth Burke, "Afterword: In Retrospective Prospect," in *Permanence and Change: An Anatomy of Purpose* (Berkeley: University of California Press, 1984), 309–10.
3. Kenneth Burke, *Attitudes Toward History*, 3rd ed. (Berkeley: University of California Press, 1984), 285.
4. Jonathan Batiste, *Social Music*. Liner notes. Razor & Tie Recordings, 2013.
5. Eric Sandler, "Jon Batiste's Social Music: Jazz Music with New Orleans

Heritage," *Revive Music*, September 24, 2013. http://revive-music.com/2013/09/24/jonathan-batistes-social-music-jazz-music-new-orleans-heritage/.

6. Jonathan Batiste, "What is Jazz?" *CNN Ideas Series*, December 28, 2012. http://www.cnn.com/2012/12/26/opinion/batiste-what-is-jazz/index.html.
7. Kenneth Burke, "Linguistic Approach to Problems of Education," in *Modern Philosophy and Education* (Chicago: The National Society for the Study of Education, 1955), 292–93.
8. Kenneth Burke, "Linguistic Approach to Problems of Education," 292.
9. Kenneth Burke, *Counter-Statement* (Berkeley: University of California Press, 1968), 224–25.
10. Kenneth Burke, "Rhetoric and Poetics," in *Language as Symbolic Action: Essays on Life, Literature, and Method* (Berkeley: University of California Press, 1966), 305.
11. Burke, *Counter-Statement*, 215.
12. Burke, *Counter-Statement*, 219.
13. Kenneth Burke, "Rhetoric and Poetics," 305.
14. Burke, *Counter-Statement*, 143.
15. Kenneth Burke, *A Grammar of Motives* (Berkeley: University of California Press, 1969), 237.
16. Burke, *Counter-Statement*, 225.
17. Kenneth Burke, "Formalist Criticism: Its Principles and Limits," in *Language as Symbolic Action: Essays on Life, Literature, and Method* (Berkeley: University of California Press, 1968), 490.
18. Kenneth Burke, "Rhetoric—Old and New," in *New Rhetorics*, ed. Martin Steinmann (New York: Scribner, 1967), 76.
19. Kenneth Burke, "Responsibilities of National Greatness," *The Nation* 205 (July 17, 1967): 50.
20. Burke, "Rhetoric—Old and New," 63.
21. Burke, "Rhetoric and Poetics," 305.
22. Burke, *Counter-Statement*, 77.
23. Burke, *Attitudes toward History*, 263, 266–67.
24. Kenneth Burke, *A Rhetoric of Motives* (Berkeley: University of California Press, 1969),
25. Burke, *A Rhetoric of Motives*, 20–21.
26. Kenneth Burke, "Art—and the First Rough Draft of Living," *Modern Age*, 8, no. 2 (spring 1964): 162–63.
27. Burke, *A Rhetoric of Motives*, 331.
28. Burke, "Rhetoric—Old and New," 76.
29. Burke, *Counter-Statement*, 130.
30. Burke, "Rhetoric—Old and New," 76.
31. Kenneth Burke, "A Theory of Terminology," in *On Human Nature: A Gathering While Everything Flows*, ed. William H. Rueckert and Angelo Bonadonna (Berkeley: University of California Press, 2003), 244.

32. Burke, *A Rhetoric of Motives*, 21.
33. Burke, *A Rhetoric of Motives*, 21
34. Its first recorded version, by the Nat King Cole Trio in 1946, is the essential one; available on *Best of Nat King Cole Trio: Vocal Classics 1942–46*, Blue Note, 1995.
35. Burke, "Rhetoric—Old and New," 76.
36. "Cross Road Blues (take 2)," American Studies at the University of Virginia, accessed 17 February 2011, http://xroads.virginia.edu/~music/blues/crb .html. 2:27. Version from *Robert Johnson: The Complete Recordings*, Sony BMG Music Entertainment, 1990.
37. Kenneth Burke, *Late Poems, 1968–1993*, ed. Julie Whitaker and David Blakesley (Columbia: University of South Carolina Press, 2005), 25.
38. Burke, *Attitudes toward History*, 217–18.
39. Burke, *The Philosophy of Literary Form*, 362.
40. Hall Johnson, *Thirty Spirituals: Arranged for Voice and Piano* (New York: Hal Leonard, 1949), 5.
41. Burke, *Late Poems*, 24–25.
42. Burke, *The Philosophy of Literary Form*, 9.
43. Albert Murray, *Stomping the Blues*, 2nd ed. (New York: Da Capo Press, 2000), 16–17.
44. Burke, *Philosophy of Literary Form*, 293.
45. Burke, *Philosophy of Literary Form*, 296–97.
46. Murray, *Stomping the Blues*, 45.
47. Murray, *Stomping the Blues*, 50.
48. Murray, *Stomping the Blues*, 68.
49. James Baldwin, "Sonny's Blues," in *Write Me a Few of Your Lines: A Blues Reader*, ed. Steven C. Tracy (Amherst: University of Massachusetts Press, 1999), 414.
50. Ali Jackson, e-mail message to author, February 18, 2011.
51. A video podcast available from iTunes or from www.wyntonmarsalis.com uses the same personnel to play a blues, and with the same elements as the performance I describe. In this podcast Marsalis is the only soloist, and the story he tells is less wrenching than the story he told at the concert I attended. But you can get the idea: "Blues," Wynton Marsalis Quintet performing at Parc Floral in Paris, July 28, 2007. Released October 20, 2007.
52. Burke, *Counter-Statement*, 174.
53. Burke, *Counter-Statement*, 167.
54. Burke, *Counter-Statement*, 41.
55. Ralph Ellison, *The Collected Essays of Ralph Ellison*, ed. John F. Callahan (New York: The Modern Library, 1995), xx.
56. Ralph Ellison, "The Art of Fiction: An Interview," in *The Collected Essays of Ralph Ellison*, ed. John F. Callahan (New York: Modern Library, 1995), 219.
57. Burke, *Philosophy of Literary Form*, 306.

58. Burke, *Philosophy of Literary Form*, 307.
59. Burke, *A Rhetoric of Motives*, 21.
60. Burke, *Attitudes toward History*, 285.
61. Burke, *Philosophy of Literary Form*, 308.
62. Burke, *Philosophy of Literary Form*, 281.

CHAPTER FOUR

1. Kenneth Burke, *Attitudes toward History*, 3rd ed. (Berkeley: University of California Press, 1984), 285.
2. Ralph Ellison, "The Little Man at Chehaw Station: The American Artist and His Audience," in *The Collected Essays of Ralph Ellison*, ed. John F. Callahan (New York: Modern Library, 1995), 500.
3. Kenneth Burke, "Responsibilities of National Greatness," *The Nation* 205 (July 17, 1967): 46, 50.
4. James P. Zappen, S. Michael Halloran, and Scott A. Wible, "Some Notes on 'Ad bellum purificandum,'" *KB Journal* (2007), n.p. http://kbjournal.org/node/201.
5. The translations are James P. Zappen's, from notes that accompany the collection of photographs he made of these inscriptions. Copies of notes and photographs in the possession of the author.
6. Kenneth Burke, *A Grammar of Motives* (Berkeley: University of California Press, 1969), 442.
7. Ellison, "The Little Man at Chehaw Station," 496. Walton Muyumba offers a penetrating explanation of the irony inherent in this phrase in *The Shadow and the Act: Black Intellectual Practice, Jazz Improvisation, and Philosophical Pragmatism* (Chicago: University of Chicago Press, 2011), 56.
8. Rick Mattingly, *The Drummer's Time: Conversations with the Great Drummers of Jazz* (Modern Drummer Publications, 1998), 60.
9. Duke Ellington, *Music Is My Mistress* (New York: De Capo Press, 1973), 447.
10. Vivian Perlis and Libby Van Cleve, *Composers' Voices from Ives to Ellington: An Oral History of American Music* (New Haven: Yale University Press, 2005), 386.
11. Ralph Ellison, "Living with Music," in *The Collected Essays of Ralph Ellison*, ed. John F. Callahan (New York: Modern Library, 1995), 228–29.
12. Kenneth Burke, "On Form," *Hudson Review* 17, no. 1 (spring 1964): 104.
13. Burke, "On Form," 109.
14. Kenneth Burke, "The Rhetorical Situation," in *Communication: Ethical and Moral Issues*, ed. Lee Thayer (London: Gordon and Breach Science Publishers, 1973), 263.
15. Kenneth Burke, *Permanence and Change: An Anatomy of Purpose*, 3rd ed. (Berkeley: University of California Press, 1984), 309–10.
16. Ralph Ellison, "The Little Man at Chehaw Station," 504.

17. Kenneth Burke, *The Philosophy of Literary Form: Studies in Symbolic Action 3rd ed.* (Berkeley: University of California Press, 1973), 306.
18. Ralph Ellison to Kenneth Burke, 23 November 1945. Cited in Bryan Crable, *Ralph Ellison and Kenneth Burke: At the Roots of the Racial Divide* (Charlottesville: University of Virginia Press, 2012), 64.
19. Kenneth Burke, *Language as Symbolic Action: Essays on Life, Literature, and Method* (Berkeley: University of California Press, 1966), 305.
20. Robert Wess, *Kenneth Burke: Rhetoric, Subjectivity, Postmodernism* (New York: Cambridge University Press, 1996), 246.
21. Burke, *Attitudes toward History*, 234.
22. Burke, *Attitudes toward History*, 337.
23. Alexis de Tocqueville, *Democracy in America*, ed. Phillips Bradley, vol. 2, (New York: Vintage, 1990), 322.
24. Tocqueville, *Democracy in America*, vol. 2, 99.
25. Kenneth Burke, "Art—and the First Rough Draft of Living," *Modern Age* 8, no. 2 (spring 1964): 158.
26. Burke, "Art—and the First Rough Draft of Living," 158–159.
27. Emerson, Ralph Waldo, "Nature," in *Nature and Selected Essays*, ed. Larzer Ziff (New York: Penguin, 1982), 81.
28. Emerson, "An Address Delivered before the Senior Class in Divinity College, Cambridge," in *Nature and Selected Essays*, ed. Larzer Ziff (New York: Penguin, 1982), 112.
29. Emerson, "An Address," 123–24.
30. Jane Tompkins, *West of Everything: The Inner Life of Westerns* (New York: Oxford University Press, 1993), 19.
31. Tompkins, *West of Everything*, 3.
32. Kenneth Burke, "Responsibilities of National Greatness," 47.
33. Kenneth Burke, *Counter-Statement* (Berkeley: University of California Press, 1968), 124, 185.
34. Burke, *The Philosophy of Literary Form*, 223.
35. Kenneth Burke, *A Rhetoric of Motives* (Berkeley: University of California Press, 1969), xiii.
36. Henry David Thoreau, *Walden and Other Writings*, ed. Brooks Atkinson (New York: Random House, 1950), 290.
37. Walt Whitman, "Democratic Vistas," in *Leaves of Grass and Selected Prose*, ed. John Kouwenhoven (New York: Modern Library, 1950), 466.
38. Whitman, "Democratic Vistas," 488.
39. Ellison, "The Little Man in Chehaw Station," 500.
40. Burke, *A Rhetoric of Motives*, 62.
41. Whitman, "Democratic Vistas," 502.
42. Whitman, "Democratic Vistas," 466.
43. Whitman, "Democratic Vistas," 488.
44. Tocqueville, *Democracy in America*, vol. 2, 138–9.

45. Tocqueville, *Democracy in America*, vol. 2, 98.
46. Tocqueville, *Democracy in America*, vol. 2, 109.
47. Jazz—Designation as an American National Treasure, H. Con. Res. 35, 101 Stat. 2013 (1987).
48. Ellen McCulloch-Lovell, "What is the Millennium Council?" The White House, accessed July 18, 2013, http://clinton4.nara.gov/Initiatives/Millennium/what.html.This statement is in an introductory letter to the public signed by Ellen McCulloch-Lovell, whose title was deputy assistant to the president and advisor to the first lady on the Millennium. There is little documentation of the series available now, though on the White House website during the Clinton years there were extensive descriptions of the program and of each evening. Videotapes of at least some of the evenings—including the evening on jazz—are available in the C-SPAN archives.
49. Bill Clinton and Hillary Clinton. "Remarks by the President and the First Lady at the White House Millennium Evening Lecture Series (9/18/98)." The White House, accessed July 18, 2013, http://clinton4.nara.gov/Initiatives/Millennium/19980921–8778.html. My source for these statements by Clinton is the transcript of the program.
50. Kenneth Burke, *The Rhetoric of Religion: Studies in Logology* (Berkeley: University of California Press, 1970), 278.
51. Ellison, "The Little Man in Chehaw Station," 501.
52. Ellison, "The Little Man in Chehaw Station," 503.
53. Clinton, "Remarks by the President."
54. Václav Havel, "Democracy's Forgotten Dimension," *Journal of Democracy* 6, no. 2 (1995): 6–7.
55. Clinton, "Remarks by the President."
56. Havel, "Democracy's Forgotten Dimension," 8.
57. Havel, "Democracy's Forgotten Dimension," 8.
58. William James, *The Varieties of Religious Experience: A Study in Human Nature, Being the Gifford Lectures on Natural Religion, Delivered at Edinburgh in 1901–1902*, (New York: New American Library, 2003), 232.
59. Kenneth Burke, "The Fate of the Union: Kennedy and After," *New York Review of Books* 1, no. 9 (December 26, 1963): 9.
60. James, *The Varieties of Religious Experience*, 232.
61. Kenneth Burke, "Musical Chronicle," *The Dial* 85 (December 1928): 529.
62. This performance is a live recording of the Gene Harris Trio (Ray Brown on bass and Mickey Roker on drums) with Stanley Turrentine on tenor saxophone. The recording is *The Gene Harris Trio Plus One* (Concord 4303), recorded at the Blue Note in New York City in the fall of 1985. It was broadcast the evening of September 12, 2001, on Salt Lake City's NPR affiliate, KUER, by jazz host Steve Williams.
63. Kenneth Burke, *A Grammar of Motives*, 339–40.
64. Burke, *A Rhetoric of Motives*, 58.

65. Gene Lees, "The Poet," 419–44, in *Reading Jazz: A Gathering of Autobiography, Reportage, and Criticism from 1919 to Now*, ed. Robert Gottlieb (New York: Vintage, 1999), 426.
66. Burke, *A Grammar of Motives*, 59–60.
67. Kenneth Burke, "'Watchful of Hermetics to Be Strong in Hermeneutics': Selections from 'Poetics, Dramatistically Considered.'" *Unending Conversations: New Writings by and about Kenneth Burke*, Ed Greig Henderson & David Cratis Williams (Carbondale: Southern Illinois University Press, 2001), 38.
68. Duke Ellington, *Music Is My Mistress* (New York: Doubleday, 1973), 465.
69. Burke, *A Grammar of Motives*, 422.
70. Kenneth Burke, "Counter-Gridlock: An Interview with Kenneth Burke," 336–89, in *On Human Nature: A Gathering while Everything Flows, 1967–1984*, ed. William H. Rueckert and Angelo Bonadonna (Berkeley: University of California Press, 2003), 367.
71. Kenneth Burke, "Ideology and Myth" manuscript, n.d. Kenneth Burke Papers, P17, Pennsylvania State University Special Collections Library. Copyright the Kenneth Burke Literary Trust, Anthony Burke and Michael Burke, trustees (15 pages, numbered 1 through 18, with some pages missing and two pages numbered 13, referenced as 13a and 13b). The quoted phrases appear on the manuscript page numbered 14. I acknowledge James P. Zappen for leading me to this source in his work, "Kenneth Burke on Dialectical-Rhetorical Transcendence, *Philosophy and Rhetoric* 42:3 (2009): 279–301.
72. Kenneth Burke, "Ideology and Myth," *Accent* 7, no. 4 (summer 1947):198.
73. Kenneth Burke, *The Rhetoric of Religion* (Berkeley: University of California Press, 1970), 166.
74. Burke, *Language as Symbolic Action*, 486.
75. Burke, *A Grammar of Motives*, 340.
76. Kenneth Burke, "'Watchful of Hermetics to Be Strong in Hermeneutics': Selections from 'Poetics, Dramatistically Considered,'" in *Unending Conversations: New Writings by and about Kenneth Burke*, ed. Greig Henderson and David Cratis Williams (Carbondale: Southern Illinois University Press, 2001), 70–71.
77. Burke, *A Grammar of Motives*, 440.
78. Burke, *The Philosophy of Literary Form*, 99–100.
79. Burke, *A Grammar of Motives*, 340.
80. Burke, "Watchful of Hermetics to be Strong in Hermeneutics," 70–71.
81. Burke, "Ideology and Myth," 14.

CHAPTER FIVE

1. Kenneth Burke, "Government in the Making," *Direction* 5 (December 19, 1942): 3.

2. Kenneth Burke, *A Grammar of Motives* (Berkeley: University of California Press, 1969), 17.
3. Burke, "Government in the Making," 3.
4. Burke, *A Grammar of Motives*, 11.
5. Alexis de Tocqueville, *Democracy in America*, ed. Phillips Bradley, vol. 1 (New York: Vintage, 1990), 7.
6. Stephen Frederick Schneck, "Habits of the Head: Tocqueville's America and Jazz," *Political Theory* 17, no. 4 (November 1989): 638–39.
7. Tocqueville, *Democracy in America*, vol. 2, 25.
8. Schneck, "Habits of the Head," 655
9. Schneck, "Habits of the Head," 639. My emphasis.
10. Bernard Crick, *Democracy: A Very Short Introduction* (New York: Oxford University Press, 2002), 113.
11. Eddie S. Glaude, Jr., *In a Shade of Blue: Pragmatism and the Politics of Black America* (Chicago: University of Chicago Press, 2007), xi–xii.
12. Kenneth Burke, "The Rhetorical Situation," in *Communication: Ethical and Moral Issues*, ed. Lee Thayer (Gordon and Breach Science, 1972), 263.
13. Kenneth Burke, "Poetics and Communication," in *Perspectives in Education, Religion, and the Arts,* ed. Howard E. Kiefer and Milton K. Munitz (Albany: State University of New York Press, 1970), 411.
14. Walter R. Fisher, "A Motive View of Communication," *Quarterly Journal of Speech* 56, no. 2 (1970): 131–32.
15. Kenneth Burke, *A Rhetoric of Motives* (Berkeley: University of California Press, 1969), 21.
16. Burke, *A Rhetoric of Motives*, 46.
17. Thomas W. Benson, preface to *Rhetorics of Display*, ed. Lawrence J. Prelli (Columbia: University of South Carolina Press, 2006), ix.
18. Ingrid Monson, *Saying Something: Jazz Improvisation and Interaction* (Chicago: University of Chicago Press, 1996), 43.
19. Ingrid Monson, *Saying Something*, 67.
20. Tocqueville, *Democracy in America*, vol. 2, 598.
21. Walt Whitman, "Democratic Vistas," in *Leaves of Grass and Selected Prose*, ed. John Kouwenhoven (New York: Modern Library, 1950), 483.
22. Bernard Crick, *Democracy: A Very Short Introduction* (New York: Oxford University Press, 2002), 113.
23. Kenneth Burke, *Counter-Statement* (Berkeley: University of California Press, 1968), 77, 143.
24. Kenneth Burke, *The Philosophy of Literary Form: Studies in Symbolic Action,* 3rd ed. (Berkeley: University of California Press, 1973), 116.
25. Burke, *The Philosophy of Literary Form*, 123.
26. Vijay Iyer, liner notes to *Accelerando*, Vijay Iyer Trio, Act Music, 2012.
27. Mark Johnson, *The Meaning of the Body: Aesthetics of Human Understanding* (Chicago: University of Chicago Press, 2007), 236, 238.

28. Johnson, *The Meaning of the Body*, 239.
29. Iyer, liner notes to *Accelerando.*
30. Kenneth Burke, "Responsibilities of National Greatness," *The Nation* 205 (July 17, 1967): 50.
31. Kenneth Burke to John Brooks Wheelwright, December 7, 1933, and Kenneth Burke to Joshua Kunitz, December 7, 1936; cited in Ann George and Jack Selzer, *Kenneth Burke in the 1930s* (Columbia: University of South Carolina Press, 2007), v.
32. Don Burks, "KB's Last Day," *Kenneth Burke Society Newsletter* 9:1 (December 1993): 24.
33. Burke, *A Rhetoric of Motives*, 41.
34. Burke, *A Rhetoric of Motives*, 25.
35. Burke, *A Rhetoric of Motives*, viii–xiv.
36. Burke, *A Rhetoric of Motives*, 45.
37. Burke, *A Rhetoric of Motives*, 43.
38. Burke, *A Rhetoric of Motives*, 44.
39. Burke, *A Rhetoric of Motives*, 58.
40. Kenneth Burke, Introduction to *Attitudes toward History*, 3rd edition (Berkeley: University of California Press, 1984), n.p.
41. W. E. B. DuBois, *The Souls of Black Folk* (New York: Bantam, 2005), 10.
42. Albert Murray, *The Omni-Americans: Black Experience and American Culture* (New York: Outerbridge & Dienstfrey, 1970), 16.
43. Ralph Ellison, "Alain Locke," in *The Collected Essays of Ralph Ellison*, ed John F. Callahan (New York: Modern Library, 1995), 442.
44. Brent Hays Edwards, "The Literary Ellington," in *Uptown Conversations: The New Jazz Studies*, ed. Robert G. O'Meally, Brent Hayes Edwards, and Farah Jasmine Griffin (New York: Columbia University Press, 2004), 326.
45. Claudia Roth Pierpont, "Black, Brown, and Beige: Duke Ellington's Music and Race in America," *New Yorker,* May 17, 2010, http://www.newyorker.com/arts/critics/atlarge/2010/05/17/100517crat_atlarge_pierpont.
46. Mark Tucker, "The Genesis of 'Black, Brown, and Beige,'" *Black Music Research Journal* 22, supplement: Best of BMRJ (2002): 136, http://www.jstor.org/stable/1519946.
47. Tucker, "The Genesis of 'Black, Brown, and Beige," 138.
48. Stanley Dance, "The Funeral Address," in *The Duke Ellington Reader,* ed. Mark Tucker (New York: Oxford University Press, 1993), 383.
49. Leonard Feather, liner notes to *The Duke Ellington Carnegie Hall Concerts, January 1943,* Prestige Records, 1977.
50. Duke Ellington, introduction to "Beige," *The Duke Ellington Carnegie Hall Concerts, January 1943*, Prestige Records, 1977.
51. Tucker, "The Genesis of 'Black, Brown, and Beige,'" 139.
52. Mark Tucker, ed., "Interview in Los Angeles: On *Jump for Joy*, Opera, and Dissonance as a 'Way of Life'" (1941), in *The Duke Ellington Reader* (New York: Oxford University Press, 1993), 149–50.

53. Duke Ellington, *Duke Ellington's "My People": The Complete Show*, Storyville Records, 2012.
54. Harvey G. Cohen, *Duke Ellington's America* (Chicago: University of Chicago Press, 2011), 395.
55. Cohen, *Duke Ellington's America*, 293.
56. Duke Ellington, *Music is My Mistress* (New York: Da Capo Press, 1976), 421.
57. Burke, *A Grammar of Motives*, 20.
58. S. Frederick Starr, *Red & Hot: The Fate of Jazz in the Soviet Union* (New York: Limelight Editions, 1994), 10.
59. Michael H. Kater, *Different Drummers: Jazz in the Culture of Nazi Germany* (New York: Oxford University Press, 1992), 29.
60. Kater, *Different Drummers*, 122–23.
61. Howard Reich, "The Sound of Freedom: Polish Jazz Comes to Chicago in Resonance Festival," *The Chicago Tribune*, February 28, 2011, http://articles.chicagotribune.com/2011–02–28/entertainment/ct-live-0301-jazz-festival-20110228_1_polish-jazz-new-jazz-zygmunt-matynia.
62. Penny M. von Eschen, *Satchmo Blows Up the World: Jazz Ambassadors Play the Cold War* (Cambridge, MA: Harvard University Press, 2004), 11.
63. Eschen, *Satchmo Blows Up the World*, 16.
64. Eschen, *Satchmo Blows Up the World*, 16.
65. Doug Ramsey, "Willis Conover Honored: A Good First Step," *Rifftides: Doug Ramsey on Jazz and Other Matters* (blog), May 1, 2009. http://www.artsjournal.com/rifftides/2009/05/the_white_house_has_yet.html.
66. Karen P. Hughes, "The Beat Goes On: Honoring Willis Conover and Celebrating the Power of Music," remarks at the Duke, Dizzy, and Diplomacy Jazz Concert, September 17, 2007. US State Department Archive, accessed March 1, 2013. http://2001–2009.state.gov/r/us/2007/93312.htm.
67. Eschen, *Satchmo Blows Up the World*, 16.
68. See S. Frederick Starr, *The Fate of Jazz in the Soviet Union*; Michael H. Kater, *Different Drummers*; Josef Skvorecky, *Talkin' Moscow Blues: Essays About Literature, Politics, Movies, and Jazz* (Toronto: University of Toronto Press, 1988).
69. Eschen, *Satchmo Blows Up the World*, 92.
70. Andrew James Kellett, "Fathers and Sons: American Blues and British Rock Music, 1960–1970" (PhD diss., University of Maryland, 2008), 14. http://hdl.handle.net/1903/8863.
71. Iola Brubeck, "World Take a Holiday Story Synopsis," 1957, Brubeck Collection, Holt-Atherton Special Collections-Digital Collections, University Library, University of the Pacific, accessed March 5, 2013. Used by permission. http://digitalcollections.pacific.edu/cdm/singleitem/collection/ambassadors/id/68/rec/1.
72. Dave Brubeck, *The Real Ambassadors: An Original Musical Production by Dave and Iola Brubeck*, Columbia Records, Sony Music Entertainment, 1994.
73. Iola Brubeck, "World Take a Holiday Story Synopsis," 1957.

74. Iola Brubeck, "They Say I Look Like God," 1961, Brubeck Collection, Holt-Atherton Special Collections-Digital Collections, University Library, University of the Pacific, accessed March 5, 2013. Used by permission. http://digitalcollections.pacific.edu/cdm/compoundobject/collection/ambassadors/id/66/rec/24
75. Terry Teachout, *Pops: A Life of Louis Armstrong* (Boston: Houghton Mifflin Harcourt, 2009,) 331.
76. Harvey G. Cohen, *Duke Ellington's America*, 251.
77. Harvey G. Cohen, *Duke Ellington's America*, 388–89.
78. Nicholas Gebhardt, *Going for Jazz: Musical Practices and American Ideology* (Chicago: University of Chicago Press, 2001), 128–29.
79. Gebhardt, *Going for Jazz*, 24.
80. Gebhardt, *Going for Jazz,* 15.
81. Maulana Ron Karenga, "Black Art," *Black Theater* 4 (April 1970): 9–10.
82. Jacques Attali, *Noise: The Political Economy of Music*, trans. Brian Massumi (St. Paul: University of Minnesota Press, 1985), 19.
83. T. J. Anderson III, *Notes to Make the Sound Come Right: Four Innovators of Jazz Poetry* (Fayetteville: University of Arkansas Press, 2004), 7.
84. The Baraka and Shepp statements were made at "Free Jazz and Its Legacies: Black Music and American Culture," a conference at Pennsylvania State University, April 5–6, 2002. From author's notes.
85. Kenneth Burke, "The Calling of the Tune," in *The Philosophy of Literary Form,* 3rd ed. (Berkeley: University of California Press, 1974), 221.
86. Eric C. Porter, *What Is This Thing Called Jazz? African American Musicians as Artists, Critics, and Activists* (Berkeley: University of California Press, 2002), 364n56.
87. Burke, *Counter-Statement*, 34.
88. Ashley Kahn, *A Love Supreme: The Story of John Coltrane's Signature Album* (New York: Penguin, 2002), 67–68.
89. Franya J. Berkman, "Appropriating Universality: The Coltranes and 1960s Spirituality," *American Studies* 48, no. 1 (Spring 2007): 43.
90. John Coltrane, *A Love Supreme*, MCA Records, 1995, liner notes.
91. Don DeMichael, "John Coltrane and Eric Dolphy Answer the Jazz Critics," in *DownBeat: The Great Jazz Interviews*, ed. Frank Alkyer, et. al. (New York: Hal Leonard, 2009), 88.
92. David Brent Johnson, "Sacred Blue: Jazz Goes to Church in the 1960s," *Indiana Public Media*, April 19, 2011, http://indianapublicmedia.org/nightlights/sacred-blue-jazz-church-1960s/.
93. Eric Reed, "Sacred Jazz," *All About Jazz* (blog), March 24, 2009, http://www.allaboutjazz.com/php/article.php?id=32072&pg=2#.UTpENKVXAuI.
94. Ashley Kahn, *A Love Supreme*, 67.
95. Jim Merod, "Jazz as a Cultural Archive," *Boundary* 2:22, no. 2 (summer 1995): 6–7.

96. John Dewey, *A Common Faith (1934)* (New Haven: Yale University Press, 1960), 26.
97. Paul Woodruff, *Reverence: Renewing a Forgotten Virtue* (New York: Oxford University Press, 2001), 48–49.
98. Woodruff, *Reverence*, 147.
99. David Ake. *Jazz Cultures* (Berkeley: University of California Press, 2002,) 108.
100. Woodruff, *Reverence*, 117.
101. Lewis Porter, *Coltrane: His Life and Music* (Ann Arbor: University of Michigan Press, 2000), 232.
102. Dan Morgenstern, quoted in Porter, *John Coltrane*, 217.
103. Porter, *John Coltrane*, 195.
104. Ian Marcus Corbin, "A Jazz Mass? The Vexing Legacy of Mary Lou Williams," *Commonweal*, December 7, 2012, http://commonwealmagazine.org/jazz-mass.
105. Dave Brubeck, *The Real Ambassadors*.
106. Kenneth Burke, "Art—and the First Rough Draft of Living," *Modern Age* 8, no. 2 (spring 1964): 158.
107. Kenneth Burke, *The Rhetoric of Religion: Studies in Logology* (Berkeley: University of California Press, 1970), 29.
108. Burke, *The Rhetoric of Religion*, 166.
109. Kenneth Burke and Malcolm Cowley, *The Selected Correspondence of Kenneth Burke and Malcolm Cowley*, ed. Paul Jay (Berkeley: University of California Press, 1988), 241.
110. Cohen, *Duke Ellington's America*, 446.
111. Cohen, *Duke Ellington's America*, 464.
112. Burke, *A Rhetoric of Motives*, xiv.
113. Janna Tull Steed, *Duke Ellington: A Spiritual Biography* (New York: The Crossroad Publishing Company, 1999), 114.
114. Steed, *Duke Ellington: A Spiritual Biography*, 148.
115. Steed, *Duke Ellington: A Spiritual Biography*, 163.
116. Cohen, *Duke Ellington's America*, 485.
117. Ellington, *Music is My Mistress*, 275.
118. Burke, *A Rhetoric of Motives*, 139.

CHAPTER SIX

1. Kenneth Burke, *Towards a Better Life* (Berkeley: University of California Press, 1984), 71.
2. Kenneth Burke, *Permanence and Change: An Anatomy of Purpose*, 3rd ed. (Berkeley: University of California Press, 1984), 266.
3. Kenneth Burke, *Attitudes toward History*, 3rd ed. (Berkeley: University of California Press, 1984), 256.

4. Kenneth Burke, "On Persuasion, Identification, and Dialectical Symmetry," ed. James Zappen, *Philosophy and Rhetoric* 39:4 (2006), 335–36.
5. Burke, *Towards a Better Life*, 67–68.
6. Ralph Waldo Emerson, *Nature and Selected Essays*, ed. Larzer Ziff (New York: Penguin, 2003), 39. The corresponding text from Jonathan Edwards is his "Personal Narrative."
7. Burke, *Towards a Better Life*, 69–71.
8. Kenneth Burke, "A Theory of Terminology," in *On Human Nature: A Gathering While Everything Flows, 1967–1984,* ed. William H. Rueckert and Angelo Bonadonna (Berkeley: University of California Press, 2003), 245. See also Kenneth Burke, "A Theory of Terms," delivered 1966, Drew Theological Seminary, Madison, NJ. http://www.americanrhetoric.com/speeches/kennethburketheoryofterms.htm. Accessed March 20, 2013.
9. Kenneth Burke, "Communication and the Human Condition," *Communication* 1, no. 2 (December 1974): 144.
10. Kenneth Burke, "The Negro's Pattern of Life," in *The Philosophy of Literary Form: Studies in Symbolic Action*, 3rd ed. (Berkeley: University of California Press, 1973), 363.
11. Burke, "The Negro's Pattern of Life," 366.
12. Kenneth Burke, *A Grammar of Motives* (Berkeley: University of California Press, 1969), 442.
13. Burke, *A Grammar of Motives*, 89.
14. Burke, *A Rhetoric of Motives* (Berkeley: University of California Press, 1969), 19.
15. Burke, "The Negro's Pattern of Life," 366.
16. Daniel J. Levitin, *This Is Your Brain on Music: The Science of a Human Obsession* (New York: Dutton, 2006), 236–37.
17. Levitin, *This Is Your Brain on Music*, 18, 178.
18. Levitin, *This Is Your Brain on Music*, 18, 168.
19. Levitin, *This Is Your Brain on Music*, 109, 238.
20. Kenneth Burke, *Counter-Statement* (Berkeley: University of California Press, 1968), 34.
21. Levitin, *This Is Your Brain on Music*, 18.
22. Cannonball Adderley, *Somethin' Else*, Blue Note, 1958.
23. Oliver Sacks, *Musicophilia: Tales of Music and the Brain* (New York: Vintage Books, 2008), 37.
24. William James, *The Principles of Psychology*, Vol. 2 (New York: Dover, 1950), 627.
25. Kenneth Burke, "On Persuasion, Identification, and Dialectical Symmetry," 336.
26. Kenneth Burke, "Art—and the First Rough Draft of Living," *Modern Age* 8, no. 2 (spring 1964): 158.
27. Kenneth Burke, *The Philosophy of Literary Form: Studies in Symbolic Action* (Berkeley: University of California Press, 1974), 116.

28. Kenneth Burke, *A Grammar of Motives*, 442.
29. Dewey, *Art as Experience* (New York: Perigee Books, 2005), 36–40.
30. Burke, *Counter-Statement*, 77,
31. Burke, *Counter-Statement*, 143.
32. Burke, *Towards a Better Life*, 71.
33. Kenneth Burke, "Archetype and Entelechy," in *On Human Nature: A Gathering While Everything Flows*, ed. William H. Rueckert and Angelo Bonadonna (Berkeley: University of California Press, 2003), 127.
34. Burke, *A Rhetoric of Motives*, 265.
35. Kenneth Burke, "'Watchful of Hermetics to Be Strong in Hermeneutics': Selections from 'Poetics, Dramatistically Considered.'" *Unending Conversations: New Writings by and about KB*, ed. Greig Henderson and David Cratis Williams (Carbondale: Southern Illinois University Press, 2001), 71.
36. Burke, *Counter-Statement*, 124.
37. Burke, *Counter-Statement*, 138.
38. Burke, "'Watchful of Hermetics,'" 38.
39. Burke, *A Rhetoric of Motives*, 232.
40. James P. Zappen, "Kenneth Burke on Dialectical-Rhetorical Transcendence," *Philosophy and Rhetoric* 42, no. 3 (2009): 81.
41. Roger Scruton, *The Aesthetics of Music* (New York: Oxford University Press, 1999), 358–59.
42. Vijay Iyer, "Exploding the Narrative in Jazz Improvisation," in *Uptown Conversation: The New Jazz Studies*, ed. Robert G. O'Meally, Brent Hayes Edwards, and Farah Jasmine Griffin (New York: Columbia University Press, 2004), 394.
43. Iyer, "Exploding the Narrative in Jazz Composition," 395.
44. Edward Strickland, "What Coltrane Wanted," *Atlantic Monthly*, December 1987, http://www.theatlantic.com/past/docs/unbound/jazz/strickla.htm.
45. *The Marsalis Family: A Jazz Celebration*, Marsalis Music, 2003.
46. Burke, *The Philosophy of Literary Form*, 107.
47. Sheila Jordan and Harvie S, *Yesterdays*, Highnote Records, 2012.
48. Interview with Harvie S, July 14, 2012.
49. Zappen, "Kenneth Burke on Dialectical-Rhetorical Transcendence," 290.
50. Zappen, "Kenneth Burke on Dialectical-Rhetorical Transcendence," 281.
51. Burke, *A Rhetoric of Motives*, 203.
52. Burke, *A Rhetoric of Motives*, 43.
53. Iyer, "Exploding the Narrative in Jazz Improvisation," 401.
54. Burke, "A Theory of Terminology," 242.
55. Burke, *A Rhetoric of Motives*, 27.
56. Kenneth Burke, "Responsibilities of National Greatness," *The Nation* 205 (July 17, 1967): 46–47, 49.
57. John Woodcock, "An Interview with Kenneth Burke," *Sewanee Review* 85, no. 4 (fall 1977): 716–17.
58. Burke, "Responsibilities of National Greatness," 50.

59. Strickland, "What Coltrane Wanted."
60. Burke, "A Theory of Terminology," 245.
61. Bill Cole, *John Coltrane* (New York: Schirmer Books, 1976), 171.
62. Frank Kofsky, *Black Nationalism and the Revolution in Music* (New York: Pathfinder Press, 1972), 227.
63. John Gennari, *Blowin' Hot and Cool: Jazz and Its Critics* (Chicago: University of Chicago Press, 2010), 263.
64. Burke, "On Persuasion," 336.
65. Burke, "A Theory of Terminology," 244.
66. Kenneth Burke, *The Letters of Kenneth Burke to William H. Rueckert*, ed. William H. Rueckert (West Lafayette: Parlor Press, 2002), 222.
67. Woodcock, "An Interview with Kenneth Burke," 713.
68. Kenneth Burke, "Rhetoric—Old and New," 59–76, in *New Rhetorics*, ed. Martin Steinmann (New York: Scribner, 1967), 76.
69. *Duke Ellington and John Coltrane*, Impulse!, 1995.
70. Ted Gioia, *The History of Jazz* (New York: Oxford University Press, 2011), 278.
71. Personal correspondence, April 9, 2013.
72. Burke, *A Rhetoric of Motives*, 58–59.
73. "It's more complicated than that," is the recurring answer that the Lord gives his protégé Satan as they contemplate the predicament of the language-using human race they are about to create, in "The Prologue in Heaven," which concludes Burke's *The Rhetoric of Religion.*
74. Burke, "A Theory of Terms," n.p.
75. Burke, *A Rhetoric of Motives*, 22.
76. Burke, *A Rhetoric of Motives*, 22–23.
77. Burke, "A Theory of Terminology," 245.

CHAPTER SEVEN

1. Kenneth Burke, "Musical Chronicle," *The Dial* 85 (December 1928): 529.
2. Kenneth Burke, *Language as Symbolic Action: Essays on Life, Literature, and Method* (Berkeley: University of California Press, 1966), 380–81.
3. Kenneth Burke, "Sin and Redemption," in *Of Symbols and Society*, ed. Joseph R. Gusfield, (Chicago: University of Chicago Press, 1989), 295–96. See also Kenneth Burke, "Identification," in *Of Symbols and Society,* ed. Joseph R. Gusfield (Chicago: University of Chicago Press, 1989), 180–81.
4. Kenneth Burke, "Myth, Poetry, and Philosophy," in *Language as Symbolic Action: Essays on Life, Literature, and Method* (Berkeley: University of California Press, 1966), 381.
5. Kenneth Burke, " 'Watchful of Hermetics to Be Strong in Hermeneutics': Selections from 'Poetics, Dramatistically Considered,' " 35–80, in *Unending Conversations: New Writings by and about Kenneth Burke*, ed. Greig Hender-

son and David Cratis Williams (Carbondale: Southern Illinois University Press, 2001), 60.

6. Kenneth Burke, *A Rhetoric of Motives* (Berkeley: University of California Press, 1969), 58.
7. Burke, *A Grammar of Motives*, 20.
8. Kenneth Burke, "*Permanence and Change*: In Retrospective Prospect," in *Permanence and Change: An Anatomy of Purpose* (Berkeley: University of California Press, 1984), 309.
9. John Woodcock, "An Interview with Kenneth Burke," *Sewanee Review* 85, no. 4 (fall 1977): 716.
10. Burke, *A Rhetoric of Motives*, 58.
11. Burke, "Afterword: In Retrospective Prospect," 309.
12. Kenneth Burke, *Permanence and Change*, 266.
13. Andrew Delbanco, *The Real American Dream: A Meditation on Hope* (Cambridge, MA: Harvard University Press, 1999), 1.
14. Delbanco, *The Real American Dream*, 6.
15. Jim Merod, "Jazz as a Cultural Archive," *Boundary* 2:22, no. 2 (summer 1995): 4–6.
16. Miles Davis, *Kind of Blue*, Sony, 1997. http://www.billevanswebpages.com/kindblue.html.
17. John Szwed, *So What: The Life of Miles Davis* (New York: Simon and Schuster, 2002), 175.
18. Bill Evans, liner notes to *Kind of Blue*, 1959, http://www.billevanswebpages.com/kindblue.html.
19. Szwed, *So What*, 175.
20. Woodcock, "An Interview with Kenneth Burke," 716.
21. Burke, *A Grammar of Motives*, 20.
22. Kenneth Burke, introduction to *Attitudes toward History*, 3rd ed. (Berkeley: University of California Press, 1984).
23. Kenneth Burke, "Art—and the First Rough Draft of Living," *Modern Age* 8, no. 2 (spring 1964), 160–61.
24. Ashley Kahn, *Kind of Blue: The Making of the Miles Davis Masterpiece* (New York: Da Capo Press, 2001), 16.
25. Burke, *Counter-Statement*, 165–67.
26. Burke, *Towards a Better Life*, 69–71.
27. Fred Kaplan, "Why the Best-Selling Jazz Album of All Time Is So Great," *Slate*, August 17, 2009. Accessed April 30, 2013. http://www.slate.com/articles/arts/music_box/2009/08/kind_of_blue.html.
28. Lewis Porter, *Coltrane: His Life and Music* (Ann Arbor: University of Michigan Press, 2000), 159.
29. Kahn, *Kind of Blue: The Making of the Miles Davis Masterpiece*, 69.
30. Paul F. Berliner, *Thinking in Jazz: The Infinite Art of Improvisation* (Chicago: University of Chicago Press, 1994), 192.

31. Vijay Iyer, "Exploding the Narrative in Jazz Improvisation," in *Uptown Conversation: The New Jazz Studies*, ed. Robert G. O'Meally, Brent Hayes Edwards, and Farah Jasmine Griffin (New York: Columbia University Press, 2004), 394–95.
32. Burke, *The Rhetoric of Religion*, 229–30.
33. Burke, *The Philosophy of Literary Form*, 100.
34. Szwed, *So What*, 174–75.
35. Berliner, *Thinking in Jazz*, 59.
36. T.J. Anderson III, *Notes to Make the Sound Come Right: Four Innovators of Jazz Poetry*. (Fayetteville: University of Arkansas Press, 2004),79.
37. Kenneth Burke and Malcolm Cowley, *The Selected Correspondence of Kenneth Burke and Malcolm Cowley, 1915–1981*, ed. Paul Jay (Berkeley: University of California Press, 1990), 24.
38. Kenneth Burke, "The Negro's Pattern of Life," in *The Philosophy of Literary Form: Studies in Symbolic Action,* 3rd ed. (Berkeley: University of California Press, 1973), 362.
39. Burke, *A Rhetoric of Motives*, 21.
40. Burke, "The Negro's Pattern of Life," 364–66.
41. Jim Maher, "Marshall Winslow Stearns: Revised Chronology": 07–22–03. By permission of the Lenox Library Association, Music Inn Archive Collection.
42. Jule Foster, "What is a Liberal Education in Music?" a panel discussion at the Berkshire Museum, February 22, 1958. By permission of the Lenox Library Association, Music Inn Archive Collection.
43. Anonymous, "The Composer in Jazz: More Time for Deep Thought," *Jazz Today* (December 1956), 19.
44. Kenneth Burke, "The Institutions of Art in America," *Arts in Society: A Journal of the Arts in Adult Education* 2 (fall–winter 1962): 59.
45. Albert Murray, *The Omni-Americans: Some Alternatives to the Folklore of White Supremacy* (New York: Avon Books, 1977), 95, 98. Burke's copy used by permission of the Kenneth Burke Literary Trust.
46. Burke, *Permanence and Change*, 309.
47. Murray, *The Omni-Americans*, 90.
48. Murray, *The Omni-Americans*, 93–94.
49. Kenneth Burke, "Ideology and Myth," *Accent* 7, no. 4 (Summer 1947): 198–99.
50. Kenneth Burke, "On Persuasion, Identification, and Dialectical Symmetry," ed. James P. Zappen. *Philosophy and Rhetoric* 39, no. 4 (2006): 336.
51. Kenneth Burke, "Music Chronicle," *The Dial* 85 (December 1928): 529.
52. Langston Hughes, "Jazz as Communication," in *The Langston Hughes Reader* (New York: George Braziller, 1958), 492–94.
53. Kenneth Burke, *Towards a Better Life* (Berkeley: University of California Press, 1984), 71.
54. *Bela Fleck and the Marcus Roberts Trio, Across the Imaginary Divide*, Rounder Records, 2012.

Bibliography

Ake, David. *Jazz Cultures*. Berkeley: University of California Press, 2002.

Anderson, Dana. *Identity's Strategy: Rhetorical Selves in Conversation*. Columbia: University of South Carolina Press, 2007.

Anderson, T. J., III. *Notes to Make the Sound Come Right: Four Innovators of Jazz Poetry*. Fayetteville: University of Arkansas Press, 2004.

Anonymous. "The Composer in Jazz: More Time for Deep Thought," *Jazz Today,* December 18–19, 1956.

Aristotle, *Politics*. Translated by T. A. Sinclair. New York: Penguin, 1985.

Attali, Jacques. *Noise: The Political Economy of Music*. Translated by Brian Massumi. St. Paul: University of Minnesota Press, 1985.

Baldwin, James. "Sonny's Blues." In *Write Me a Few of Your Lines: A Blues Reader*, edited by Steven C. Tracy, 394–415. Amherst: University of Massachusetts Press, 1999.

Benson, Thomas W. Preface to *Rhetorics of Display*, edited by Lawrence J. Prelli, ix–x. Columbia: University of South Carolina Press, 2006.

Berkman, Franya J. "Appropriating Universality: The Coltranes and 1960s Spirituality." *American Studies* 48, no. 1 (spring 2007): 41–62.

Berliner, Paul. *Thinking in Jazz: The Infinite Art of Improvisation*. Chicago: University of Chicago Press, 1994.

Brubeck, Iola. "They Say I Look Like God," 1961. Brubeck Collection, Holt-Atherton Special Collections-Digital Collections, University Library, University of the Pacific. Used by permission of the Brubeck Collection, Holt-Atherton Special Collections, University Library, University of the Pacific. Accessed

March 5, 2013. http://digitalcollections.pacific.edu/cdm/compoundobject/collection/ambassadors/id/66/rec/24.

———. "World Take a Holiday Story Synopsis," 1957. Brubeck Collection, Holt-Atherton Special Collections-Digital Collections, University Library, University of the Pacific. Used by permission of the Brubeck Collection, Holt-Atherton Special Collections, University Library, University of the Pacific. Accessed March 5, 2013. http://digitalcollections.pacific.edu/cdm/singleitem/collection/ambassadors/id/68/rec/1.

Burke, Kenneth. "Art—and the First Rough Draft of Living." *Modern Age* 8, no. 2 (spring 1964): 155–65.

———. *Attitudes toward History*. 3rd ed. Berkeley: University of California Press, 1984.

———. "Communication and the Human Condition," *Communication* 1, no. 2 (December 1974): 135–52.

———. *Counter-Statement*. Berkeley: University of California Press, 1968.

———. "The Fate of the Union: Kennedy and After." *New York Review of Books* 1, no. 9 (December 26, 1963): 9–10.

———. "Government in the Making." *Direction* 5 (December 19, 1942): 3–4.

———. *A Grammar of Motives*. Berkeley: University of California Press, 1969.

———. "Ideology and Myth," typescript. Kenneth Burke Papers, P17, n.d. Eberly Family Special Collections Library, Pennsylvania State University. Used by permission of the Kenneth Burke Literary Trust.

———. "Ideology and Myth." *Accent* 7, no. 4 (summer 1947): 195–205.

———. "The Institutions of Art in America." *Arts in Society: A Journal of the Arts in Adult Education* 2 (fall-winter 1962): 57–60.

———. *Language as Symbolic Action: Essays on Life, Literature, and Method*. Berkeley: University of California Press, 1966.

———. *Late Poems, 1968–1993*. Edited by Julie Whitaker and David Blakesley. Columbia: University of South Carolina Press, 2005.

———. Letter to Dutchie (Elspeth) Burke, February 21, 1989. Used by permission of the Kenneth Burke Literary Trust.

———. Letter to Jim Chesebro, September 24, 1987. Used by permission of the Kenneth Burke Literary Trust.

———. *The Letters of Kenneth Burke to William H. Rueckert*. Edited by William H. Rueckert. West Lafayette: Parlor Press, 2002.

———. "Musical Chronicle." *The Dial* 84 (April 1928): 356–58.

———. "Musical Chronicle." *The Dial* 85 (December 1928): 529–32.

———. "On Form." *Hudson Review* 17, no. 1 (spring 1964): 103–9.

———. *On Human Nature: A Gathering While Everything Flows*. Edited by William H. Rueckert and Angelo Bonadonna. Berkeley: University of California Press, 2003.

———. "On Persuasion, Identification, and Dialectical Symmetry," ed. James Zappen. *Philosophy and Rhetoric* 39, no. 4 (2006): 333–39.

———. *Permanence and Change: An Anatomy of Purpose*. 3rd edition. Berkeley: University of California Press, 1984.

———. *The Philosophy of Literary Form: Studies in Symbolic Action*. 3rd ed. Berkeley: University of California Press, 1973.

———. "Poetics and Communication." In *Perspectives in Education, Religion, and the Arts*, edited by Howard E. Kiefer and Milton K. Munitz, 401–18. Albany: State University of New York Press, 1970.

———. "Responsibilities of National Greatness." *The Nation* 205 (July 17, 1967): 46–50.

———. *A Rhetoric of Motives*. Berkeley: University of California Press, 1969.

———. *The Rhetoric of Religion: Studies in Logology*. Berkeley: University of California Press, 1970.

———. "Rhetoric—Old and New." In *New Rhetorics*, edited by Martin Steinmann, 59–76. New York: Scribner, 1967.

———. "The Rhetorical Situation." In *Communication: Ethical and Moral Issues*, edited by Lee Thayer, 263–75. London: Gordon and Breach Science Publishers, 1973.

———. *Of Symbols and Society*. Edited by Joseph R. Gusfield. Chicago: University of Chicago Press, 1989.

———. "A Theory of Terms." Lecture delivered 1966, Drew Theological Seminary, Madison, NJ. http://www.americanrhetoric.com/speeches/kennethburketheoryofterms.htm. Accessed March 20, 2013.

———. *Towards a Better Life*. Berkeley: University of California Press, 1894.

———. "'Watchful of Hermetics to Be Strong in Hermeneutics': Selections from 'Poetics, Dramatistically Considered.'" In *Unending Conversations: New Writings by and about Kenneth Burke*, edited by Greig Henderson and David Cratis Williams, 35–80. Carbondale: Southern Illinois University Press, 2001.

Burke, Kenneth, and Malcolm Cowley. *The Selected Correspondence of Kenneth Burke and Malcolm Cowley, 1915–1981*. Edited by Paul Jay. Berkeley: University of California Press, 1990.

Burks, Don. "KB's Last Day." *The Kenneth Burke Society Newsletter* 9:1 (December 1993): 10, 24.

Callahan, John F. Introduction to *The Collected Essays of Ralph Ellison*, edited by John F. Callahan, xvii–xxix. New York: Modern Library, 1994.

Carroll, Jeffrey. "The Song above Catastrophe: Kenneth Burke on Music." *KB Journal* 7, no. 2 (spring 2011). http://kbjournal.org/carroll.

Clark, Gregory. *Rhetorical Landscapes in America: Variations on a Theme from Kenneth Burke*. Columbia: University of South Carolina Press, 2004.

Clinton, Bill, and Hillary Clinton. "Remarks by the President and the First Lady at the White House Millennium Evening Lecture Series (9/18/98)." The White House, accessed July 18, 2013. http://clinton4.nara.gov/Initiatives/Millennium/19980921–8778.html.

Cohen, Harvey G. *Duke Ellington's America*. Chicago: University of Chicago Press, 2011.

Cole, Bill. *John Coltrane*. New York: Schirmer Books, 1976.

Coltrane, John. Liner notes to *A Love Supreme*, MCA Records, 1964.

Corbin, Ian Marcus. "A Jazz Mass? The Vexing Legacy of Mary Lou Williams." *Commonweal*, December 7, 2012. http://commonwealmagazine.org/jazz-mass.

Crable, Bryan. *Ralph Ellison and Kenneth Burke at the Roots of the Racial Divide*. Charlottesville: University of Virginia Press, 2012.

Crick, Bernard. *Democracy: A Very Short Introduction*. New York: Oxford University Press, 2002.

Crouch, Stanley. "Blues to Be Constitutional." In *Considering Genius: Writings on Jazz*, 166–205. New York: Basic Books, 2006.

Crucius, Timothy W. *Kenneth Burke and the Conversation after Philosophy*. Carbondale: Southern Illinois University Press, 1999.

Dance, Stanley. "The Funeral Address." In *The Duke Ellington Reader*, edited by Mark Tucker, 381–84. New York: Oxford University Press, 1993.

Delbanco, Andrew. *The Real American Dream: A Meditation on Hope*. Cambridge, MA: Harvard University Press, 1999.

DeMichael, Don. "John Coltrane and Eric Dolphy Answer the Jazz Critics." In *DownBeat: The Great Jazz Interviews*, edited by Frank Alkyer et al., 86–90. New York: Hal Leonard, 2009.

Dewey, John. *Art as Experience*. New York: Perigee Books, 2005.

———. *A Common Faith*. New Haven: Yale University Press, 1960.

Douglas, Ann. *Terrible Honesty: Mongrel Manhattan in the 1920s*. New York: Noonday, 1995.

DuBois, W. E. B. *The Souls of Black Folk*. New York: Bantam, 2005.

Eagleton, Terry. *The Ideology of the Aesthetic*. Oxford: Blackwell,1991.

———. *The Meaning of Life: A Very Short Introduction*. New York: Oxford University Press, 2008.

Eddy, Beth. *The Rites of Identity: The Religious Naturalism and Cultural Criticism of Kenneth Burke and Ralph Ellison*. Princeton, NJ: Princeton University Press, 2003.

Edwards, Brent Hays. "The Literary Ellington." In *Uptown Conversations: The New Jazz Studies*, edited by Robert G. O'Meally, Brent Hayes Edwards, and Farah Jasmine Griffin, 326–65. New York: Columbia University Press, 2004.

Ellington, Duke. *Music is My Mistress*. New York: Da Capo Press, 1973.

Ellison, Ralph. *The Collected Essays of Ralph Ellison*. Edited by John F. Callahan. New York: Modern Library, 1995.

———. Letter to Kenneth Burke, November 23, 1945. Kenneth Burke Papers, Eberly Family Special Collections Library, Pennsylvania State University. Used by permission of the Kenneth Burke Literary Trust.

Emerson, Ralph Waldo. *Nature and Selected Essays*. Edited by Larzer Ziff. New York: Penguin, 1982.

Eschen, Penny M. von. *Satchmo Blows Up the World: Jazz Ambassadors Play the Cold War*. Cambridge, MA: Harvard University Press, 2004.

Evans, Bill. Liner notes to *Conversations with Myself*, Polygram Records, 1959. http://www.billevanswebpages.com/kindblue.html.

Feather, Leonard. Liner notes to *The Duke Ellington Carnegie Hall Concerts, January 1943*, Prestige Records, 1977.

Fisher, Walter R. "A Motive View of Communication." *Quarterly Journal of Speech* 56, no. 2 (1970): 131–39.

Foster, Jule. "What Is a Liberal Education in Music," Panel discussion at the Berkshire Museum, February 22, 1958. By permission of the Lenox Library Association, Music Inn Archive Collection.

Gebhardt, Nicholas. *Going for Jazz: Musical Practices and American Ideology*. Chicago: University of Chicago Press, 2001.

Gennari, John. *Blowin' Hot and Cool: Jazz and Its Critics*. Chicago: University of Chicago Press, 2010.

George, Ann, and Jack Selzer. *Kenneth Burke in the 1930s*. Columbia, SC: University of South Carolina Press, 2007.

Gioia, Ted. *The History of Jazz*. New York: Oxford University Press, 2011.

Glaude, Eddie S., Jr. *In a Shade of Blue: Pragmatism and the Politics of Black America*. Chicago: University of Chicago Press, 2007.

Havel, Václav. "Democracy's Forgotten Dimension." *Journal of Democracy* 6, no. 2 (1995): 3–10.

Hawhee, Debra. *Moving Bodies: Kenneth Burke at the Edges of Language*. Columbia, SC: University of South Carolina Press, 2012.

Hughes, Karen P. "The Beat Goes On: Honoring Willis Conover and Celebrating the Power of Music." Remarks at the Duke, Dizzy, and Diplomacy Jazz Concert, September 17, 2007. US State Department Archive, accessed March 1, 2013. http://2001–2009.state.gov/r/us/2007/93312.htm.

Hughes, Langston. *The First Book of Jazz*. Hopewell, NJ: Ecco Press, 1982.

———. "Jazz as Communication." In *The Langston Hughes Reader*, 492–94. New York: George Braziller, 1958.

Hughes, Langston, and Carl Van Vechten. *Remember Me to Harlem: The Letters of Langston Hughes and Carl Van Vechten*. Edited by Emily Bernard. New York: Vintage, 2001.

Iyer, Vijay. Liner notes to *Accelerando*, Vijay Iyer Trio, Act Music, 2012.

———. "Exploding the Narrative in Jazz Improvisation." In *Uptown Conversation: The New Jazz Studies*, edited by Robert G. O'Meally, Brent Hayes Edwards, and Farah Jasmine Griffin, 393–403. New York: Columbia University Press, 2004.

James, William. *The Principles of Psychology*, Vol 2. New York: Dover, 1950.

———. "Report on Mrs. Piper's Hodgson-Control." In *Collected Essays and Reviews*, 484–90. New York: Longmans, Green and Co., 1920.

———. *The Varieties of Religious Experience: A Study in Human Nature, Being the Gifford Lectures on Natural Religion, Delivered at Edinburgh in 1901–1902*. New York: New American Library, 2003.

Jazz: Designation as an American National Treasure, H. Con. Res. 35, 101 Stat. 2013 (1987).

Johnson, David Brent. "Sacred Blue: Jazz Goes to Church in the 1960s." *Indiana Public Media*, April 19, 2011. http://indianapublicmedia.org/nightlights/sacred-blue-jazz-church-1960s/.

Johnson, Hall. *Thirty Spirituals Arranged for Voice and Piano*. New York: Hal Leonard, 1949.

Johnson, Mark. *The Meaning of the Body: Aesthetics of Human Understanding*. Chicago: University of Chicago Press, 2007.

Kahn, Ashley. *Kind of Blue: The Making of the Miles Davis Masterpiece*. New York: Da Capo Press, 2001.

———. *A Love Supreme: The Story of John Coltrane's Signature Album*. New York: Penguin, 2002.

Kaplan, Fred. "Why the Best-Selling Jazz Album of All Time is So Great." *Slate*, August 17, 2009. Accessed April 30, 2013. http://www.slate.com/articles/arts/music_box/2009/08/kind_of_blue.html.

Karenga, Maulana Ron. "Black Art." *Black Theater* 4 (April 1970): 9–10.

Kater, Michael H. *Different Drummers: Jazz in the Culture of Nazi Germany*. New York: Oxford University Press, 1992.

Kellett, Andrew James. "Fathers and Sons: American Blues and British Rock Music, 1960–1970." PhD dissertation, University of Maryland, 2008. http://hdl.handle.net/1903/8863.

Kofsky, Frank. *Black Nationalism and the Revolution in Music*. New York: Pathfinder Press, 1972.

Langer, Susanne. *Feeling and Form: A Theory of Art*. New York: Scribner, 1953.

Lees, Gene. "The Poet." In *Reading Jazz: A Gathering of Autobiography, Reportage, and Criticism from 1919 to Now*, edited by Robert Gottlieb, 419–44. New York: Vintage, 1999.

Levitin, Daniel J. *This Is Your Brain on Music: The Science of a Human Obsession*. New York: Dutton, 2006.

Maher, Jim. "Marshall Winslow Stearns: Revised Chronology, by JTM: 07–22–03." By permission of the Lenox Library Association, Music Inn Archive Collection.

Marsalis, Wynton, and Carl Vigeland. *Jazz in the Bittersweet Blues of Life*. New York: Da Capo Press, 2001.

Marsalis, Wynton, and Geoffrey C. Ward. *Moving to Higher Ground: How Jazz Can Change Your Life*. New York: Random House, 2009.

Mattingly, Rick. *The Drummer's Time: Conversations with the Great Drummers of Jazz*. Cedar Grove, NJ: Modern Drummer Publications, 1998.

McCulloch-Lovell, Ellen. "What is the Millennium Council?" The White House, accessed July 18, 2013. http://clinton4.nara.gov/Initiatives/Millennium/what.html.

Merod, Jim. "Jazz as a Cultural Archive." *Boundary* 2:22, no. 2 (summer 1995): 1–18.

Monson, Ingrid. *Saying Something: Jazz Improvisation and Interaction*. Chicago: University of Chicago Press, 1996.

Murray, Albert. *The Omni-Americans: Black Experience and American Culture*. New York: Outerbridge & Dienstfrey, 1970.

———. *The Omni-Americans: Some Alternatives to the Folklore of White Supremacy.* New York: Avon Books, 1977. Kenneth Burke's copy used by permission of the Kenneth Burke Literary Trust.

———. *Stomping the Blues.* 2nd ed. New York: Da Capo Press, 2000.

Muyumba, Walton. *The Shadow and the Act: Black Intellectual Practice, Jazz Improvisation, and Philosophical Pragmatism.* Chicago: University of Chicago Press, 2011.

O'Meally, Robert G. Afterword to *The Book of Rhythms* by Langston Hughes, 50–55. New York: Oxford University Press, 1995.

———. "Introduction: Jazz Shapes." In *Living with Music: Ralph Ellison's Jazz Writings*, edited by Robert G. O'Meally, ix–xxxv. New York: Modern Library, 2001.

Nisensen, Eric. *Kind of Blue: The Making of the Miles Davis Masterpiece.* New York: Da Capo Press, 2001.

Pauley, Garth. "Criticism in Context: Kenneth Burke's 'The Rhetoric of Hitler's Battle.'" *KB Journal* 6, no. 1 (fall 2009). http://kbjournal.org/content/criticism-context-kenneth-burkes-rhetoric-hitlers-battle.

Perlis, Vivian, and Libby Van Cleve. *Composers' Voices from Ives to Ellington: An Oral History of American Music.* New Haven: Yale University Press, 2005.

Pierpont, Claudia Roth. "Black, Brown, and Beige: Duke Ellington's Music and Race in America." *The New Yorker*, May 17, 2010. http://www.newyorker.com/arts/critics/atlarge/2010/05/17/100517crat_atlarge_pierpont.

Porter, Eric C. *What Is This Thing Called Jazz? African American Musicians as Artists, Critics, and Activists.* Berkeley: University of California Press, 2002.

Porter, Lewis. *Coltrane: His Life and Music.* Ann Arbor: University of Michigan Press, 2000.

Ramsey, Doug. "Willis Conover Honored: A Good First Step," *Rifftides: Doug Ramsey on Jazz and Other Matters* (blog), May 1, 2009. http://www.artsjournal.com/rifftides/2009/05/the_white_house_has_yet.html.

Ratliff, Ben. *The New York Times Essential Library: A Critic's Guide to the 100 Most Important Recordings.* New York: Times Books, 2002.

Reed, Eric. "Sacred Jazz." *All About Jazz* (blog). March 24, 2009. http://www.allaboutjazz.com/php/article.php?id=32072&pg=2#.UTpENKVXAuI.

Reich, Howard. "The Sound of Freedom: Polish Jazz Comes to Chicago in Resonance Festival," *Chicago Tribune*, February 28, 2011. http://articles.chicagotribune.com/2011–02–28/entertainment/ct-live-0301-jazz-festival-20110228_1_polish-jazz-new-jazz-zygmunt-matynia.

Sacks, Oliver. *Musicophilia: Tales of Music and the Brain.* New York: Vintage Books, 2008.

Schneck, Stephen Frederick. "Habits of the Head: Tocqueville's America and Jazz." *Political Theory* 17, no. 4 (November 1989): 638–62.

Schudel, Matt. "Jazz Musician Max Roach Dies at 83." *Washington Post*, August 16, 2007. http://www.washingtonpost.com/wpdyn/content/article/2007/08/16/AR2007081601092.html.

Scruton, Roger. *The Aesthetics of Music*. New York: Oxford University Press, 1999.

Selzer, Jack. *Kenneth Burke in Greenwich Village: Conversing with the Moderns, 1915–1931*. Madison: University of Wisconsin Press, 1996.

Skvorecky, Josef. *Talkin' Moscow Blues: Essays about Literature, Politics, Movies, and Jazz*. Toronto: University of Toronto Press, 1988.

Starr, S. Frederick. *Red and Hot: The Fate of Jazz in the Soviet Union*. New York: Limelight Editions, 1994.

Steed, Janna Tull. *Duke Ellington: A Spiritual Biography*. New York: Crossroad Publishing Company, 1999.

Strickland, Edward. "What Coltrane Wanted." *Atlantic Monthly*, December 1987. http://www.theatlantic.com/past/docs/unbound/jazz/strickla.htm.

Szwed, John. *So What: The Life of Miles Davis*. New York: Simon and Schuster, 2002.

Teachout, Terry. *Pops: A Life of Louis Armstrong*. Boston: Houghton Mifflin Harcourt, 2009.

Thoreau, Henry David. *Walden and Other Writings*. Edited by Brooks Atkinson. New York: Random House, 1950.

Tocqueville, Alexis de. *Democracy in America*. Edited by Phillips Bradley. New York: Vintage Press, 1990.

Tompkins, Jane. *West of Everything: The Secret Life of Westerns*. New York: Oxford University, 1992.

Tucker, Mark. "The Genesis of 'Black, Brown, and Beige,'" *Black Music Research Journal* 22, supplement: Best of BMRJ (2002): 136. http://www.jstor.org/stable/1519946.

Tucker, Mark, ed. "Interview in Los Angeles: On *Jump for Joy*, Opera, and Dissonance as a 'Way of Life, (1941),'" in *The Duke Ellington Reader,* 148–51. New York: Oxford University Press, 1993.

Wess, Robert. *Kenneth Burke: Rhetoric, Subjectivity, Postmodernism*. New York: Cambridge University Press, 1996.

Whitman, Walt. "Democratic Vistas." In *Leaves of Grass and Selected Prose*, edited by John Kouwenhoven, 466–516. New York: Modern Library, 1950.

Williams, Martin. *The Jazz Tradition*. 2nd ed. New York: Oxford University Press, 1993.

Woodcock, John. "An Interview with Kenneth Burke." *The Sewanee Review* 85, no. 4 (fall 1977): 704–18.

Woodruff, Paul. *Reverence: Renewing a Forgotten Virtue*. New York: Oxford University Press, 2001.

Zappen, James P. "Kenneth Burke on Dialectical-Rhetorical Transcendence." *Philosophy and Rhetoric* 42, no. 3 (2009): 279–301.

Discography

Adderley, Cannonball. *Somethin' Else*. Blue Note, 1958.

Armstrong, Louis. *The Essential Louis Armstrong*. Sony, 2004.

Batiste, Jon, and Stay Human. *Social Music*. Razor & Tie Recordings, 2013.

Brubeck, Dave. *The Real Ambassadors: An Original Musical Production by Dave and Iola Brubeck*. Columbia Records, Sony Music Entertainment, 1994.

Carrington, Terri Lyne. *Money Jungle: Provocative in Blue*. GrooveJazz Media/Hebert-Carrington Media, 2013.

Cole, Nat King. *Best of Nat King Cole Trio: Vocal Classics 42–46*. Blue Note, 1995.

Cole, Natalie. *Unforgettable*. Elektra/Wea, 1991.

Davis, Miles. *Kind of Blue*. Sony, 1997.

Ellington, Duke. *The Duke Ellington Carnegie Hall Concerts, January 1943*. Prestige, 1977.

———. *Duke Ellington's "My People": The Complete Show*. Storyville, 2012.

Ellington, Duke, and John Coltrane. *Duke Ellington and John Coltrane*. Impulse!, 1995.

Ellington, Duke, Charlie Mingus, and Max Roach. *Money Jungle*. Blue Note, 1963.

Evans, Bill. *Conversations with Myself*, Polygram, 1997.

Fleck, Bela, and the Marcus Roberts Trio. *Across the Imaginary Divide*. Rounder, 2012.

Harris, Gene. *The Gene Harris Trio Plus One*. Concord, 1990.

Johnson, Robert. "Cross Road Blues (Take 2)," American Studies at the University of Virginia. Accessed February 17, 2011, at http://xroads.virginia.edu/~music/blues/crb.html. Version from *Robert Johnson: The Complete Recordings*, Sony BMG Music Entertainment, 1990.

Jordan, Sheila, and Harvie S. *Yesterdays*. Highnote, 2012.

Lloyd, Charles, and Jason Moran. *Hagar's Song*. ECM, 2013.

The Marsalis Family: A Jazz Celebration. Marsalis Music, 2003.

Mingus, Charles. *The Black Saint and the Sinner Lady*. GRP, 1995.

Moran, Jason. *The Bandwagon*. Blue Note, 2010.

———. *Ten*. Blue Note, 2010.

Marsalis, Wynton Quintet. "Blues." Live performance at Parc Floral, Paris, July 28, 2007. Podcast released Oct 20, 2007, at wyntonmarsalis.org/marsalis_podcast.xml.

NEXT Collective. *Cover Art*. Concord Music Group, 2013.

Roach, Max. *We Insist! Max Roach's Freedom Now Suite*. Candid, *1988*.

———. *It's Time*. Impulse!, *1996*.

Salvant, Cecile McLorin. *Woman Child*. Mack Avenue, 2013.

Index